THE WORKS OF WILLIAM SHAKESPEARE

VOLUME FOUR

WILLIAM SHAKESPEARE

From the Statue by Lord Ronald Gower in the Grounds of The Memorial Theatre at Stratford-on-Avon

THE WORKS OF WILLIAM SHAKESPEARE

VOLUME FOUR

King Henry VI: Second Part
King Henry VI: Third Part
The Famous History of King Henry VIII
The Life and Death of King John

THE PEEBLES CLASSIC LIBRARY

SANDY LESBERG, *Editor*

ISBN 0-85690-042-7

Published by Peebles Press International
U.S.A.: 10 Columbus Circle, New York, NY 10019
U.K.: 12 Thayer Street, London W1M 5LD

Distributed by WHS Distributors

PRINTED AND BOUND IN THE U.S.A.

CONTENTS

KING HENRY THE SIXTH

SECOND PART

DRAMATIS PERSONÆ

KING HENRY THE SIXTH
HUMPHREY, *Duke of Gloster, his uncle*
CARDINAL BEAUFORT, *Bishop of Winchester, great-uncle to the King*
RICHARD PLANTAGENET, *Duke of York*
EDWARD *and* RICHARD, *his sons*

DUKE OF SOMERSET DUKE OF SUFFOLK DUKE OF BUCKINGHAM LORD CLIFFORD YOUNG CLIFFORD, *his son*	*Of the King's party*
EARL OF SALISBURY EARL OF WARWICK	*Of the York faction*

LORD SCALES, *Governor of the Tower*
LORD SAY
SIR HUMPHREY STAFFORD, *and* WILLIAM STAFFORD, *his brother*
SIR JOHN STANLEY
WALTER WHITMORE
A Sea Captain, Master, and Master's-Mate
Two Gentlemen, prisoners with Suffolk
VAUX
JOHN HUME, *and* JOHN SOUTHWELL, *Priests*
ROGER BOLINGBROKE, *a conjurer. A Spirit raised by him*
THOMAS HORNER, *an armourer*
PETER, *his man*
Clerk of Chatham
Mayor of Saint Albans
SAUNDER SIMPCOX, *an impostor*
JACK CADE
GEORGE BEVIS, JOHN HOLLAND, DICK *the butcher*, SMITH *the weaver*, MICHAEL, *etc., Cade's followers*
ALEXANDER IDEN, *a Kentish gentleman*
Two Murderers

MARGARET, *Queen to King Henry*
ELEANOR, *Duchess of Gloster*
MARGERY JOURDAIN, *a witch*
Wife to Simpcox

Lords, Ladies, and Attendants; Herald; Petitioners, Aldermen, a Beadle, Sheriff, and Officers; Citizens, 'Prentices, Falconers, Guards, Soldiers, Messengers, etc.

SCENE—*In various parts of England*

THE SECOND PART OF

KING HENRY VI

ACT ONE

SCENE I.—London. A Room of State in the Palace

Flourish of trumpets: then hautboys. Enter, on one side, KING HENRY, DUKE OF GLOSTER, SALISBURY, WARWICK, *and* CARDINAL BEAUFORT; *on the other,* QUEEN MARGARET, *led in by* SUFFOLK; YORK, SOMERSET, BUCKINGHAM, *and others, following*

Suf. As by your high imperial majesty
I had in charge at my depart for France,
As procurator to your excellence,
To marry Princess Margaret for your grace;
So, in the famous ancient city, Tours,
In the presence of the Kings of France and Sicil,
The Dukes of Orleans, Calaber, Bretagne, and Alençon,
Seven earls, twelve barons, and twenty reverend bishops,
I have performed my task, and was espoused:
And humbly now upon my bended knee,
In sight of England and her lordly peers,
Deliver up my title in the queen
To your most gracious hands, that are the substance
Of that great shadow I did represent;
The happiest gift that ever marquess gave,
The fairest queen that ever king received.
K. Hen. Suffolk, arise.—Welcome, Queen Margaret:
I can express no kinder sign of love
Than this kind kiss.—O Lord! that lends me life,
Lend me a heart replete with thankfulness;
For thou hast given me, in this beauteous face,
A world of earthly blessings to my soul,
If sympathy of love unite our thoughts.
Q. Mar. Great King of England, and my gracious lord,
The mutual conference that my mind hath had
By day, by night, waking, and in my dreams,
In courtly company, or at my beads,

With you mine alderliefest sovereign,
Makes me the bolder to salute my king
With ruder terms, and as my wit affords,
And over-joy of heart doth minister.

K. Hen. Her sight did ravish, but her grace in speech,
Her words y-clad with wisdom's majesty,
Makes me from wondering fall to weeping joys;
Such is the fulness of my heart's content.
Lords, with one cheerful voice welcome my love.

All. Long live Queen Margaret, England's happiness!

Q. Mar. We thank you all. [*Flourish*

Suf. My lord Protector, so it please your grace,
Here are the articles of contracted peace,
Between our sovereign, and the French king Charles,
For eighteen months concluded by consent.

Glo. [*Reads*] 'Imprimis, It is agreed between the French king, Charles, and William de la Poole, Marquess of Suffolk, ambassador for Henry King of England, that the said Henry shall espouse the Lady Margaret, daughter unto Reignier King of Naples, Sicilia, and Jerusalem; and crown her Queen of England ere the thirtieth of May next ensuing.—Item,—That the duchy of Anjou and the county of Maine shall be released and delivered to the king her father'— [*Duke Humphrey lets the paper fall*

K. Hen. Uncle, how now?

Glo. Pardon me, gracious lord;
Some sudden qualm hath struck me at the heart,
And dimmed mine eyes, that I can read no further.

K. Hen. Uncle of Winchester, I pray, read on.

Win. 'Item,—It is further agreed between them,—that the duchies of Anjou and Maine shall be released and delivered over to the king her father; and she sent over of the King of England's own proper cost and charges, without having any dowry.'

K. Hen. They please us well.—Lord marquess, kneel down:
We here create thee the first Duke of Suffolk,
And girt thee with the sword.—Cousin of York,
We here discharge your grace from being regent
I' the parts of France, till term of eighteen months
Be full expired.—Thanks, uncle Winchester,
Gloster, York, Buckingham, Somerset,
Salisbury, and Warwick;
We thank you all for this great favour done,
In entertainment to my princely queen.
Come, let us in; and with all speed provide
To see her coronation be performed.
[*Exeunt King, Queen, and Suffolk*

Glo. Brave peers of England, pillars of the state,
To you Duke Humphrey must unload his grief,

Your grief, the common grief of all the land.
What! did my brother Henry spend his youth,
His valour, coin, and people, in the wars?
Did he so often lodge in open field,
In winter's cold, and summer's parching heat,
To conquer France, his true inheritance?
And did my brother Bedford toil his wits,
To keep by policy what Henry got?
Have you, ourselves, Somerset, Buckingham,
Brave York, Salisbury, and victorious Warwick,
Received deep scars in France and Normandy?
Or hath mine uncle Beaufort, and myself,
With all the learned council of the realm,
Studied so long, sat in the council-house
Early and late, debating to and fro
How France and Frenchmen might be kept in awe?
And hath his highness in his infancy
Been crowned in Paris, in despite of foes?
And shall these labours, and these honours, die?
Shall Henry's conquest, Bedford's vigilance,
Your deeds of war, and all our counsel, die?
O peers of England! shameful is this league;
Fatal this marriage; cancelling your fame,
Blotting your names from books of memory,
Razing the characters of your renown,
Defacing monuments of conquered France,
Undoing all, as all had never been!
Car. Nephew, what means this passionate discourse,
This peroration with such circumstance?
For France, 't is ours; and we will keep it still.
Glo. Ay, uncle; we will keep it, if we can;
But now it is impossible we should.
Suffolk, the new-made duke that rules the roast,
Hath given the duchy of Anjou, and Maine,
Unto the poor King Reignier, whose large style
Agrees not with the leanness of his purse.
Sal. Now, by the death of him that died for all,
These counties were the keys of Normandy.—
But wherefore weeps Warwick, my valiant son?
War. For grief, that they are past recovery;
For, were there hope to conquer them again,
My sword should shed hot blood, mine eyes no tears.
Anjou and Maine! myself did win them both;
Those provinces these arms of mine did conquer:
And are the cities, that I got with wounds,
Delivered up again with peaceful words?
Mort Dieu!
York. For Suffolk's duke, may he be suffocate,
That dims the honour of this warlike isle!
France should have torn and rent my very heart,

Before I would have yielded to this league.
I never read but England's kings have had
Large sums of gold, and dowries, with their wives;
And our King Henry gives away his own,
To match with her that brings no vantages.
Glo. A proper jest, and never heard before,
That Suffolk should demand a whole fifteenth,
For costs and charges in transporting her!
She should have stayed in France, and starved in France,
Before—
Car. My Lord of Gloster, now you grow too hot.
It was the pleasure of my lord the king.
Glo. My Lord of Winchester, I know your mind:
'T is not my speeches that you do mislike,
But 't is my presence that doth trouble ye.
Rancour will out: proud prelate, in thy face
I see thy fury. If I longer stay,
We shall begin our ancient bickerings.—
Lordings, farewell; and say, when I am gone,
I prophesied, France will be lost ere long. [*Exit*
Car. So, there goes our Protector in a rage.
'T is known to you he is mine enemy;
Nay, more, an enemy unto you all,
And no great friend, I fear me, to the king.
Consider, lords, he is the next of blood,
And heir-apparent to the English crown:
Had Henry got an empire by his marriage,
And all the wealthy kingdoms of the west,
There's reason he should be displeased at it.
Look to it, lords: let not his smoothing words
Bewitch your hearts; be wise, and circumspect.
What though the common people favour him,
Calling him 'Humphrey, the good Duke of Gloster;'
Clapping their hands, and crying with loud voice—
'Jesu maintain your royal excellence!'
With—'God preserve the good Duke Humphrey!'
I fear me, lords, for all this flattering gloss,
He will be found a dangerous Protector.
Buck. Why should he then protect our sovereign,
He being of age to govern of himself?—
Cousin of Somerset, join you with me,
And all together, with the Duke of Suffolk,
We'll quickly hoise Duke Humphrey from his seat.
Car. This weighty business will not brook delay;
I'll to the Duke of Suffolk presently. [*Exit*
Som. Cousin of Buckingham, though Humphrey's pride,
And greatness of his place, be grief to us,
Yet let us watch the haughty cardinal.
His insolence is more intolerable
Than all the princes' in the land beside:

If Gloster be displaced, he'll be Protector.
Buck. Or thou, or I, Somerset, will be Protector,
Despite Duke Humphrey, or the cardinal.
[*Exeunt Buckingham and Somerset*
Sal. Pride went before, ambition follows him.
While these do labour for their own preferment,
Behoves it us to labour for the realm.
I never saw but Humphrey, Duke of Gloster,
Did bear him like a noble gentleman.
Oft have I see the haughty cardinal,
More like a soldier than a man o' the church,
As stout and proud, as he were lord of all,
Swear like a ruffian, and demean himself
Unlike the ruler of a commonweal.—
Warwick, my son, the comfort of my age,
Thy deeds, thy plainness, and thy housekeeping,
Hath won the greatest favour of the commons,
Excepting none but good Duke Humphrey;
And brother York, thy acts in Ireland,
In bringing them to civil discipline,
Thy late exploits, done in the heart of France,
When thou wert regent for our sovereign,
Have made thee feared and honoured of the people.—
Join we together, for the public good,
In what we can, to bridle and suppress
The pride of Suffolk, and the cardinal,
With Somerset's and Buckingham's ambition;
And, as we may, cherish Duke Humphrey's deeds,
While they do tend the profit of the land.
War. So God help Warwick, as he loves the land,
And common profit of his country.
York. [*Aside*] And so says York, for he hath greatest cause.
Sal. Then let's make haste away, and look unto the main.
War. Unto the main! O father, Maine is lost;
That Maine, which by main force Warwick did win,
And would have kept, so long as breath did last:
Main chance, father, you meant; but I meant Maine,
Which I will win from France, or else be slain.
[*Exeunt Warwick and Salisbury*
York. Anjou and Maine are given to the French;
Paris is lost: the state of Normandy
Stands on a tickle point, now they are gone.
Suffolk concluded on the articles,
The peers agreed, and Henry was well pleased,
To change two dukedoms for a duke's fair daughter.
I cannot blame them all: what is 't to them?
'T is thine they give away, and not their own.
Pirate may make cheap pennyworths of their pillage,

And purchase friends, and give to courtesans,
Still revelling, like lords, till all be gone;
Whileas the silly owner of the goods
Weeps over them, and wrings his hapless hands,
And shakes his head, and trembling stands aloof,
While all is shared, and all is borne away,
Ready to starve, and dare not touch his own:
So York must sit, and fret, and bite his tongue,
While his own lands are bargained for, and sold.
Methinks, the realms of England, France, and Ireland,
Bear that proportion to my flesh and blood,
As did the fatal brand Althæa burned,
Unto the prince's heart of Calydon.
Anjou and Maine, both given unto the French!
Cold news for me; for I had hope of France,
Even as I have of fertile England's soil.
A day will come when York shall claim his own;
And therefore I will take the Nevils' parts,
And make a show of love to proud Duke Humphrey,
And, when I spy advantage, claim the crown,
For that's the golden mark I seek to hit.
Nor shall proud Lancaster usurp my right,
Nor hold the sceptre in his childish fist,
Nor wear the diadem upon his head,
Whose church-like humours fit not for a crown.
Then, York, be still awhile, till time do serve:
Watch thou, and wake, when others be asleep,
To pry into the secrets of the state,
Till Henry, surfeiting in joys of love,
With his new bride, and England's dear-bought queen,
And Humphrey with the peers be fall'n at jars:
Then will I raise aloft the milk-white rose,
With whose sweet smell the air shall be perfumed,
And in my standard bear the arms of York,
To grapple with the house of Lancaster;
And, force perforce, I'll make him yield the crown,
Whose bookish rule hath pulled fair England down. [*Exit*

SCENE II.—London. A Room in the DUKE OF GLOSTER'S House

Enter GLOSTER *and the* DUCHESS

Duch. Why droops my lord, like over-ripened corn,
Hanging the head at Ceres' plenteous load?
Why doth the great Duke Humphrey knit his brows,
As frowning at the favours of the world?
Why are thine eyes fixed to the sullen earth,
Gazing on that which seems to dim thy sight?

What seest thou there? King Henry's diadem,
Enchased with all the honours of the world?
If so, gaze on, and grovel on thy face,
Until thy head be circled with the same.
Put forth thy hand; reach at the glorious gold.—
What, is't too short? I'll lengthen it with mine;
And, having both together heaved it up,
We'll both together lift our heads to heaven,
And never more abase our sight so low,
As to vouchsafe one glance unto the ground.

Glo. O Nell, sweet Nell, if thou dost love thy lord,
Banish the canker of ambitious thoughts:
And may that thought, when I imagine ill
Against my king and nephew, virtuous Henry,
Be my last breathing in this mortal world.
My troublous dream this night doth make me sad.

Duch. What dreamed my lord? tell me, and I'll requite it
With sweet rehearsal of my morning's dream.

Glo. Methought, this staff, mine office-badge in court,
Was broke in twain: by whom, I have forgot,
But, as I think, 't was by the cardinal;
And on the pieces of the broken wand
Were placed the heads of Edmund Duke of Somerset,
And William de la Poole, first Duke of Suffolk.
This was my dream: what it doth bode, God knows.

Duch. Tut! this was nothing but an argument,
That he that breaks a stick of Gloster's grove,
Shall lose his head for his presumption.
But list to me, my Humphrey, my sweet duke:
Methought, I sat in seat of majesty,
In the cathedral church of Westminster,
And in that chair where kings and queens are crowned;
Where Henry, and Dame Margaret, kneeled to me,
And on my head did set the diadem.

Glo. Nay, Eleanor, then must I chide outright.
Presumptuous dame! ill-nurtured Eleanor!
Art thou not second woman in the realm,
And the Protector's wife, beloved of him?
Hast thou not worldly pleasure at command,
Above the reach or compass of thy thought?
And wilt thou still be hammering treachery,
To tumble down thy husband, and thyself,
From top of honour to disgrace's feet?
Away from me, and let me hear no more.

Duch. What, what, my lord! are you so choleric
With Eleanor, for telling but her dream?
Next time I'll keep my dreams unto myself,
And not be checked.

Glo. Nay, be not angry, I am pleased again.

Enter a Messenger

Mess. My lord protector, 't is his highness' pleasure,
You do prepare to ride unto Saint Albans,
Whereas the king and queen do mean to hawk.
Glo. I go.—Come, Nell; thou wilt ride with us?
Duch. Yes, my good lord, I'll follow presently.
[*Exeunt Gloster and Messenger*
Follow I must; I cannot go before,
While Gloster bears this base and humble mind.
Were I a man, a duke, and next of blood,
I would remove these tedious stumbling-blocks,
And smooth my way upon their headless necks:
And, being a woman, I will not be slack
To play my part in Fortune's pageant.
Where are you there? Sir John! nay, fear not, man,
We are alone: here's none but thee, and I.

Enter JOHN HUME

Hume. Jesus preserve your royal majesty.
Duch. What say'st thou? majesty! I am but grace.
Hume. But, by the grace of God, and Hume's advice,
Your grace's title shall be multiplied.
Duch. What say'st thou, man? hast thou as yet conferred
With Margery Jourdain, the cunning witch,
And Roger Bolingbroke, the conjurer?
And will they undertake to do me good?
Hume. This they have promiséd,—to show your highness
A spirit raised from depth of under-ground,
That shall make answer to such questions,
As by your grace shall be propounded him.
Duch. It is enough: I'll think upon the questions.
When from Saint Albans we do make return,
We'll see these things effected to the full.
Here, Hume, take this reward; make merry, man,
With thy confederates in this weighty cause. [*Exit*
Hume. Hume must make merry with the duchess' gold:
Marry, and shall. But how now, Sir John Hume?
Seal up your lips, and give no words but—mum:
The business asketh silent secrecy.
Dame Eleanor gives gold to bring the witch:
Gold cannot come amiss, were she a devil.
Yet have I gold, flies from another coast:
I dare not say, from the rich cardinal,
And from the great and new-made Duke of Suffolk;
Yet I do find it so; for, to be plain,
They, knowing Dame Eleanor's aspiring humour,

Have hired me to undermine the duchess,
And buz these conjurations in her brain.
They say, a crafty knave does need no broker;
Yet am I Suffolk and the cardinal's broker.
Hume, if you take not heed, you shall go near
To call them both a pair of crafty knaves.
Well, so it stands; and thus, I fear, at last,
Hume's knavery will be the duchess' wrack,
And her attainture will be Humphrey's fall.
Sort how it will, I shall have gold for all. [*Exit*

Scene III.—London. A Room in the Palace

Enter Peter, *and others, with petitions*

First Pet. My masters, let's stand close: my lord Protector will come this way by-and-by, and then we may deliver our supplications in the quill.

Sec. Pet. Marry, the Lord protect him, for he's a good man! Jesu bless him!

Enter Suffolk *and* Queen Margaret

First Pet. Here 'a comes, methinks, and the queen with him. I'll be the first, sure.

Sec. Pet. Come back, fool! this is the Duke of Suffolk, and not my lord Protector.

Suf. How now, fellow? wouldst anything with me?

First Pet. I pray, my lord, pardon me: I took ye for my lord Protector.

Q. Mar. 'To my lord Protector!' are your supplications to his lordship? Let me see them. What is thine?

First Pet. Mine is, an't please your grace, against John Goodman, my lord cardinal's man, for keeping my house, and lands, and wife, and all, from me.

Suf. Thy wife too? that is some wrong indeed.—What's yours?—What's here! [*Reads*] 'Against the Duke of Suffolk, for enclosing the commons of Melford.'—How now, sir knave?

Sec. Pet. Alas! sir, I am but a poor petitioner of our whole township.

Peter. [*Presenting his petition*] Against my master, Thomas Horner, for saying, that the Duke of York was rightful heir to the crown.

Q. Mar. What say'st thou? did the Duke of York say he was rightful heir to the crown?

Pet. That my master was? No, forsooth: my master said, that he was; and that the king was an usurper.

Suf. Who is there?

Enter Servant

Take this fellow in, and send for his master with a pursuivant presently.—We'll hear more of your matter before the king. [*Exeunt Servant with Peter*

Q. Mar. And as for you, that love to be protected
Under the wings of our Protector's grace,
Begin your suits anew, and sue to him.
[*Tears the petition*
Away, base cullions!—Suffolk, let them go.

All. Come, let's be gone. [*Exeunt Petitioners*

Q. Mar. My Lord of Suffolk, say, is this the guise,
Is this the fashion in the court of England?
Is this the government of Britain's isle,
And this the royalty of Albion's king?
What! shall King Henry be a pupil still,
Under the surly Gloster's governance?
Am I a queen in title and in style,
And must be made a subject to a duke?
I tell thee, Poole, when in the city Tours
Thou rann'st a tilt in honour of my love,
And stol'st away the ladies' hearts of France,
I thought King Henry had resembled thee,
In courage, courtship, and proportion:
But all his mind is bent to holiness,
To number *Ave-Maries* on his beads;
His champions are the prophets and apostles;
His weapons, holy saws of sacred writ;
His study is his tilt-yard, and his loves
Are brazen images of canónised saints.
I would the college of the cardinals
Would choose him pope, and carry him to Rome,
And set the triple crown upon his head:
That were a state fit for his holiness.

Suf. Madam, be patient; as I was cause
Your highness came to England, so will I
In England work your grace's full content.

Q. Mar. Beside the haughty Protector, have we Beaufort,
The imperious churchman, Somerset, Buckingham,
And grumbling York: and not the least of these
But can do more in England than the king.

Suf. And he of these that can do most of all,
Cannot no more in England than the Nevils:
Salisbury and Warwick are no simple peers.

Q. Mar. Not all these lords do vex me half so much,
As that proud dame, the lord Protector's wife:
She sweeps it through the court with troops of ladies,
More like an empress than Duke Humphrey's wife.
Strangers in court do take her for the queen:

She bears a duke's revenues on her back,
And in her heart she scorns our poverty.
Shall I not live to be avenged on her?
Contemptuous base-born callat as she is,
She vaunted 'mongst her minion t' other day,
The very train of her worst wearing-gown
Was better worth than all my father's lands,
Till Suffolk gave two dukedoms for his daughter.
Suf. Madam, myself have limed a bush for her;
And placed a quire of such enticing birds,
That she will light to listen to the lays,
And never mount to trouble you again.
So, let her rest, and, madam, list to me;
For I am bold to counsel you in this.
Although we fancy not the cardinal,
Yet must we join with him, and with the lords,
Till we have brought Duke Humphrey in disgrace.
As for the Duke of York, this late complaint
Will make but little for his benefit:
So, one by one, we'll weed them all at last,
And your yourself shall steer the happy helm.

Enter KING HENRY, YORK, *and* SOMERSET; DUKE *and* DUCHESS OF GLOSTER, CARDINAL BEAUFORT, BUCKINGHAM, SALISBURY, *and* WARWICK

K. Hen. For my part, noble lords, I care not which;
Or Somerset, or York, all's one to me.
York. If York have ill demeaned himself in France,
Then let him be denayed the regentship.
Som. If Somerset be unworthy of the place,
Let York be regent; I will yield to him.
War. Whether your grace be worthy, yea or no,
Dispute not that: York is the worthier.
Car. Ambitious Warwick, let thy betters speak.
War. The cardinal's not my better in the field.
Buck. All in this presence are thy betters, Warwick.
War. Warwick may live to be the best of all.
Sal. Peace, son!—and show some reason, Buckingham,
Why Somerset should be preferred in this.
Q. Mar. Because the king, forsooth, will have it so.
Glo. Madam, the king is old enough himself
To give his censure. These are no women's matters.
Q. Mar. If he be old enough, what needs your grace
To be Protector of his excellence?
Glo. Madam, I am Protector of the realm,
And at his pleasure will resign my place.
Suf. Resign it then, and leave thine insolence.
Since thou wert king,—as who is king but thou?—
The commonwealth hath daily run to wrack;

The Dauphin hath prevailed beyond the seas;
And all the peers and nobles of the realm
Have been as bondmen to thy sovereignty.
Car. The commons hast thou racked; the clergy's bags
Are lank and lean with thy extortions.
Som. Thy sumptuous buildings, and thy wife's attire,
Have cost a mass of public treasury.
Buck. Thy cruelty in execution
Upon offenders hath exceeded law,
And left thee to the mercy of the law.
Q. Mar. Thy sale of offices, and towns in France,
If they were known, as the suspect is great,
Would make thee quickly hop without thy head.
[*Exit Gloster. The Queen drops her fan*
Give me my fan: what, minion! can you not?
[*Giving the Duchess a box on the ear*
I cry you mercy, madam: was it you?
Duch. Was 't I? yea, I it was, proud Frenchwoman:
Could I come near your beauty with my nails,
I 'd set my ten commandments in your face.
K. Hen. Sweet aunt, be quiet: 't was against her will.
Duch. Against her will! Good king, look to 't in time;
She'll hamper thee, and dandle thee like a baby:
Though in this place most master wear no breeches,
She shall not strike Dame Eleanor unrevenged. [*Exit*
Buck. Lord Cardinal, I will follow Eleanor,
And listen after Humphrey, how he proceeds:
She's tickled now; her fume needs no spurs,
She'll gallop far enough to her destruction. [*Exit*

Re-enter GLOSTER

Glo. Now, lords, my choler being overblown
With walking once about the quadrangle,
I come to talk of commonwealth affairs.
As for your spiteful false objections,
Prove them, and I lie open to the law;
And God in mercy so deal with my soul,
As I in duty love my king and country.
But, to the matter that we have in hand.—
I say, my sovereign, York is meetest man
To be your regent in the realm of France.
Suf. Before we make election, give me leave
To show some reason, of no little force,
That York is most unmeet of any man.
York. I'll tell thee, Suffolk, why I am unmeet:
First, for I cannot flatter thee in pride;
Next, if I be appointed for the place,
My lord of Somerset will keep me here,
Without discharge, money, or furniture,

Till France be won into the Dauphin's hands.
Last time I danced attendance on his will
Till Paris was besieged, famished, and lost.
War. That can I witness; and a fouler fact
Did never traitor in the land commit.
Suf. Peace, headstrong Warwick!
War. Image of pride, why should I hold my peace?

Enter Servants of SUFFOLK, *bringing in* HORNER *and* PETER

Suf. Because here is a man accused of treason:
Pray God, the Duke of York excuse himself!
York. Doth any one accuse York for a traitor?
K. Hen. What mean'st thou, Suffolk? Tell me, what are these?
Suf. Please it your majesty, this is the man
That doth accuse his master of high treason.
His words were these:—That Richard, Duke of York,
Was rightful heir unto the English crown,
And that your majesty was an usurper.
K. Hen. Say, man, were these thy words?
Hor. An 't shall please your majesty, I never said nor thought any such matter. God is my witness, I am falsely accused by the villain.
Pet. By these ten bones, my lords, he did speak them to me in the garret one night, as we were scouring my Lord of York's armour.
York. Base dunghill villain, and mechanical,
I'll have thy head for this thy traitor's speech.—
I do beseech your royal majesty,
Let him have all the rigour of the law.
Hor. Alas! my lord, hang me, if ever I spake the words. My accuser is my prentice; and when I did correct him for his fault the other day, he did vow upon his knees, he would be even with me. I have good witness of this: therefore, I beseech your majesty, do not cast away an honest man for a villain's accusation.
K. Hen. Uncle, what shall we say to this in law?
Glo. This doom, my lord, if I may judge:
Let Somerset be regent o'er the French,
Because in York this breeds suspicion;
And let these have a day appointed them
For single combat in convenient place;
For he hath witness of his servant's malice.
This is the law, and this Duke Humphrey's doom.
Som. I humbly thank your royal majesty.
Hor. And I accept the combat willingly.
Pet. Alas! my lord, I cannot fight: for God's sake, pity my case! the spite of man prevaileth against me. O Lord, have mercy upon me! I shall never be able to fight a blow. O Lord, my heart!

Glo. Sirrah, or you must fight or else be hanged.
K. Hen. Away with them to prison; and the day
Of combat shall be the last of the next month.—
Come, Somerset, we'll see thee sent away. [*Exeunt*

SCENE IV.—The Same. The DUKE OF GLOSTER'S Garden

Enter MARGERY JOURDAIN, JOHN HUME, JOHN SOUTHWELL, *and* BOLINGBROKE

Hume. Come, my masters; the duchess, I tell you, expects performance of your promises.

Boling. Master Hume, we are therefore provided. Will her ladyship behold and hear our exorcisms?

Hume. Ay; what else? fear you not her courage.

Boling. I have heard her reported to be a woman of an invincible spirit: but it shall be convenient, Master Hume, that you be by her aloft, while we be busy below; and so, I pray you, go in God's name, and leave us. [*Exit Hume*] Mother Jourdain, be you prostrate, and grovel on the earth:—John Southwell, read you, and let us to our work.

Enter DUCHESS *above*

Duch. Well said, my masters, and welcome all.
To this gear; the sooner, the better.
Boling. Patience, good lady; wizards know their times.
Deep night, dark night, the silent of the night,
The time of night when Troy was set on fire;
The time when screech-owls cry, and ban-dogs howl,
And spirits walk, and ghosts break up their graves,
That time best fits the work we have in hand.
Madam, sit you, and fear not: whom we raise,
We will make fast within a hallowed verge.

[*Here they perform the ceremonies belonging, and make the circle; Bolingbroke, or Southwell, reads,* Conjuro te, etc. *It thunders and lightens terribly; then the Spirit riseth*

Spir. Adsum.
M. Jourd. Asmath!
By the eternal God, whose name and power
Thou tremblest at, answer that I shall ask;
For till thou speak, thou shalt not pass from hence.
Spir. Ask what thou wilt.—That I had said and done!
Boling. First, of the king. What shall of him become?
Spir. The Duke yet lives that Henry shall depose;

But him outlive, and die a violent death.
[*As the Spirit speaks, Southwell writes the answer*
Boling. What fates await the Duke of Suffolk?
Spir. By Water shall he die, and take his end.
Boling. What shall befall the Duke of Somerset?
Spir. Let him shun castles:
Safer shall he be upon the sandy plains,
Than where castles mounted stand.
Have done, for more I hardly can endure.
Boling. Descend to darkness and the burning lake:
False fiend, avoid!
[*Thunder and lightning. Spirit descends*

Enter YORK *and* BUCKINGHAM, *hastily, with their Guards*

York. Lay hands upon these traitors, and their trash.
Beldam, I think, we watched you at an inch.
What! madam, are you there? the king and commonweal
Are deeply indebted for this piece of pains:
My lord Protector will, I doubt it not,
See you well guerdoned for these good deserts.
Duch. Not half so bad as thine to England's king,
Injurious duke, that threat'st where is no cause.
Buck. True, madam, none at all. What call you this?
[*Showing her the papers*
Away with them! let them be clapped up close,
And kept asunder.—You, madam, shall with us:
Stafford, take her to thee.—
[*Exit Duchess from above*
We'll see your trinkets here all forthcoming;
All, away! [*Exeunt Guards, with Southwell, Bolingbroke, etc.*
York. Lord Buckingham, methinks, you watched her well:
A pretty plot, well chosen to build upon!
Now, pray, my lord, let's see the devil's writ.
What have we here?
[*Reads*] 'The duke yet lives that Henry shall depose;
But him outlive, and die a violent death.'
Why, this is just,
Aio te, Æacida, Romanos vincere posse.
Well, to the rest:
'Tell me, what fate awaits the Duke of Suffolk?
By Water shall he die, and take his end.
What shall betide the Duke of Somerset?
Let him shun castles:
Safer shall he be upon the sandy plains,
Than where castles mounted stand.'
Come, come, my lords;
These oracles are hardly attained,
And hardly understood.

The king is now in progress towards Saint Albans;
With him the husband of this lovely lady:
Thither go these news, as fast as horse can carry them;
A sorry breakfast for my lord Protector.
Buck. Your grace shall give me leave, my Lord of York,
To be the post, in hope of his reward.
York. At your pleasure, my good lord.—
Who's within there, ho!

Enter a Servant

Invite my Lords of Salisbury and Warwick,
To sup with me to-morrow night.—Away! [*Exeunt*

ACT TWO

Scene I.—Saint Albans

Enter King Henry, Queen Margaret, Gloster, Cardinal, *and* Suffolk, *with Falconers halloing*

Q. Mar. Believe me, lords, for flying at the brook,
I saw not better sport these seven years' day:
Yet, by your leave, the wind was very high,
And, ten to one, old Joan had not gone out.
K. Hen. But what a point, my lord, your falcon made,
And what a pitch she flew above the rest!—
To see how God in all his creatures works!
Yes, man and birds are fain of climbing high.
Suf. No marvel, an it like your majesty,
My lord Protector's hawks do tower so well:
They know their master loves to be aloft,
And bears his thoughts above his falcon's pitch.
Glo. My lord, 't is but a base ignoble mind,
That mounts no higher than a bird can soar.
Car. I thought as much: he'd be above the clouds.
Glo. Ay, my lord cardinal: how think you by that?
Were it not good your grace could fly to heaven?
K. Hen. The treasury of everlasting joy.
Car. Thy heaven is on earth; thine eyes and thoughts
Beat on a crown, the treasure of thy heart:
Pernicious Protector, dangerous peer,
That smooth'st it so with king and commonweal.
Glo. What, cardinal, is your priesthood grown peremptory?
Tantæne animis cœlestibus iræ?
Churchmen so hot? good uncle, hide such malice;
With such holiness can you do it?

Suf. No malice, sir; no more than well becomes
So good a quarrel, and so bad a peer.
Glo. As who, my lord?
Suf. Why, as you, my lord;
An't like your lordly lord-protectorship.
Glo. Why, Suffolk, England knows thine insolence.
Q. Mar. And thy ambition, Gloster.
K. Hen. I pr'ythee, peace,
Good queen; and whet not on these furious peers,
For blessèd are the peacemakers on earth.
Car. Let me be blessèd for the peace I make
Against this proud Protector with my sword.
Glo. [*Aside to the Cardinal*] 'Faith, holy uncle, 'would 't were come to that!
Car. [*Aside*] Marry, when thou dar'st.
Glo. [*Aside*] Make up no factious numbers for the matter;
In thine own person answer thy abuse.
Car. [*Aside*] Ay, where thou dar'st not peep: an. if thou dar'st,
This evening on the east side of the grove.
K. Hen. How now, my lords!
Car. Believe me, cousin Gloster,
Had not your man put up the fowl so suddenly,
We had had more sport.—[*Aside to Gloster*] Come with thy two-hand sword.
Glo. True, uncle.
Car. [*Aside*] Are you advised?—the east side of the grove.
Glo. [*Aside*] Cardinal, I am with you.
K. Hen. Why, how now, uncle Gloster?
Glo. Talking of hawking; nothing else, my lord.—
[*Aside*] Now, by God's mother, priest, I'll shave your crown
For this, or all my fence shall fail.
Car. [*Aside*] *Medice, teipsum*—
Protector, see to 't well, protect yourself.
K. Hen. The winds grow high; so do your stomachs, lords.
How irksome is this music to my heart!
When such strings jar, what hope of harmony?
I pray, my lords, let me compound this strife.

Enter one, crying, 'A miracle!'

Glo. What means this noise?
Fellow, what miracle dost thou proclaim?
One. A miracle! a miracle!
Suf. Come to the king, and tell him what miracle.
One. Forsooth, a blind man, at Saint Alban's shrine,
Within this half hour hath received his sight;

A man that ne'er saw in his life before.
K. Hen. Now, God be praised, that to believing souls
Gives light in darkness, comfort in despair!

Enter the MAYOR OF SAINT ALBANS *and his Brethren; and* SIMPCOX, *borne between two persons in a chair; his* WIFE *and a great multitude following*

Car. Here comes the townsmen in procession,
To present your highness with the man.
K. Hen. Great is his comfort in this earthly vale,
Although by 's sight his sin be multiplied.
Glo. Stand by, my masters; bring him near the king:
His highness' pleasure is to talk with him.
K. Hen. Good fellow, tell us here the circumstance,
That we for thee may glorify the Lord.
What! hast thou been long blind, and now restored?
Simp. Born blind, an 't please your grace.
Wife. Ay, indeed, was he.
Suf. What woman is this?
Wife. His wife, an 't like your worship.
Glo. Hadst thou been his mother, thou couldst have better told.
K. Hen. Where wert thou born?
Simp. At Berwick in the north, an't like your grace.
K. Hen. Poor soul! God's goodness hath been great to thee:
Let never day nor night unhallowed pass,
But still remember what the Lord hath done.
Q. Mar. Tell me, good fellow, cam'st thou here by chance,
Or of devotion, to this holy shrine?
Simp. God knows, of pure devotion; being called
A hundred times, and oft'ner, in my sleep,
By good Saint Alban; who said,—'Simpcox, come;
Come, offer at my shrine, and I will help thee.'
Wife. Most true, forsooth; and many time and oft
Myself have heard a voice to call him so.
Car. What! art thou lame?
Simp. Ay, God Almighty help me!
Suf. How cam'st thou so?
Simp. A fall off a tree.
Wife. A plum-tree, master.
Glo. How long hast thou been blind?
Simp. O, born so, master.
Glo. What! and wouldst climb a tree?
Simp. But that in all my life, when I was a youth.
Wife. Too true; and bought his climbing very dear.
Glo. 'Mass, thou lov'dst plums well, that wouldst venture so.

Simp. Alas, master, my wife desired some damsons,
And made me climb with danger of my life.

Glo. A subtle knave; but yet it shall not serve.—
Let me see thine eyes:—wink now;—now open them.—
In my opinion yet thou seest not well.

Simp. Yes, master, clear as day; I thank God, and Saint Alban.

Glo. Say'st thou me so? What colour is this cloak of?

Simp. Red, master; red as blood.

Glo. Why, that's well said. What colour is my gown of?

Simp. Black, forsooth; coal-black as jet.

K. Hen. Why then, thou know'st what colour jet is of?

Suf. And yet, I think, jet did he never see.

Glo. But cloaks, and gowns, before this day a many.

Wife. Never, before this day, in all his life.

Glo. Tell me, sirrah, what's my name?

Simp. Alas! master, I know not.

Glo. What's his name?

Simp. I know not.

Glo. Nor his?

Simp. No, indeed, master.

Glo. What's thine own name?

Simp. Saunder Simpcox, an if it please you, master.

Glo. Then, Saunder, sit there, the lyingest knave in Christendom. If thou hadst been born blind, thou mightst as well have known all our names, as thus to name the several colours we do wear. Sight may distinguish of colours; but suddenly to nominate them all, it is impossible. —My lords, Saint Alban here hath done a miracle: and would ye not think his cunning to be great that could restore this cripple to his legs again?

Simp. O master, that you could!

Glo. My masters of Saint Albans, have you not beadles in your town, and things called whips?

May. Yes, my lord, if it please your grace.

Glo. Then send for one presently.

May. Sirrah, go fetch the beadle hither straight.
[*Exit an Attendant*

Glo. Now fetch me a stool hither by-and-by. [*A stool brought out.*] Now, sirrah, if you mean to save yourself from whipping, leap over this stool, and run away.

Simp. Alas! master, I am not able to stand alone:
You go about to torture me in vain.

Re-enter Attendant, and a Beadle with a whip

Glo. Well, sir, we must have you find your legs.
Sirrah beadle, whip him till he leap over that same stool.

Bead. I will, my lord.—Come on, sirrah; off with your doublet quickly.

Simp. Alas! master, what shall I do? I am not able to stand.

[*After the Beadle had hit him once, he leaps over the stool and runs away; and the People follow and cry*, 'A miracle!'

K. Hen. O God! seest thou this, and bearest so long?
Q. Mar. It made me laugh to see the villain run.
Glo. Follow the knave, and take this drab away.
Wife. Alas! sir, we did it for pure need.
Glo. Let them be whipped through every market-town, till they come to Berwick, from whence they came.

[*Exeunt Mayor, Beadle, Wife, etc.*

Car. Duke Humphrey has done a miracle to-day.
Suf. True; made the lame to leap, and fly away.
Glo. But you have done more miracles than I;
You made in a day, my lord, whole towns to fly.

Enter BUCKINGHAM

K. Hen. What tidings with our cousin Buckingham?
Buck. Such as my heart doth tremble to unfold.
A sort of naughty persons, lewdly bent,
Under the countenance and confederacy
Of Lady Eleanor, the Protector's wife,
The ringleader and head of all this rout,
Have practised dangerously against your state,
Dealing with witches, and with conjurers,
Whom we have apprehended in the fact;
Raising up wicked spirits from under-ground,
Demanding of King Henry's life and death,
And other of your highness' privy council,
As more at large your grace shall understand.
Car. And so, my lord Protector, by this means
Your Lady is forthcoming yet at London.
This news, I think, hath turned your weapon's edge;
'T is like, my lord, you will not keep your hour.
Glo. Ambitious churchman, leave to afflict my heart.
Sorrow and grief have vanquished all my powers;
And, vanquished as I am, I yield to thee,
Or to the meanest groom.
K. Hen. O God! what mischiefs work the wicked ones;
Heaping confusion on their own heads thereby.
Q. Mar. Gloster, see here the tainture of thy nest;
And look thyself be faultless, thou wert best.
Glo. Madam, for myself, to Heaven I do appeal,
How I have loved my king and commonweal;
And, for my wife, I know not how it stands.
Sorry I am to hear what I have heard;
Noble she is, but if she have forgot
Honour, and virtue, and conversed with such

As, like to pitch, defile nobility,
I banish her my bed and company,
And give her, as a prey, to law and shame,
That hath dishonoured Gloster's honest name.
K. Hen. Well, for this night, we will repose us here:
To-morrow toward London, back again,
To look into this business thoroughly,
And call these foul offenders to their answers;
And poise the cause in justice' equal scales,
Whose beam stands sure, whose rightful cause prevails.
[*Flourish. Exeunt*

SCENE II.—London. The DUKE OF YORK'S Garden

Enter YORK, SALISBURY, *and* WARWICK

York. Now, my good Lords of Salisbury and Warwick,
Our simple supper ended, give me leave,
In this close walk, to satisfy myself,
In craving your opinion of my title,
Which is infallible, to England's crown.
Sal. My lord, I long to hear it at full.
War. Sweet York, begin; and if thy claim be good,
The Nevils are thy subjects to command.
York. Then thus:—
Edward the Third, my lords, had seven sons:
The first, Edward the Black Prince, Prince of Wales;
The second, William of Hatfield; and the third,
Lionel, Duke of Clarence; next to whom
Was John of Gaunt, the Duke of Lancaster.
The fifth was Edmund Langley, Duke of York;
The sixth was Thomas of Woodstock, Duke of Gloster;
William of Windsor was the seventh and last.
Edward, the Black Prince, died before his father,
And left behind him Richard, his only son;
Who, after Edward the Third's death, reigned as king,
Till Henry Bolingbroke, Duke of Lancaster,
The eldest son and heir of John of Gaunt,
Crowned by the name of Henry the Fourth,
Seized on the realm; deposed the rightful king;
Sent his poor queen to France from whence she came,
And him to Pomfret; where, as all you know,
Harmless Richard was murdered traitorously.
War. Father, the duke hath told the truth;
Thus got the house of Lancaster the crown.
York. Which now they hold by force, and not by right;
For Richard, the first son's heir, being dead,
The issue of the next son should have reigned.
Sal. But William of Hatfield died without an heir.

York. The third son, Duke of Clarence, from whose line
I claim the crown, had issue—Philippe, a daughter,
Who married Edmund Mortimer, Earl of March;
Edmund had issue—Roger, Earl of March;
Roger had issue—Edmund, Anne, and Eleanor.
Sal. This Edmund, in the reign of Bolingbroke,
As I have read, laid claim unto the crown;
And, but for Owen Glendower, had been king,
Who kept him in captivity till he died.
But to the rest.
York. His eldest sister, Anne,
My mother, being heir unto the crown,
Married Richard, Earl of Cambridge, who was son
To Edmund Langley, Edward the Third's fifth son.
By her I claim the kingdom: she was heir
To Roger, Earl of March, who was the son
Of Edmund Mortimer, who married Philippe,
Sole daughter unto Lionel, Duke of Clarence:
So, if the issue of the elder son
Succeed before the younger, I am king.
War. What plain proceeding is more plain than this?
Henry doth claim the crown from John of Gaunt,
The fourth son; York claims it from the third.
Till Lionel's issue fails, his should not reign:
It fails not yet, but flourishes in thee,
And in thy sons, fair slips of such a stock.
Then, father Salisbury, kneel we together
And, in this private plot, be we the first,
That shall salute our rightful sovereign
With honour of his birthright to the crown.
Both. Long live our sovereign Richard, England's king!
York. We thank you, lords! But I am not your king
Till I be crowned, and that my sword be stained
With heart-blood of the house of Lancaster;
And that's not suddenly to be performed,
But with advice, and silent secrecy.
Do you, as I do, in these dangerous days
Wink at the Duke of Suffolk's insolence,
At Beaufort's pride, at Somerset's ambition,
At Buckingham, and all the crew of them,
Till they have snared the shepherd of the flock,
That virtuous prince, the good Duke of Humphrey.
'T is that they seek: and they, in seeking that,
Shall find their deaths, if York can prophesy.
Sal. My lord, break we off: we know your mind at full.
War. My heart assures me, that the Earl of Warwick
Shall one day make the Duke of York a king.
York. And, Nevil, this I do assure myself:
Richard shall live to make the Earl of Warwick
The greatest man in England but the king. [*Exeunt*

Scene III.—London. A Hall of Justice

Trumpets sounded. Enter King Henry, Queen Margaret, Gloster, York, Suffolk, *and* Salisbury; *the* Duchess of Gloster, Margery Jourdain, Southwell, Hume, *and* Bolingbroke, *under guard*

K. Hen. Stand forth, Dame Eleanor Cobham, Gloster's wife.
In sight of God, and us, your guilt is great:
Receive the sentence of the law, for sins
Such as by God's book are adjudged to death.—
[*To Jourdain, etc.*] You four, from hence to prison back again;
From thence, unto the place of execution:
The witch in Smithfield shall be burned to ashes,
And you three shall be strangled on the gallows.—
You, madam, for you are more nobly born,
Despoilèd of your honour in your life,
Shall, after three days' open penance done,
Live in your country here in banishment,
With Sir John Stanley in the Isle of Man.

Duch. Welcome is banishment; welcome were my death.

Glo. Eleanor, the law, thou seest, hath judgèd thee:
I cannot justify whom the law condemns.—
[*Exeunt the Duchess and other prisoners, guarded*
Mine eyes are full of tears, my heart of grief.
Ah, Humphrey! this dishonour in thine age
Will bring thy head with sorrow to the ground.—
I beseech your majesty, give me leave to go;
Sorrow would solace, and mine age would ease.

K. Hen. Stay, Humphrey, Duke of Gloster. Ere thou go,
Give up thy staff: Henry will to himself
Protector be; and God shall be my hope,
My stay, my guide, and lantern to my feet.
And go in peace, Humphrey; no less beloved,
Than when thou wert Protector to thy king.

Q. Mar. I see no reason why a king of years
Should be to be protected like a child.—
God and King Henry govern England's helm!—
Give up your staff, sir, and the king his realm.

Glo. My staff?—here, noble Henry, is my staff:
As willingly do I the same resign,
As e'er thy father Henry made it mine;
And even as willingly at thy feet I leave it,
As others would ambitiously receive it.
Farewell, good king: when I am dead and gone,

May honourable peace attend thy throne. [*Exit*

Q. Mar. Why, now is Henry king, and Margaret queen;
And Humphrey, Duke of Gloster, scarce himself,
That bears so shrewd a maim: two pulls at once,—
His lady banished, and a limb lopped off;
This staff of honour raught:—there let it stand.
Where it best fits to be, in Henry's hand.

Suf. Thus droops this lofty pine, and hangs his sprays;
Thus Eleanor's pride dies in her youngest days.

York. Lords, let him go.—Please it your majesty,
This is the day appointed for the combat;
And ready are the appellant and defendant,
The armourer and his man, to enter the lists,
So please your highness to behold the fight.

Q. Mar. Ay, good my lord; for purposely therefore
Left I the court, to see this quarrel tried.

K. Hen. O' God's name, see the lists and all things fit:
Here let them end it, and God defend the right!

York. I never saw a fellow worse bested,
Or more afraid to fight, than is the appellant,
The servant of this armourer, my lords.

Enter, on one side, HORNER, *and his Neighbours, drinking to him so much that he is drunk; and he enters bearing his staff with a sand-bag fastened to it; a drum before him: at the other side,* PETER, *with a drum and a similar staff; accompanied by 'Prentices drinking to him*

First Neigh. Here, neighbour Horner, I drink to you in a cup of sack. And fear not, neighbour, you shall do well enough.

Sec. Neigh. And here, neighbour, here's a cup of charneco.

Third Neigh. And here's a pot of good double beer, neighbour: drink, and fear not your man.

Hor. Let it come, i' faith, and I'll pledge you all; and a fig for Peter!

First Pren. Here, Peter, I drink to thee; and be not afraid.

Sec. Pren. Be merry, Peter, and fear not thy master: fight for credit of the prentices.

Peter. I thank you all: drink, and pray for me, I pray you; for, I think, I have taken my last draught in this world.—Here, Robin, an if I die, I give thee my apron; and, Will, thou shalt have my hammer:—and here, Tom, take all the money that I have.—O Lord, bless me! I pray God, for I am never able to deal with my master, he hath learnt so much fence already.

Sal. Come, leave your drinking, and fall to blows.—Sirrah, what's thy name?

Peter. Peter, forsooth.

Sal. Peter! what more?

Peter. Thump.

Sal. Thump! then see thou thump thy master well.

Hor. Masters, I am come hither, as it were, upon my man's instigation, to prove him a knave, and myself an honest man: and touching the Duke of York, I will take my death, I never meant him any ill, nor the queen: and therefore, Peter, have at thee with a downright blow.

York. Despatch: this knave's tongue begins to double.
Sound, trumpets, alarum to the combatants.

[*Alarum. They fight, and Peter strikes down his master*

Hor. Hold, Peter hold! I confess, I confess treason. [*Dies*

York. Take away his weapon.—Fellow, thank God, and the good wine in thy master's way.

Peter. O God! have I overcome mine enemies in this presence? O Peter! thou hast prevailed in right.

K. Hen. Go, take hence that traitor from our sight;
For, by his death, we do perceive his guilt.
And God in justice hath revealed to us
The truth and innocence of this poor fellow
Which he had thought to have murdered wrongfully.—
Come, fellow; follow us for thy reward. [*Exeunt*

SCENE IV.—London. A Street

Enter GLOSTER *and Servants, in mourning cloaks*

Glo. Thus, sometimes hath the brightest day a cloud;
And after summer evermore succeeds
Barren winter, with his wrathful nipping cold:
So cares and joys abound, as seasons fleet.—
Sirs, what's o'clock?

Serv. Ten, my lord.

Glo. Ten is the hour that was appointed me
To watch the coming of my punished duchess:
Uneath may she endure the flinty streets,
To tread them with her tender-feeling feet.
Sweet Nell, ill can thy noble mind abrook
The abject people, gazing on thy face,
With envious looks, laughing at thy shame,
That erst did follow thy proud chariot wheels,
When thou didst ride in triumph through the streets.
But soft! I think, she comes; and I'll prepare
My tear-stained eyes to see her miseries.

Enter the Duchess of Gloster, *in a white sheet with papers pinned upon her back, her feet bare, and a taper burning in her hand;* Sir John Stanley, *a Sheriff, and Officers*

Serv. So please your grace, we'll take her from the sheriff.
Glo. No, stir not, for your lives: let her pass by.
Duch. Come you, my lord, to see my open shame?
Now thou dost penance too. Look, how they gaze:
See, how the giddy multitude do point,
And nod their heads, and throw their eyes on thee.
Ah, Gloster, hide thee from their hateful looks,
And, in thy closet pent up, rue my shame,
And ban thine enemies, both mine and thine.
Glo. Be patient, gentle Nell: forget this grief.
Duch. Ah, Gloster, teach me to forget myself;
For, whilst I think I am thy married wife,
And thou a prince, Protector of this land,
Methinks, I should not thus be led along,
Mailed up in shame, with papers on my back,
And followed with a rabble, that rejoice
To see my tears, and hear my deep-fet groans.
The ruthless flint doth cut my tender feet;
And when I start, the envious people laugh,
And bid me be advisèd how I tread.
Ah, Humphrey, can I bear this shameful yoke?
Trow'st thou, that e'er I'll look upon the world,
Or count them happy that enjoy the sun?
No; dark shall be my light, and night my day:
To think upon my pomp shall be my hell.
Sometime I'll say, I am Duke Humphrey's wife,
And he a prince, and ruler of the land;
Yet so he ruled, and such a prince he was,
As he stood by, whilst I, his forlorn duchess,
Was made a wonder, and a pointing-stock,
To every idle rascal follower.
But be thou mild, and blush not at my shame;
Nor stir at nothing, till the axe of death
Hang over thee, as, sure, it shortly will:
For Suffolk,—he that can do all in all
With her that hateth thee, and hates us all,—
And York, and impious Beaufort, that false priest,
Have all limed bushes to betray thy wings;
And, fly thou how thou canst, they'll tangle thee.
But fear not thou, until thy foot be snared,
Nor never seek prevention of thy foes.
Glo. Ah, Nell! forbear: thou aimest all awry;
I must offend before I be attainted;
And had I twenty times so many foes,
And each of them had twenty times their power,

All these could not procure me any scath,
So long as I am loyal, true, and crimeless.
Wouldst have me rescue thee from this reproach?
Why, yet thy scandal were not wiped away,
But I in danger for the breach of law.
Thy greatest help is quiet, gentle Nell;
I pray thee, sort thy heart to patience:
These few days' wonder will be quickly worn.

Enter a Herald

Her. I summon your grace to his majesty's parliament, holden at Bury the first of this next month.

Glo. And my consent ne'er asked herein before?
This is close dealing.—Well, I will be there. [*Exit Herald*
My Nell, I take my leave:—and, master sheriff,
Let not her penance exceed the king's commission.

Sher. An 't please your grace, here my commission stays,
And Sir John Stanley is appointed now
To take her with him to the Isle of Man.

Glo. Must you, Sir John, protect my lady here?

Stan. So am I given in charge, may 't please your grace.

Glo. Entreat her not the worse, in that I pray
You use her well. The world may laugh again;
And I may live to do you kindness, if
You do it her: and so, Sir John, farewell.

Duch. What, gone, my lord, and bid me not farewell?

Glo. Witness my tears, I cannot stay to speak.
[*Exeunt Gloster and Servants*

Duch. Art thou gone too? All comfort go with thee,
For none abides with me: my joy is death,—
Death, at whose name I oft have been afeared,
Because I wished this world's eternity.—
Stanley, I pr'ythee, go, and take me hence;
I care not whither, for I beg no favour,
Only convey me where thou art commanded.

Stan. Why, madam, that is to the Isle of Man;
There to be used according to your state.

Duch. That's bad enough, for I am but reproach:
And shall I then be used reproachfully?

Stan. Like to a duchess, and Duke Humphrey's lady:
According to that state you shall be used.

Duch. Sheriff, farewell, and better than I fare,
Although thou hast been conduct of my shame.

Sher. It is my office; and, madam, pardon me.

Duch. Ay, ay, farewell: thy office is discharged.—
Come, Stanley, shall we go?

Stan. Madam, your penance done, throw off this sheet,
And go we to attire you for our journey.

Duch. My shame will not be shifted with my sheet:
No; it will hang upon my richest robes,
And show itself, attire me how I can.
Go, lead the way: I long to see my prison. [*Exeunt*

ACT THREE

Scene I.—The Abbey at Bury

A Sennet. Enter to the Parliament, King Henry, Queen Margaret, Cardinal Beaufort, Suffolk, York Buckingham, *and others*

K. Hen. I muse, my Lord of Gloster is not come:
'T is not his wont to be the hindmost man,
Whate'er occasion keeps him from us now.
Q. Mar. Can you not see? or will you not observe
The strangeness of his altered countenance?
With what a majesty he bears himself;
How insolent of late he is become,
How proud, how peremptory, and unlike himself?
We know the time, since he was mild and affable;
And if we did but glance a far-off look,
Immediately he was upon his knee,
That all the court admired him for submission:
But meet him now, and, be it in the morn,
When every one will give the time of day,
He knits his brow, and shows an angry eye,
And passeth by with stiff unbowéd knee,
Disdaining duty that to us belongs.
Small curs are not regarded when they grin,
But great men tremble when the lion roars;
And Humphrey is no little man in England.
First, note, that he is near you in descent,
And should you fall, he is the next will mount.
Me seemeth then, it is no policy,
Respecting what a rancorous mind he bears,
And his advantage following your decease,
That he should come about your royal person
Or be admitted to your highness' council.
By flattery hath he won the commons' hearts,
And, when he please to make commotion,
'T is to be feared they all will follow him.
Now 't is the spring, and weeds are shallow-rooted;
Suffer them now, and they'll o'ergrow the garden,
And choke the herbs for want of husbandry.
The reverent care I bear unto my lord

Made me collect these dangers in the duke.
If it be fond, call it a woman's fear;
Which fear if better reasons can supplant,
I will subscribe and say, I wronged the duke.
My Lord of Suffolk,—Buckingham and York,—
Reprove my allegation, if you can,
Or else conclude my words effectual.

Suf. Well hath your highness seen into this duke;
And had I first been put to speak my mind,
I think, I should have told your grace's tale.
The duchess, by his subornation,
Upon my life, began her devilish practices:
Or if he were not privy to those faults,
Yet, by reputing of his high descent,
(As next the king he was successive heir,)
And such high vaunts of his nobility,
Did instigate the bedlam brain-sick duchess
By wicked means to frame our sovereign's fall.
Smooth runs the water where the brook is deep,
And in his simple show he harbours treason.
The fox barks not when he would steal the lamb:
No, no, my sovereign; Gloster is a man
Unsounded yet, and full of deep deceit.

Car. Did he not, contrary to form of law,
Devise strange deaths for small offences done?

York. And did he not, in his protectorship,
Levy great sums of money through the realm
For soldiers' pay in France, and never sent it?
By means whereof the towns each day revolted.

Buck. Tut! these are petty faults to faults unknown,
Which time will bring to light in smooth Duke Humphrey.

K. Hen. My lords, at once: the care you have of us,
To mow down thorns that would annoy our foot,
Is worthy praise; but shall I speak my conscience?
Our kinsman Gloster is as innocent
From meaning treason to our royal person,
As is the sucking lamb, or harmless dove.
The duke is virtuous, mild, and too well given,
To dream on evil, or to work my downfall.

Q. Mar. Ah! what's more dangerous than this fond affiance?
Seems he a dove! his feathers are but borrowed,
For he's disposéd as the hateful raven.
Is he a lamb? his skin is surely lent him,
For he's inclined as is the ravenous wolf.
Who cannot steal a shape, that means deceit?
Take heed, my lord; the welfare of us all
Hangs on the cutting short that fraudful man.

Enter SOMERSET

Som. All health unto my gracious sovereign!
K. Hen. Welcome, Lord Somerset. What news from France?
Som. That all your interest in those territories
Is utterly bereft you: all is lost.
K. Hen. Cold news, Lord Somerset; but God's will be done.
York. [*Aside*] Cold news for me; for I had hope of France,
As firmly as I hope for fertile England.
Thus are my blossoms blasted in the bud,
And caterpillars eat my leaves away;
But I will remedy this gear ere long,
Or sell my title for a glorious grave.

Enter GLOSTER

Glo. All happiness unto my lord the king!
Pardon, my liege, that I have stayed so long.
Suf. Nay, Gloster, know, that thou art come too soon,
Unless thou wert more loyal than thou art.
I do arrest thee of high treason here.
Glo. Well, Suffolk's duke, thou shalt not see me blush,
Nor change my countenance for this arrest:
A heart unspotted is not easily daunted.
The purest spring is not so free from mud,
As I am clear from treason to my sovereign.
Who can accuse me? wherein am I guilty?
York. 'T is thought, my lord, that you took bribes of France,
And, being Protector, stayed the soldiers' pay;
By means whereof his highness hath lost France.
Glo. Is it but thought so? What are they that think it?
I never robbed the soldiers of their pay,
Nor ever had one penny bribe from France.
So help me God, as I have watched the night,
Ay, night by night, in studying good for England!
That doit that e'er I wrested from the king,
Or any groat I hoarded to my use,
Be brought against me at my trial-day!
No; many a pound of mine own proper store,
Because I would not tax the needy commons,
Have I disbursèd to the garrisons,
And never asked for restitution.
Car. It serves you well, my lord, to say so much.
Glo. I say no more than truth, so help me God!
York. In your protectorship you did devise.

Strange tortures for offenders, never heard of,
That England was defamed by tyranny.
Glo. Why, 't is well known, that whiles I was Protector,
Pity was all the fault that was in me;
For I should melt at an offender's tears,
And lowly words were ransom for their fault.
Unless it were a bloody murderer,
Or foul felonious thief that fleeced poor passengers,
I never gave them condign punishment.
Murder, indeed, that bloody sin, I tortured
Above the felon, or what trespass else.
Suf. My lord, these faults are easy, quickly answered;
But mightier crimes are laid unto your charge,
Whereof you cannot easily purge yourself.
I do arrest you in his highness' name;
And here commit you to my lord cardinal
To keep, until your further time of trial.
K. Hen. My Lord of Gloster, 't is my special hope,
That you will clear yourself from all suspect;
My conscience tells me you are innocent.
Glo. Ah, gracious lord, these days are dangerous.
Virtue is choked with foul ambition,
And charity chased hence by rancour's hand;
Foul subornation is predominant,
And equity exiled your highness' land.
I know, their complot is to have my life;
And if my death might make this island happy
And prove the period of their tyranny,
I would expend it with all willingness;
But mine is made the prologue to their play;
For thousands more, that yet suspect no peril,
Will not conclude their plotted tragedy.
Beaufort's red sparkling eyes blab his heart's malice,
And Suffolk's cloudy brow his stormy hate;
Sharp Buckingham unburdens with his tongue
The envious load that lies upon his heart;
And doggéd York, that reaches at the moon,
Whose overweening arm I have plucked back,
By false accuse doth level at my life:
And you, my sovereign lady, with the rest,
Causeless have laid disgraces on my head,
And with your best endeavour have stirred up
My liefest liege to be mine enemy.
Ay, all of you have laid your heads together;
Myself had notice of your cónventicles;
And all to make away my guiltless life.
I shall not want false witness to condemn me,
Nor store of treason to augment my guilt;
The ancient proverb will be well effected,—
A staff is quickly found to beat a dog.

Car. My liege, his railing is intolerable.
If those that care to keep your royal person
From treason's secret knife, and traitor's rage,
Be thus upbraided, chid, and rated at,
And the offender granted scope of speech,
'T will make them cool in zeal unto your grace.
Suf. Hath he not twit our sovereign lady here
With ignominious words, though clerkly couched,
As if she had suborned some to swear
False allegations to o'erthrow his state?
Q. Mar. But I can give the loser leave to chide.
Glo. Far truer spoke, than meant: I lose, indeed;
Beshrew the winners, for they played me false!
And well such losers may have leave to speak.
Buck. He'll wrest the sense, and hold us here all day.—
Lord cardinal, he is your prisoner.
Car. Sirs, take away the duke, and guard him sure.
Glo. Ah, thus King Henry throws away his crutch,
Before his legs be firm to bear his body:
Thus is the shepherd beaten from thy side,
And wolves are gnarling who shall gnaw thee first.
Ah, that my fear were false! ah, that it were!
For, good King Henry, thy decay I fear.
[*Exeunt Attendants with Gloster*
K. Hen. My lords, what to your wisdoms seemeth best,
Do, or undo, as if ourself were here.
Q. Mar. What! will your highness leave the parliament?
K. Hen. Ay, Margaret, my heart is drowned with grief,
Whose flood begins to flow within mine eyes;
My body round engirt with misery,
For what's more miserable than discontent?—
Ah, uncle Humphrey! in thy face I see
The map of honour, truth, and loyalty;
And yet, good Humphrey, is the hour to come,
That e'er I proved thee false, or feared thy faith.
What low'ring star now envies thy estate,
That these great lords, and Margaret our queen,
Do seek subversion of thy harmless life!
Thou never didst them wrong, nor no man wrong;
And as the butcher takes away the calf,
And binds the wretch, and beats it when it strays,
Bearing it to the bloody slaughter-house;
Even so, remorseless, have they borne him hence;
And as the dam runs lowing up and down,
Looking the way her harmless young one went,
And can do nought but wail her darling's loss;
Even so myself bewails good Gloster's case,
With sad unhelpful tears; and with dimmed eyes
Look after him, and cannot do him good;

So mighty are his vowèd enemies.
His fortunes I will weep; and, 'twixt each groan,
Say—'Who's a traitor? Gloster he is none.' [*Exit*

Q. Mar. Fair lords, cold snow melts with the sun's hot beams.
Henry my lord is cold in great affairs,
Too full of foolish pity; and Gloster's show
Beguiles him, as the mournful crocodile
With sorrow snares relenting passengers;
Or as the snake, rolled in a flowering bank,
With shining checkered slough, doth sting a child
That for the beauty thinks it excellent.
Believe me, lords, were none more wise than I
(And yet herein I judge mine own wit good),
This Gloster should be quickly rid the world,
To rid us from the fear we have of him.

Car. That he should die is worthy policy,
But yet we want a colour for his death.
'T is meet he be condemned by course of law.

Suf. But, in my mind that were no policy;
The king will labour still to save his life;
The commons haply rise to save his life;
And yet we have but trivial argument,
More than distrust, that shows him worthy death.

York. So that, by this, you would not have him die.

Suf. Ah, York, no man alive so fain as I.

York. 'T is York that hath more reason for his death.—
But, my lord cardinal, and you, my Lord of Suffolk,
Say, as you think, and speak it from your souls,
Were't not all one, an empty eagle were set
To guard the chicken from a hungry kite,
As place Duke Humphrey for the king's protector?

Q. Mar. So the poor chicken should be sure of death.

Suf. Madam, 't is true: and were't not madness then,
To make the fox surveyor of the fold?
Who, being accused a crafty murderer,
His guilt should be but idly posted over,
Because his purpose is not executed.
No; let him die, in that he is a fox,
By nature proved an enemy to the flock,
Before his chaps be stained with crimson blood,
As Humphrey proved by reasons to my liege.
And do not stand on quillets how to slay him:
Be it by gins, by snares, by subtilty,
Sleeping, or waking, 't is no matter how,
So he be dead; for that is good deceit
Which mates him first, that first intends deceit.

Q. Mar. Thrice-noble Suffolk, 't is resolutely spoke.

Suf. Not resolute, except so much were done,
For things are often spoke, and seldom meant;

But, that my heart accordeth with my tongue,—
Seeing the deed is meritorious,
And to preserve my sovereign from his foe,—
Say but the word, and I will be his priest.
Car. But I would have him dead, my Lord of Suffolk,
Ere you can take due orders for a priest.
Say, you consent, and censure well the deed,
And I'll provide his executioner;
I tender so the safety of my liege.
Suf. Here is my hand; the deed is worthy doing.
Q. Mar. And so say I.
York. And I; and now we three have spoken it,
It skills not greatly who impugns our doom.

Enter a Messenger

Mess. Great lords, from Ireland am I come amain,
To signify that rebels there are up,
And put the Englishmen unto the sword.
Send succours, lords, and stop the rage betime,
Before the wound do grow incurable;
For being green, there is great hope of help.
Car. A breach that craves a quick expedient stop!
What counsel give you in this weighty cause?
York. That Somerset be sent as regent thither.
'T is meet, that lucky ruler be employed;
Witness the fortune he hath had in France.
Som. If York, with all his far-fet policy,
Had been the regent there instead of me,
He never would have stayed in France so long.
York. No, not to lose it all, as thou hast done.
I rather would have lost my life betimes,
Than bring a burden of dishonour home,
By staying there so long, till all were lost.
Show me one scar charáctered on thy skin:
Men's flesh preserved so whole do seldom win.
Q. Mar. Nay then, this spark will prove a raging fire.
If wind and fuel be brought to feed it with.—
No more, good York;—sweet Somerset, be still:—
Thy fortune, York, hadst thou been regent there,
Might happily have proved far worse than his.
York. What, worse than nought? nay, then a shame take all!
Som. And, in the number, thee, that wishest shame.
Car. My Lord of York, try what your fortune is.
The uncivil kerns of Ireland are in arms,
And temper clay with blood of Englishmen:
To Ireland will you lead a band of men,
Collected choicely, from each county some,
And try your hap against the Irishmen?

York. I will, my lord, so please his majesty.
Suf. Why, our authority is his consent,
And what we do establish, he confirms:
Then, noble York, take thou this task in hand.
York. I am content. Provide me soldiers, lords,
Whiles I take order for mine own affairs.
Suf. A charge, Lord York, that I will see performed.
But now return we to the false Duke Humphrey.
Car. No more of him; for I will deal with him,
That henceforth he shall trouble us no more:
And so break off; the day is almost spent.
Lord Suffolk, you and I must talk of that event.
York. My Lord of Suffolk, within fourteen days,
At Bristol I expect my soldiers,
For there I'll ship them all for Ireland.
Suf. I'll see it truly done, my Lord of York.
[*Exeunt all but York*
York. Now, York, or never, steel thy fearful thoughts,
And change misdoubt to resolution:
Be that thou hop'st to be, or what thou art
Resign to death; it is not worth the enjoying.
Let pale-faced fear keep with the mean-born man,
And find no harbour in a royal heart.
Faster than spring-time showers comes thought on thought,
And not a thought but thinks on dignity.
My brain, more busy than the labouring spider,
Weaves tedious snares to trap mine enemies.
Well, nobles, well; 't is politicly done,
To send me packing with an host of men:
I fear me, you but warm the starvéd snake,
Who, cherished in your breasts, will sting your hearts.
'T was men I lacked, and you will give them me:
I take it kindly; yet, be well assured,
You put sharp weapons in a madman's hands.
Whiles I in Ireland nourish a mighty band,
I will stir up in England some black storm,
Shall blow ten thousand souls to heaven, or hell;
And this fell tempest shall not cease to rage,
Until the golden circuit on my head,
Like to the glorious sun's transparent beams,
Do calm the fury of this mad-bred flaw.
And, for a minister of my intent,
I have seduced a headstrong Kentishman,
John Cade of Ashford,
To make commotion, as full well he can,
Under the title of John Mortimer.
In Ireland have I seen this stubborn Cade
Oppose himself against a troop of kerns;
And fought so long, till that his thighs with darts
Were almost like a sharp-quilled porpentine:

And, in the end being rescued, I have seen
Him caper upright, like a wild Morisco,
Shaking the bloody darts, as he his bells.
Full often, like a shag-haired crafty kern,
Hath he conversèd with the enemy,
And undiscovered come to me again,
And given me notice of their villainies.
This devil here shall be my substitute;
For that John Mortimer, which now is dead,
In face, in gait, in speech, he doth resemble:
By this I shall perceive the commons' mind,
How they affect the house and claim of York.
Say, he be taken, racked, and torturèd,
I know, no pain they can inflict upon him
Will make him say, I moved him to those arms.
Say, that he thrive, as't is great like he will,
Why, then from Ireland come I with my strength,
And reap the harvest which that rascal sowed;
For, Humphrey being dead, as he shall be,
And Henry put apart, the next for me. [*Exit*

Scene II.—Bury. A Room in the Palace

Enter certain Murderers, hastily

First Mur. Run to my Lord of Suffolk; let him know,
We have despatched the duke, as he commanded.
Sec. Mur. O that it were to do!—What have we done?
Didst ever hear a man so penitent?
First Mur. Here comes my lord.

Enter Suffolk

Suf. Now, sirs, have you despatched this thing?
First Mur. Ay, my good lord, he's dead.
Suf. Why, that's well said. Go, get you to my house;
I will reward you for this venturous deed.
The king and all the peers are here at hand.
Have you laid fair the bed? Is all things well,
According as I gave directions?
First Mur. 'T is, my good lord.
Suf. Away, be gone. [*Exeunt Murderers*

Sound Trumpets. Enter King Henry, Queen Margaret, Cardinal Beaufort, Somerset, *Lords, and others*

K. Hen. Go, call our uncle to our presence straight:
Say, we intend to try his grace to-day,
If he be guilty, as't is publishèd.

Suf. I'll call him presently, my noble lord. [*Exit*
K. Hen. Lords, take your places; and, I pray you all,
Proceed no straiter 'gainst our uncle Gloster,
Than from true evidence, of good esteem,
He be approved in practice culpable.
Q. Mar. God forbid any malice should prevail,
That faultless may condemn a nobleman!
Pray God, he may acquit him of suspicion!
K. Hen. I thank thee, Meg; these words content me much.

Re-enter SUFFOLK

How now? why look'st thou pale? why tremblest thou?
Where is our uncle? what's the matter, Suffolk?
Suf. Dead in his bed, my lord; Gloster is dead.
Q. Mar. Marry, God forfend!
Car. God's secret judgment!—I did dream to-night,
The duke was dumb, and could not speak a word.
[*The King swoons*
Q. Mar. How fares my lord?—Help, lords! the king is dead.
Som. Rear up his body: wring him by the nose.
Q. Mar. Run, go, help, help!—O Henry, ope thine eyes!
Suf. He doth revive again.—Madam, be patient.
K. Hen. O heavenly God!
Q. Mar. How fares my gracious lord?
Suf. Comfort, my sovereign! gracious Henry, comfort!
K. Hen. What! doth my Lord of Suffolk comfort me?
Came he right now to sing a raven's note,
Whose dismal tune bereft my vital powers,
And thinks he that the chirping of a wren,
By crying comfort from a hollow breast,
Can chase away the first conceivéd sound?
Hide not thy poison with such sugared words;
Lay not thy hands on me; forbear, I say:
Their touch affrights me as a serpent's sting.
Thou baleful messenger, out of my sight!
Upon thy eye-balls murderous tyranny
Sits in grim majesty to fright the world.
Look not upon me, for thine eyes are wounding.
Yet do not go away:—come, basilisk,
And kill the innocent gazer with thy sight;
For in the shade of death I shall find joy,
In life but double death, now Gloster's dead.
Q. Mar. Why do you rate my Lord of Suffolk thus?
Although the duke was enemy to him,
Yet he, most Christian-like, laments his death:
And for myself, foe as he was to me,
Might liquid tears, or heart-offending groans

Or blood-consuming sighs, recall his life,
I would be blind with weeping, sick with groans,
Look pale as primrose with blood-drinking sighs,
And all to have the noble duke alive.
What know I how the world may deem of me?
For it is known, we were but hollow friends;
It may be judged, I made the duke away:
So shall my name with slander's tongue be wounded,
And princes' courts be filled with my reproach.
This get I by his death. Ah me, unhappy!
To be a queen, and crowned with infamy!

K. Hen. Ah, woe is me for Gloster, wretched man!

Q. Mar. Be woe for me, more wretched than he is.
What, dost thou turn away, and hide thy face?
I am no loathsome leper; look on me.
What, art thou, like the adder, waxen deaf?
Be poisonous too, and kill thy forlorn queen.
Is all thy comfort shut in Gloster's tomb?
Why, then Dame Margaret was ne'er thy joy:
Erect his statua, and worship it,
And make my image but an ale-house sign.
Was I for this nigh wracked upon the sea,
And twice by awkward wind from England's bank
Drove back again unto my native clime?
What boded this, but well-forewarning wind
Did seem to say,—Seek not a scorpion's nest,
Nor set no footing on this unkind shore?
What did I then, but cursed the gentle gusts,
And he that loosed them from their brazen caves;
And bid them blow towards England's blessed shore,
Or turn our stern upon a dreadful rock.
Yet Æolus would not be a murderer,
But let that hateful office unto thee:
The pretty-vaulting sea refused to drown me,
Knowing that thou wouldst have me drowned on shore
With tears as salt as sea through thy unkindness:
The splitting rocks cowered in the sinking sands
And would not dash me with their ragged sides,
Because thy flinty heart, more hard than they,
Might in thy palace perish Margaret.
As far as I could ken thy chalky cliffs,
When from the shore the tempest beat us back,
I stood upon the hatches in the storm;
And when the dusky sky began to rob
My earnest-gaping sight of thy land's view,
I took a costly jewel from my neck,—
A heart it was, bound in with diamonds,—
And threw it towards thy land. The sea received it,
And so I wished thy body might my heart:
And even with this I lost fair England's view,

And bid mine eyes be packing with my heart:
And called them blind and dusky spectacles,
For losing ken of Albion's wishèd coast.
How often have I tempted Suffolk's tongue
(The agent of thy foul inconstancy),
To sit and witch me, as Ascanius did,
When he to madding Dido would unfold
His father's acts, commenced in burning Troy!
Am I not witched like her? or thou not false like him?
Ah me! I can no more. Die, Margaret,
For Henry weeps that thou dost live so long.

Noise within. Enter WARWICK *and* SALISBURY. *The Commons press to the door*

War. It is reported, mighty sovereign,
That good Duke Humphrey traitorously is murdered
By Suffolk and the Cardinal Beaufort's means.
The commons, like an angry hive of bees,
That want their leader, scatter up and down,
And care not whom they sting in his revenge.
Myself have calmed their spleenful mutiny,
Until they hear the order of his death.

K. Hen. That he is dead, good Warwick, 't is too true;
But how he died, God knows, not Henry.
Enter his chamber, view his breathless corse,
And comment then upon his sudden death.

War. That I shall do, my liege.—Stay, Salisbury,
With the rude multitude, till I return.

[*Warwick goes into an inner room, and Salisbury retires*

K. Hen. O Thou that judgest all things, stay my thoughts!
My thoughts that labour to persuade my soul
Some violent hands were laid on Humphrey's life.
If my suspect be false, forgive me, God,
For judgment only doth belong to Thee.
Fain would I go to chafe his paly lips
With twenty thousand kisses, and to drain
Upon his face an ocean of salt tears,
To tell my love unto his dumb deaf trunk,
And with my finger, feel his hand unfeeling;
But all in vain are these mean obsequies,
And to survey his dead and earthy image,
What were it but to make my sorrow greater?

The doors of an inner chamber are thrown open, and GLOSTER *is discovered dead in his bed;* WARWICK *and others standing by it*

War. Come hither, gracious sovereign, view this body.

K. Hen. That is to see how deep my grave is made;
For with his soul fled all my worldly solace,
For seeing him, I see my life in death.
War. As surely as my soul intends to live
With that dread King, that took our state upon Him
To free us from His Father's wrathful curse,
I do believe that violent hands were laid
Upon the life of this thrice-faméd duke.
Suf. A dreadful oath, sworn with a solemn tongue!
What instance gives Lord Warwick for his vow?
War. See, how the blood is settled in his face.
Oft have I seen a timely-parted ghost,
Of ashy semblance, meagre, pale, and bloodless,
Being all descended to the labouring heart;
Who, in the conflict that it holds with death,
Attracts the same for aidance 'gainst the enemy;
Which with the heart there cools, and ne'er returneth
To blush and beautify the cheek again.
But see, his face is black, and full of blood;
His eye-balls further out than when he lived,
Staring full ghastly like a strangled man:
His hair upreared, his nostrils stretched with struggling;
His hands abroad displayed, as one that grasped
And tugged for life, and was by strength subdued.
Look, on the sheets, his hair, you see, is sticking;
His well-proportioned beard made rough and rugged
Like to the summer's corn by tempest lodged.
It cannot be but he was murdered here;
The least of all these signs were probable.
Suf. Why, Warwick, who should do the duke to death?
Myself and Beaufort had him in protection,
And we, I hope, sir, are no murderers.
War. But both of you were vowed Duke Humphrey's foes,
And you, forsooth, had the good duke to keep:
'T is like you would not feast him like a friend,
And't is well seen he found an enemy.
Q. Mar. Then you, belike, suspect these noblemen
As guilty of Duke Humphrey's timeless death.
War. Who finds the heifer dead, and bleeding fresh,
And sees fast by a butcher with an axe,
But will suspect 't was he that made the slaughter?
Who finds the partridge in the puttock's nest,
But may imagine how the bird was dead,
Although the kite soar with unbloodied beak?
Even so suspicious is this tragedy.
Q. Mar. Are you the butcher, Suffolk? where's your knife?
Is Beaufort termed a kite? where are his talons?
Suf. I wear no knife, to slaughter sleeping men;

But here's a vengeful sword, rusted with ease,
That shall be scourèd in his rancorous heart
That slanders me with murder's crimson badge.—
Say, if thou dar'st, proud Lord of Warwickshire,
That I am faulty in Duke Humphrey's death.
[*Exeunt Cardinal, Somerset, and others*

War. What dares not Warwick, if false Suffolk dare him?

Q. Mar. He dares not calm his contumelious spirit,
Nor cease to be an arrogant controller,
Though Suffolk dare him twenty thousand times.

War. Madam, be still, with reverence may I say;
For every word you speak in his behalf
Is slander to your royal dignity.

Suf. Blunt-witted lord, ignoble in demeanour,
If ever lady wronged her lord so much,
Thy mother took into her blameful bed
Some stern untutored churl, and noble stock
Was graft with crab-tree slip; whose fruit thou art,
And never of the Nevils' noble race.

War. But that the guilt of murder bucklers thee,
And I should rob the deathsman of his fee,
Quitting thee thereby of ten thousand shames,
And that my sovereign's presence makes me mild,
I would, false murderous coward, on thy knee
Make thee beg pardon for thy passèd speech,
And say, it was thy mother that thou meant'st;
That thou thyself was born in bastardy:
And, after all this fearful homage done,
Give thee thy hire, and send thy soul to hell,
Pernicious bloodsucker of sleeping men.

Suf. Thou shalt be waking while I shed thy blood,
If from this presence thou dar'st go with me.

War. Away even now, or I will drag thee hence.
Unworthy though thou art, I'll cope with thee,
And do some service to Duke Humphrey's ghost.
[*Exeunt Suffolk and Warwick*

K. Hen. What stronger breastplate than a heart untainted?
Thrice is he armed that hath his quarrel just;
And he but naked, though locked up in steel,
Whose conscience with injustice is corrupted.
[*A noise within*

Q. Mar. What noise is this?

Re-enter SUFFOLK *and* WARWICK, *with their weapons drawn*

K. Hen. Why, how now, lords? your wrathful weapons drawn

Here in our presence? dare you be so bold?—
Why, what tumultuous clamour have we here?
Suf. The traitorous Warwick, with the men of Bury,
Set all upon me, mighty sovereign.

Noise of a crowd within. Re-enter SALISBURY

Sal. [*Speaking to those within*] Sirs, stand apart; the king shall know your mind.—
Dread lord, the commons send you word by me,
Unless false Suffolk straight be done to death,
Or banishéd fair England's territories,
They will by violence tear him from your palace,
And torture him with grievous lingering death.
They say, by him the good Duke Humphrey died
They say, in him they fear your highness' death;
And mere instinct of love, and loyalty,
Free from a stubborn opposite intent,
As being thought to contradict your liking,
Makes them thus forward in his banishment.
They say, in care of your most royal person,
That, if your highness should intend to sleep,
And charge, that no man should disturb your rest,
In pain of your dislike, or pain of death,
Yet, notwithstanding such a strait edict,
Were there a serpent seen, with forkéd tongue,
That slily glided towards your majesty,
It were but necessary, you were waked;
Lest, being suffered in that harmful slumber,
The mortal worm might make the sleep eternal:
And therefore do they cry, though you forbid,
That they will guard you, whe'r you will or no,
From such fell serpents as false Suffolk is;
With whose envenoméd and fatal sting,
Your loving uncle, twenty times his worth,
They say, is shamefully bereft of life.
Commons. [*Within*] An answer from the king, my Lord of Salisbury!
Suf. 'T is like, the commons, rude unpolished hinds,
Could send such message to their sovereign!
But you, my lord, were glad to be employed,
To show how quaint an orator you are:
But all the honour Salisbury hath won,
Is, that he was the lord ambassador
Sent from a sort of tinkers to the king.
Commons. [*Within*] An answer from the king, or we will all break in!
K. Hen. Go, Salisbury, and tell them all from me,
I thank them for their tender loving care;
And had I not been cited so by them,

Yet did I purpose as they do entreat;
For sure, my thoughts do hourly prophesy
Mischance unto my state by Suffolk's means:
And therefore, by His Majesty I swear,
Whose far unworthy deputy I am,
He shall not breathe infection in this air
But three days longer, on the pain of death. [*Exit Salisbury*
Q. Mar. O Henry, led me plead for gentle Suffolk.
K. Hen. Ungentle queen, to call him gentle Suffolk.
No more, I say; if thou dost plead for him,
Thou wilt but add increase unto my wrath.
Had I but said, I would have kept my word;
But when I swear, it is irrevocable.—
If after three days' space thou here be'st found
On any ground that I am ruler of,
The world shall not be ransom for thy life.—
Come, Warwick, come, good Warwick, go with me;
I have great matters to impart to thee.
[*Exeunt all but Queen and Suffolk*
Q. Mar. Mischance and sorrow go along with you!
Heart's discontent, and sour affliction,
Be playfellows to keep you company!
There's two of you; the devil make a third,
And threefold vengeance tend upon your steps!
Suf. Cease, gentle queen, these execrations,
And let thy Suffolk take his heavy leave.
Q. Mar. Fie, coward woman, and soft-hearted wretch!
Hast thou not spirit to curse thine enemy?
Suf. A plague upon them! wherefore should I curse them!
Would curses kill, as doth the mandrake's groan,
I would invent as bitter-searching terms,
As curst, as harsh, and horrible to hear,
Delivered strongly through my fixéd teeth,
With full as many signs of deadly hate,
As lean-faced Envy in her loathsome cave.
My tongue should stumble in mine earnest words;
Mine eyes should sparkle like the beaten flint;
My hair be fixed on end, as one distract;
Ay, every joint should seem to curse and ban:
And even now my burdened heart would break;
Should I not curse them. Poison be their drink!
Gall, worse than gall, the daintiest that they taste!
Their sweetest shade a grove of cypress trees!
Their chiefest prospect murdering basilisks!
Their softest touch as smart as lizard's stings!
Their music frightful as the serpent's hiss,
And boding screech-owls make the concert full!
All the foul terrors in dark-seated hell—
Q. Mar. Enough, sweet Suffolk: though torment'st thyself;

And these dread curses, like the sun 'gainst glass,
Or like an overchargéd gun, recoil,
And turn the force of them upon thyself.

Suf. You bade me ban, and will you bid me leave?
Now, by the ground that I am banished from,
Well could I curse away a winter's night,
Though standing naked on a mountain top,
Where biting cold would never let grass grow,
And think it but a minute spent in sport.

Q. Mar. O! let me entreat thee, cease. Give me thy hand,
That I may dew it with my mournful tears;
Nor let the rain of heaven wet this place,
To wash away my woful monuments.
O! could this kiss be printed in thy hand,
That thou mightst think upon these by the seal,
Through whom a thousand sighs are breathed for thee.
So, get thee gone, that I may know my grief;
'T is but surmised whilst thou art standing by,
As one that surfeits, thinking on a want.
I will repeal thee, or, be well assured,
Adventure to be banishéd myself;
And banishéd I am, if but from thee.
Go, speak not to me; even now be gone.—
O, go not yet.—Even thus two friends condemned
Embrace, and kiss, and take ten thousand leaves,
Loather a hundred times to part than die.
Yet now farewell; and farewell life with thee!

Suf. Thus is poor Suffolk ten times banishéd,
Once by the king, and three times thrice by thee.
'T is not the land I care for, wert thou thence;
A wilderness is populous enough,
So Suffolk had thy heavenly company:
For where thou art, there is the world itself,
With every several pleasure in the world,
And where thou art not, desolation.
I can no more.—Live thou to joy thy life;
Myself no joy in nought, but that thou liv'st.

Enter VAUX

Q. Mar. Whither goes Vaux so fast? what news, pr'ythee?

Vaux. To signify unto his majesty,
That Cardinal Beaufort is at point of death;
For suddenly a grievous sickness took him,
That makes him gasp, and stare, and catch the air,
Blaspheming God, and cursing men on earth.
Sometimes he talks as if Duke Humphrey's ghost
Were by his side; sometime he calls the king,
And whispers to his pillow, as to him,

The secrets of his overchargéd soul:
And I am sent to tell his majesty,
That even now he cries aloud for him.

Q. Mar. Go, tell this heavy message to the king.
[*Exit Vaux*

Ah me! what is this world? what news are these?
But wherefore grieve I at an hour's poor loss,
Omitting Suffolk's exile, my soul's treasure?
Why only, Suffolk, mourn I not for thee,
And with the southern clouds content in tears?
Theirs for the earth's increase, mine for my sorrows.
Now, get thee hence: the king, thou know'st, is coming;
If thou be found by me, thou art but dead.

Suf. If I depart from thee, I cannot live;
And in thy sight to die, what were it else
But like a pleasant slumber in thy lap?
Here could I breathe my soul into the air,
As mild and gentle as the cradle-babe,
Dying with mother's dug between its lips;
Where, from thy sight, I should be raging mad,
And cry out for thee to close up mine eyes,
To have thee with thy lips to stop my mouth:
So shouldst thou either turn my flying soul,
Or I should breathe it so into thy body,
And then it lived in sweet Elysium.
To die by thee, were but to die in jest;
From thee to die, were torture more than death.
O, let me stay, befall what may befall.

Q. Mar. Away! though parting be a fretful corsive,
It is appliéd to a deathful wound.
To France, sweet Suffolk: let me hear from thee;
For wheresoe'er thou art in this world's globe,
I'll have an Iris that shall find thee out.

Suf. I go.

Q. Mar. And take my heart with thee.

Suf. A jewel, locked into the wofull'st cask
That ever did contain a thing of worth.
Even as a splitted bark, so sunder we:
This way fall I to death.

Q. Mar. This way for me.
[*Exeunt severally*

SCENE III.—London. CARDINAL BEAUFORT'S Bedchamber

Enter KING HENRY, SALISBURY, WARWICK, *and others.*
The CARDINAL *in bed; Attendants with him*

K. Hen. How fares my lord? speak, Beaufort, to thy sovereign.

Car. If thou be'st death, I'll give thee England's treasure,
Enough to purchase such another island,
So thou wilt let me live, and feel no pain.
K. Hen. Ah, what a sign it is of evil life,
Where death's approach is seen so terrible!
War. Beaufort, it is thy sovereign speaks to thee.
Car. Bring me unto my trial when you will.
Died he not in his bed? where should he die?
Can I make men live, whe'r they will or no?—
O! torture me no more, I will confess.—
Alive again? then show me where he is:
I'll give a thousand pound to look upon him.—
He hath no eyes, the dust hath blinded them.—
Comb down his hair: look! look! it stands upright,
Like lime-twigs set to catch my wingéd soul.—
Give me some drink; and bid the apothecary
Bring the strong poison that I bought of him.
K. Hen. O Thou eternal Mover of the heavens,
Look with a gentle eye upon this wretch!
O, beat away the busy meddling fiend,
That lay strong siege unto this wretch's soul,
And from his bosom purge this black despair.
War. See, how the pangs of death do make him grin.
Sal. Disturb him not, let him pass peaceably.
K. Hen. Peace to his soul, if God's good pleasure be.
Lord cardinal, if thou think'st on heaven's bliss,
Hold up thy hand, make signal of thy hope.—
He dies, and makes no sign. O God, forgive him!
War. So bad a death argues a monstrous life.
K. Hen. Forbear to judge, for we are sinners all.—
Close up his eyes, and draw the curtain close,
And let us all to meditation. [*Exeunt*

ACT FOUR

Scene I.—Kent. The Sea-shore near Dover

Firing heard at sea. Then enter from a boat, a Captain, a Master, a Master's-Mate, Walter Whitmore, *and others; with them* Suffolk, *disguised, and other Gentlemen, prisoners*

Cap. The gaudy, blabbing, and remorseful day
Is crept into the bosom of the sea,
And now loud-howling wolves arouse the jades
That drag the tragic melancholy night;
Who with their drowsy, slow, and flagging wings

Clip dead men's graves, and from their misty jaws
Breathe foul contagious darkness in the air.
Therefore, bring forth the soldiers of our prize;
For, whilst our pinnace anchors in the Downs,
Here shall they make their ransom on the sand,
Or with their blood stain this discoloured shore.—
Master, this prisoner freely give I thee;—
And thou that art his mate, make boot of this;—
The other [*pointing to Suffolk*], Walter Whitmore, is thy share.

First Gent. What is my ransom, master? let me know.

Mast. A thousand crowns, or else lay down your head.

Mate. And so much shall you give, or off goes yours.

Cap. What! think you much to pay two thousand crowns,
And bear the name and port of gentlemen?
Cut both the villains' throats!—for die you shall:
The lives of those which we have lost in fight,
Be counterpoised with such a petty sum!

First Gen. I'll give it, sir; and therefore spare my life.

Sec. Gent. And so will I, and write home for it straight.

Whit. I lost mine eye in laying the prize aboard.
[*To Suffolk*] And, therefore, to revenge it shalt thou die;
And so should these, if I might have my will.

Cap. Be not so rash: take ransom; let him live.

Suf. Look on my George: I am a gentleman.
Rate me at what thou wilt, thou shalt be paid.

Whit. And so am I; my name is Walter Whitmore.
How now? why start'st thou? what! doth death affright?

Suf. Thy name affrights me, in whose sound is death.
A cunning man did calculate my birth,
And told me that by *Water* I should die:
Yet let not this make thee be bloody-minded;
Thy name is *Gaultier*, being rightly sounded.

Whit. *Gaultier*, or *Walter*, which it is, I care not;
Never yet did base dishonour blur our name,
But with our sword we wiped away the blot:
Therefore, when merchant-like I sell revenge,
Broke be my sword, my arms torn and defaced,
And I proclaimed a coward through the world!
[*Lays hold on Suffolk*

Suf. Stay, Whitmore; for thy prisoner is a prince,
The Duke of Suffolk, William de la Poole.

Whit. The Duke of Suflolk muffied up in rags!

Suf. Ay, but these rags are no part of the duke:
Jove sometime went disguised, and why not I?

Cap. But Jove was never slain, as thou shalt be.

Suf. Obscure and lowly swain, King Henry's blood,
The honourable blood of Lancaster,
Must not be shed by such a jaded groom.

Hast thou not kissed thy hand, and held my stirrup?
Bare-headed plodded by my foot-cloth mule.
And thought thee happy when I shook my head?
How often hast thou waited at my cup,
Fed from my trencher, kneeled down at the board,
When I have feasted with Queen Margaret?
Remember it, and let it make thee crestfall'n;
Ay, and allay this thy abortive pride.
How in our voiding lobby hast thou stood,
And duly waited for my coming forth?
This hand of mine hath writ in thy behalf,
And therefore shall it charm thy riotous tongue.

Whit. Speak, captain, shall I stab the forlorn swain?

Cap. First let my words stab him, as he hath me.

Suf. Base slave, thy words are blunt, and so art thou.

Cap. Convey him hence, and on our long-boat's side
Strike off his head.

Suf. Thou dar'st not for thy own.

Cap. Yes, Poole.

Suf. Poole?

Cap. Poole? Sir Poole? lord?
Ay, kennel, puddle, sink; whose filth and dirt
Troubles the silver spring where England drinks.
Now will I dam up this thy yawning mouth,
For swallowing the treasure of the realm:
Thy lips, that kissed the queen, shall sweep the ground;
And thou, that smil'dst at good Duke Humphrey's death,
Against the senseless winds shalt grin in vain,
Who in contempt shall hiss at thee again:
And wedded be thou to the hags of hell,
For daring to affy a mighty lord
Unto the daughter of a worthless king,
Having neither subject, wealth, nor diadem.
By devilish policy art thou grown great,
And, like ambitious Sylla, overgorged
With gobbets of thy mother's bleeding heart.
By thee Anjou and Maine were sold to France;
The false revolting Normans thorough thee
Disdain to call us lord; and Picardy
Hath slain their governors, surprised our forts,
And sent the ragged soldiers wounded home.
The princely Warwick and the Nevils all,
Whose dreadful swords were never drawn in vain,
As hating thee, are rising up in arms:
And now the house of York—thrust from the crown,
By shameful murder of a guiltless king,
And lofty proud encroaching tyranny—
Burns with revenging fire; whose hopeful colours
Advance our half-faced sun, striving to shine,
Under the which is writ—*Invitis nubibus.*

The commons, here in Kent, are up in arms;
And, to conclude, reproach and beggary
Is crept into the palace of our king,
And all by thee.—Away!—convey him hence.

Suf. O, that I were a god, to shoot forth thunder
Upon these paltry, servile, abject drudges!
Small things make base men proud: this villain here,
Being captain of a pinnace, threatens more
Than Bargulus the strong Illyrian pirate.
Drones suck not eagles' blood, but rob beehives.
It is impossible, that I should die
By such a lowly vassal as thyself.
Thy words move rage, and not remorse, in me:
I go of message from the queen to France;
I charge thee, waft me safely cross the Channel.

Cap. Walter!—

Whit. Come, Suffolk; I must waft thee to thy death.

Suf. *Gelidus timor occupat artus*:—it is thee I fear.

Whit. Thou shalt have cause to fear, before I leave thee.
What! are ye daunted now? now will ye stoop?

First Gent. My gracious lord, entreat him, speak him fair.

Suf. Suffolk's imperial tongue is stern and rough,
Used to command, untaught to plead for favour.
Far be it we should honour such as these
With humble suit: no, rather let my head
Stoop to the block than these knees bow to any,
Save to the God of heaven, and to my king:
And sooner dance upon a bloody pole,
Than stand uncovered to the vulgar groom.
True nobility is exempt from fear:
More can I bear than you dare execute.

Cap. Hale him away, and let him talk no more.

Suf. Come, soldiers, show what cruelty ye can,
That this my death may never be forgot.—
Great men oft die by vile Bezonians.
A Roman sworder and banditto slave
Murdered sweet Tully; Brutus' bastard hand
Stabbed Julius Cæsar; savage islanders
Pompey the Great; and Suffolk dies by pirates.
[*Exit Suffolk, with Whitmore and others*

Cap. And as for these whose ransom we have set,
It is our pleasure one of them depart:
Therefore, come you with us, and let him go.
[*Exeunt all but the First Gentleman*

Re-enter WHITMORE, *with* SUFFOLK'S *body*

Whit. There let his head and lifeless body lie,
Until the queen, his mistress, bury it. [*Exit*

First Gen. O barbarous and bloody spectacle!
His body will I bear unto the king:
If he revenge it not, yet will his friends;
So will the queen, that living held him dear.
[*Exit, with the body*

SCENE II.—Blackheath

Enter GEORGE BEVIS *and* JOHN HOLLAND

Geo. Come, and get thee a sword, though made of a lath: they have been up these two days.

John. They have the more need to sleep now then.

Geo. I tell thee, Jack Cade the clothier means to dress the commonwealth, and turn it, and set a new nap upon it.

John. So he had need, for't is threadbare. Well, I say, it was never merry world in England, since gentlemen came up.

Geo. O miserable age! Virtue is not regarded in handicraftsmen.

John. The nobility think scorn to go in leather aprons.

Geo. Nay, more; the king's council are no good workmen.

John. True; and yet it is said, Labour in thy vocation: which is as much to say as,—let the magistrates be labouring men: and therefore should we be magistrates.

Geo. Thou hast hit it; for there's no better sign of a brave mind than a hard hand.

John. I see them! I see them! There's Best's son, the tanner of Wingham,—

Geo. He shall have the skins of our enemies to make dog's-leather of.

John. And Dick the butcher,—

Geo. Then is sin struck down like an ox, and iniquity's throat cut like a calf.

John. And Smith the weaver,—

Geo. *Argo,* their thread of life is spun.

John. Come, come; let's fall in with them.

Drum. *Enter* CADE, DICK *the Butcher,* SMITH *the Weaver, and others in great number*

Cade. We John Cade, so termed of our supposed father,—

Dick. [*Aside*] Or rather, of stealing a cade of herrings.

Cade. For our enemies shall fall before us, inspired with the spirit of putting down kings and princes,—Command silence.

Dick. Silence!

Cade. My father was a Mortimer,—

Dick. [*Aside*] He was an honest man, and a good bricklayer.

Cade. My mother a Plantagenet,—

Dick [*Aside*] I knew her well; she was a midwife,

Cade. My wife descended of the Lacies,—

Dick. [*Aside*] She was, indeed, a pedlar's daughter, and sold many laces.

Smith. [*Aside*] But, now of late, not able to travel with her furred pack, she washes bucks here at home.

Cade. Therefore am I of an honourable house.

Dick. [*Aside*] Ay, by my faith, the field is honourable, and there was he born, under a hedge; for his father had never a house, but the cage.

Cade. Valiant I am.

Smith. [*Aside*] 'A must needs, for beggary is valiant.

Cade. I am able to endure much.

Dick. [*Aside*] No question of that, for I have seen him whipped three market-days together.

Cade. I fear neither sword nor fire.

Smith. [*Aside*] He need not fear the sword, for his coat is of proof.

Dick. [*Aside*] But, methinks, he should stand in fear of fire, being burnt i' the hand for stealing of sheep.

Cade. Be brave then; for your captain is brave, and vows reformation. There shall be in England seven halfpenny loaves sold for a penny; the three-hooped pot shall have ten hoops; and I will make it felony to drink small beer. All the realm shall be in common, and in Cheapside shall my palfrey go to grass. And, when I am king (as king I will be),—

All. God save your majesty!

Cade. I thank you, good people:—there shall be no money; all shall eat and drink on my score; and I will apparel them all in one livery, that they may agree like brothers, and worship me their lord.

Dick. The first thing we do, let's kill all the lawyers.

Cade. Nay, that I mean to do. Is not this a lamentable thing, that of the skin of an innocent lamb should be made parchment? that parchment, being scribbled o'er, should undo a man? Some say, the bee stings; but I say, 't is the bee's wax, for I did but seal once to a thing, and I was never mine own man since. How now, who's there?

Enter some, bringing in the Clerk of Chatham

Smith. The clerk of Chatham: he can write and read, and cast accompt.

Cade. O monstrous!

Smith. We took him setting of boys' copies.

Cade. Here's a villain!

Smith. H' as a book in his pocket, with red letters in't.

Cade. Nay, then he is a conjurer.

Dick. Nay, he can make obligations, and write court-hand.

Cade. I am sorry for't: the man is a proper man, of mine honour; unless I find him guilty, he shall not die.—Come hither, sirrah, I must examine thee. What is thy name?

Clerk. Emmanuel.

Dick. They use to write it on the top of letters.—'T will go hard with you.

Cade. Let me alone.—Dost thou use to write thy name, or hast thou a mark to thyself, like an honest plain-dealing man?

Clerk. Sir, I thank God, I have been so well brought up, that I can write my name.

All. He hath confessed: away with him! he's a villain and a traitor.

Cade. Away with him, I say: hang him with his pen and ink-horn about his neck. [*Exeunt some with the Clerk*

Enter MICHAEL

Mich. Where's our general?

Cade. Here I am, thou particular fellow.

Mich. Fly, fly, fly! Sir Humphrey Stafford and his brother are hard by, with the king's forces.

Cade. Stand, villain, stand, or I'll fell thee down. He shall be encountered with a man as good as himself: he is but a knight, is 'a?

Mich. No.

Cade. To equal him, I will make myself a knight presently. [*Kneels*]—Rise up Sir John Mortimer. Now have at him.

Enter SIR HUMPHREY STAFFORD, *and* WILLIAM *his Brother, with drum and Forces*

Staf. Rebellious hinds, the filth and scum of Kent,
Marked for the gallows, lay your weapons down;
Home to your cottages, forsake this groom,
The king is merciful, if you revolt.

W. Staf. But angry, wrathful, and inclined to blood,
If you go forward: therefore yield, or die.

Cade. As for these silken-coated slaves, I pass not:
It is to you, good people, that I speak,
O'er whom in time to come I hope to reign;
For I am rightful heir unto the crown.

Staf. Villain! thy father was a plasterer;

And thou thyself a shearman, art thou not?

Cade. And Adam was a gardener.

W. Staf. And what of that?

Cade. Marry, this:—Edmund Mortimer, Earl of March,
Married the Duke of Clarence' daughter, did he not?

Staf. Ay, sir.

Cade. By her he had two children at one birth.

W. Staf. That's false.

Cade. Ay, there's the question; but I say, 't is true.
The elder of them, being put to nurse,
Was by a beggar-woman stol'n away;
And, ignorant of his birth and parentage,
Became a bricklayer when he came to age.
His son am I: deny it, if you can.

Dick. Nay, 't is too true; therefore, he shall be king.

Smith. Sir, he made a chimney in my father's house, and the bricks are alive at this day to testify it: therefore, deny it not.

Staf. And will you credit this base drudge's words,
That speaks he knows not what?

All. Ay, marry, will we; therefore get ye gone.

W. Staf. Jack Cade, the Duke of York hath taught you this.

Cade. [*Aside*] He lies, for I invented it myself.—Go to, sirrah: tell the king from me, that for his father's sake, Henry the Fifth, in whose time boys went to span-counter for French crowns, I am content he shall reign; but I'll be protector over him.

Dick. And, furthermore, we'll have the Lord Say's head, for selling the dukedom of Maine.

Cade. And good reason; for thereby is England mained, and fain to go with a staff, but that my puissance holds it up. Fellow kings, I tell you that that Lord Say hath gelded the commonwealth, and made it an eunuch; and more than that, he can speak French, and therefore he is a traitor.

Staf. O gross and miserable ignorance!

Cade. Nay, answer, if you can: the Frenchmen are our enemies; go to then, I ask but this: can he that speaks with the tongue of an enemy be a good counsellor, or no?

All. No, no; and therefore we'll have his head.

W. Staf. Well, seeing gentle words will not prevail,
Assail them with the army of the king.

Staf. Herald, away; and, throughout every town,
Proclaim them traitors that are up with Cade;
That those which fly before the battle ends,
May, even in their wives' and children's sight,
Be hanged up for example at their doors.—

And you that be the king's friends, follow me.
[*Exeunt the two Staffords and forces*

Cade. And you that love the commons, follow me.—
Now show yourselves men: 't is for liberty.
We will not leave one lord, one gentleman:
Spare none but such as go in clouted shoon,
For they are thrifty honest men, and such
As would (but that they dare not) take our parts.

Dick. They are all in order, and march toward us.

Cade. But then are we in order, when we are most out of order. Come: march! forward! [*Exeunt*

Scene III.—Another Part of Blackheath

Alarums. The two parties enter, and fight, and both the Staffords *are slain*

Cade. Where's Dick, the butcher of Ashford?

Dick. Here, sir.

Cade. They fell before thee like sheep and oxen, and thou behavedst thyself as if thou hadst been in thine own slaughter-house: therefore thus will I reward thee,—the Lent shall be as long again as it is; and thou shalt have a license to kill for a hundred lacking one.

Dick. I desire no more.

Cade. And, to speak truth, thou deservest no less. This monument of the victory will I bear; and the bodies shall be dragged at my horse' heels, till I do come to London, where we will have the mayor's sword borne before us.

Dick. If we mean to thrive and do good, break open the gaols, and let out the prisoners.

Cade. Fear not that, I warrant thee. Come; let's march towards London. [*Exeunt*

Scene IV.—London. A Room in the Palace

Enter King Henry, *reading a supplication; the* Duke of Buckingham, *and* Lord Say, *with him : at a distance,* Queen Margaret, *mourning over Suffolk's head*

Q. Mar. Oft have I heard that grief softens the mind,
And makes it fearful and degenerate;
Think therefore on revenge, and cease to weep.
But who can cease to weep, and look on this?
Here may his head lie on my throbbing breast;
But where's the body that I should embrace?

Buck. What answer makes your grace to the rebels' supplication?

K. Hen. I'll send some holy bishop to entreat;
For God forbid, so many simple souls
Should perish by the sword! And I myself,
Rather than bloody war shall cut them short,
Will parley with Jack Cade, their general.—
But stay, I'll read it over once again.
Q. Mar. Ah, barbarous villains! hath this lovely face
Ruled like a wandering planet over me,
And could it not enforce them to relent,
That were unworthy to behold the same?
K. Hen. Lord Say, Jack Cade hath sworn to have thy head.
Say. Ay, but I hope, your highness shall have his.
K. Hen. How now, madam?
Still lamenting, and mourning for Suffolk's death?
I fear me, love, if that I had been dead,
Thou wouldst not have mourned so much for me.
Q. Mar. No, my love; I should not mourn, but die for thee.

Enter a Messenger

K. Hen. How now! what news? why com'st thou in such haste?
Mess. The rebels are in Southwark. Fly, my lord!
Jack Cade proclaims himself Lord Mortimer,
Descended from the Duke of Clarence' house,
And calls your grace usurper openly,
And vows to crown himself in Westminster.
His army is a ragged multitude
Of hinds and peasants, rude and merciless.
Sir Humphrey Stafford and his brother's death
Hath given them heart and courage to proceed.
All scholars, lawyers, courtiers, gentlemen,
They call false caterpillars, and intent their death.
K. Hen. O graceless men! they know not what they do.
Buck. My gracious lord, retire to Killingworth,
Until a power be raised to put them down.
Q. Mar. Ah! were the Duke of Suffolk now alive,
These Kentish rebels would be soon appeased.
K. Hen. Lord Say, the traitors hate thee,
Therefore away with us to Killingworth.
Say. So might your grace's person be in danger.
The sight of me is odious in their eyes;
And therefore in this city will I stay,
And live alone as secret as I may.

Enter another Messenger

Sec. Mes. Jack Cade hath gotten London Bridge;
The citizens fly and forsake their houses;

The rascal people, thirsting after prey,
Join with the traitor; and they jointly swear,
To spoil the city, and your royal court.
Buck. Then linger not, my lord: away, take horse.
K. Hen. Come, Margaret: God, our hope, will succour us.
Q. Mar. My hope is gone, now Suffolk is deceased.
K. Hen. [*To Lord Say*] Farewell, my lord: trust not the Kentish rebels.
Buck. Trust nobody, for fear you be betrayed.
Say. The trust I have is in mine innocence,
And therefore am I bold and resolute. [*Exeunt*

Scene V.—The Same. The Tower

Enter Lord Scales, *and others, walking on the walls. Then enter certain Citizens, below*

Scales. How now! is Jack Cade slain?

First Cit. No, my lord, nor likely to be slain; for they have won the bridge, killing all those that withstand them. The lord mayor craves aid of your honour from the Tower, to defend the city from the rebels.

Scales. Such aid as I can spare, you shall command;
But I am troubled here with them myself:
The rebels have essayed to win the Tower.
But get you to Smithfield, and gather head,
And thither I will send you Matthew Gough.
Fight for your king, your country, and your lives;
And so farewell, for I must hence again. [*Exeunt*

Scene VI.—The Same. Cannon Street

Enter Jack Cade *and his Followers. He strikes his staff on London Stone*

Cade. Now is Mortimer lord of this city. And here, sitting upon London Stone, I charge and command, that, of the city's cost, the pissing-conduit run nothing but claret wine this first year of our reign. And now, henceforward, it shall be treason for any that calls me other than Lord Mortimer.

Enter a Soldier, running

Sold. Jack Cade! Jack Cade!
Cade. Knock him down there. [*They kill him*

Smith. If this fellow be wise, he'll never call you Jack Cade more: I think, he hath a very fair warning.

Dick. My lord, there's an army gathered together in Smithfield.

Cade. Come then, let's go fight with them. But first, go and set London Bridge on fire, and, if you can, burn down the Tower too. Come, let's away. [*Exeunt*

SCENE VII.—The Same. Smithfield

Alarum. Enter, on one side, CADE *and his company; on the other, the Citizens, and the King's Forces, headed by* MATTHEW GOUGH. *They fight; the Citizens are routed, and* MATTHEW GOUGH *is slain*

Cade. So, Sirs.—Now go home and pull down the Savoy; others to the inns of court: down with them all.

Dick. I have a suit unto your lordship.

Cade. Be it a lordship, thou shalt have it for that word.

Dick. Only, that the laws of England may come out of your mouth.

John. [*Aside*] Mass, 't will be sore law then; for he was thrust in the mouth with a spear, and 't is not whole yet.

Smith. [*Aside*] Nay, John, it will be stinking law; for his breath stinks with eating toasted cheese.

Cade. I have thought upon it; it shall be so. Away! burn all the records of the realm: my mouth shall be the parliament of England.

John. [*Aside*] Then we are like to have biting statutes, unless his teeth be pulled out.

Cade. And henceforward all things shall be in common.

Enter a Messenger

Mess. My lord, a prize, a prize! here's the Lord Say, which sold the towns in France; he that made us pay one-and-twenty fifteens, and one shilling to the pound, the last subsidy.

Enter GEORGE BEVIS, *with the* LORD SAY

Cade. Well, he shall be beheaded for it ten times.—Ah, thou say, thou serge, nay, thou buckram lord! now art thou within point-blank of our jurisdiction regal. What canst thou answer to my majesty, for giving up of Normandy unto Monsieur Basimecu, the dauphin of France? Be it known unto thee by these presence, even the presence of Lord Mortimer, that I am the besom that must sweep the court clean of such filth as thou art. Thou hast most traitorously corrupted the youth of the realm in erecting a grammar-school: and whereas, before, our forefathers had no other books but the score and the tally, thou hast caused printing to be used; and, contrary to the king, his crown, and dignity, thou hast built a paper-mill. It will be proved to thy face, that thou hast men about thee, that usually talk of a noun, and a verb, and such abominable words, as no Christian ear can endure to hear. Thou hast appointed justices of peace, to call poor men before them about matters they were not able to answer. Moreover, thou hast put them in prison; and because they could not read, thou hast hanged them; when, indeed, only for that cause they have been most worthy to live. Thou dost ride in a foot-cloth, dost thou not?

Say. What of that?

Cade. Marry, thou oughtest not to let thy horse wear a cloak, when honester men than thou go in their hose and doublets.

Dick. And work in their shirt too; as myself, for example, that am a butcher.

Say. You men of Kent,—

Dick. What say you of Kent?

Say. Nothing but this: 't is *bona terra, mala gens.*

Cade. Away with him! away with him! he speaks Latin.

Say. Hear me but speak, and bear me where you will.
Kent, in the Commentaries Cæsar writ,
Is termed the civil'st place of all this isle:
Sweet is the country, because full of riches;
The people liberal, valiant, active, wealthy;
Which makes me hope you are not void of pity.
I sold not Maine, I lost not Normandy;
Yet, to recover them, would lose my life.
Justice with favour have I always done;
Prayers and tears have moved me, gifts could never.
When have I aught exacted at your hands,
But to maintain the king, the realm, and you?
Large gifts have I bestowed on learned clerks,
Because my book preferred me to the king;
And seeing ignorance is the curse of God,
Knowledge the wing wherewith we fly to heaven,
Unless you be possessed with devilish spirits,
You cannot but forbear to murder me.
This tongue hath parleyed unto foreign kings
For your behoof.—

Cade. Tut! when struck'st thou one blow in the field?

Say. Great men have reaching hands: oft have I struck
Those that I never saw, and struck them dead.

Geo. O monstrous coward! what, to come behind folks?

Say. These cheeks are pale for watching for your good.

Cade. Give him a box o' the ear, and that will make 'em red again.

Say. Long sitting, to determine poor men's causes,
Hath made me full of sickness and diseases.

Cade. Ye shall have a hempen caudle then, and the help of hatchet.

Dick. Why dost thou quiver, man?

Say. The palsy, and not fear, provokes me.

Cade. Nay, he nods at us; as who should say, I'll be even with you. I'll see if his head will stand steadier on a pole, or no. Take him away, and behead him.

Say. Tell me, wherein have I offended most?
Have I affected wealth, or honour? speak.
Are my chests filled up with extorted gold?
Is my apparel sumptuous to behold?
Whom have I injured, that ye seek my death?
These hands are free from guiltless blood-shedding,
This breast from harbouring foul deceitful thoughts.
O, let me live!

Cade. I feel remorse in myself with his words; but I'll bridle it: he shall die, an it be but for pleading so well for his life. Away with him! he has a familiar under his tongue: he speaks not o' God's name. Go, take him away, I say, and strike off his head presently; and then break into his son-in-law's house, Sir James Cromer, and strike off his head, and bring them both upon two poles hither.

All. It shall be done.

Say. Ah, countrymen! if when you make your prayers,
God should be so obdurate as yourselves,
How would it fare with your departed souls?
And therefore yet relent, and save my life.

Cade. Away with him, and do as I command ye.
[*Exeunt some, with Lord Say*
The proudest peer in the realm shall not wear a head on his shoulders, unless he pay me tribute: there shall not a maid be married, but she shall pay to me her maidenhead, ere they have it. Men shall hold of me *in capite*; and we charge and command, that their wives be as free as heart can wish, or tongue can tell.

Dick. My lord, when shall we go to Cheapside, and take up commodities upon our bills?

Cade. Marry, presently.

All. O, brave!

Re-enter Rebels, with the heads of LORD SAY *and his Son-in-law*

Cade. But is not this braver?—Let them kiss one another, for they loved well, when they were alive. Now part them again, lest they consult about the giving up of some more towns in France. Soldiers, defer the spoil of the city until night; for with these borne before us, instead of maces, will we ride through the streets; and at every corner have them kiss.—Away! [*Exeunt*

SCENE VIII.—Southwark

Alarum. Enter CADE *and all his rabblement*

Cade. Up Fish Street! down Saint Magnus' Corner! kill and knock down! throw them into Thames!—[*A parley sounded, then a retreat*] What noise is this I hear? Dare any be so bold to sound retreat or parley, when I command them kill?

Enter BUCKINGHAM, *and Old* CLIFFORD, *with Forces*

Buck. Ay, here they be that dare and will disturb thee.
Know, Cade, we come ambassadors from the king
Unto the commons whom thou hast misled;
And here pronounce free pardon to them all
That will forsake thee, and go home in peace.
Clif. What say ye, countrymen? will ye relent,
And yield to mercy, whilst 't is offered you,
Or let a rabble lead you to your deaths?
Who loves the king, and will embrace his pardon,
Fling up his cap, and say—God save his majesty!
Who hateth him, and honours not his father,
Henry the Fifth, that made all France to quake,
Shake he his weapon at us, and pass by.
All. God save the king! God save the king!
Cade. What! Buckingham, and Clifford, are ye so brave?—And you, base peasants, do ye believe him? will you needs be hanged with your pardons about your necks? Hath my sword therefore broke through London gates, that you should leave me at the White Hart in Southwark? I thought, ye would never have given out these arms, till you had recovered your ancient freedom; but you are all recreants, and dastards, and delight to live in slavery to the nobility. Let them break your backs with burdens, take your houses over your heads, ravish your wives and daughters before your faces: for me,—I will make shift for one, and so,—God's curse light upon you all!
All. We'll follow Cade, we'll follow Cade.
Clif. Is Cade the son of Henry the Fifth,
That thus you do exclaim, you'll go with him?
Will he conduct you through the heart of France
And make the meanest of you earls and dukes?
Alas, he hath no home, no place to fly to;
Nor knows he how to live, but by the spoil,
Unless by robbing of your friends, and us.

Were't not a shame, that whilst you live at jar,
The fearful French, whom you late vanquishéd,
Should make a start o'er seas, and vanquish you?
Methinks, already, in this civil broil,
I see them lording it in London streets,
Crying—'Villiago!' unto all they meet.
Better ten thousand base-born Cades miscarry,
Than you should stoop unto a Frenchman's mercy.
To France, to France! and get what you have lost.
Spare England, for it is your native coast.
Henry hath money, you are strong and manly:
God on our side, doubt not of victory.

All. A Clifford! a Clifford! we'll follow the king, and Clifford.

Cade. Was ever feather so lightly blown to and fro, as this multitude? The name of Henry the Fifth hales them to an hundred mischiefs, and makes them leave me desolate. I see them lay their heads together to surprise me: my sword make way for me, for here is no staying.—In despite of the devils and hell, have through the very midst of you; and heavens and honour be witness, that no want of resolution in me, but only my followers' base and ignominious treasons, makes me betake me to my heels. [*Exit*

Buck. What! is he fled? go some, and follow him;
And he, that brings his head unto the king,
Shall have a thousand crowns for his reward.— [*Exeunt some of them*
Follow me, soldiers: we'll devise a mean
To reconcile you all unto the king. [*Exeunt*

Scene IX.—Kenilworth Castle

Sound Trumpets. Enter King Henry, Queen Margaret, *and* Somerset, *on the Terrace of the Castle*

K. Hen. Was ever king that joyed an earthly throne,
And could command no more content than I?
No sooner was I crept out of my cradle,
But I was made a king, at nine months old;
Was never subject longed to be a king,
As I do long and wish to be a subject.

Enter Buckingham *and* Clifford

Buck. Health, and glad tidings, to your majesty!

K. Hen. Why, Buckingham, is the traitor, Cade, surprised?
Or is he but retired to make him strong?

Enter below, a number of Cade's Followers, with halters about their necks

Clif. He's fled, my lord, and all his powers do yield,
And humbly thus, with halters on their necks,
Expect your highness' doom, of life, or death.
K. Hen. Then, heaven, set ope thy everlasting gates,
To entertain my vows of thanks and praise!—
Soldiers, this day have you redeemed your lives,
And showed how well you love your prince and country:
Continue still in this so good a mind,
And Henry, though he be infortunate,
Assure yourselves, will never be unkind:
And so, with thanks and pardon to you all,
I do dismiss you to your several countries.
All. God save the king! God save the king!

Enter a Messenger

Mess. Please it your grace to be advértiséd,
The Duke of York is newly come from Ireland,
And with a puissant and a mighty power
Of gallowglasses and stout kernes,
Is marching hitherward in proud array;
And still proclaimeth, as he comes along,
His arms are only to remove from thee
The Duke of Somerset, whom he terms a traitor.
K. Hen. Thus stands my state, 'twixt Cade and York distressed,
Like to a ship, that, having scaped a tempest,
Is straightway calmed and boarded with a pirate.
But now is Cade driven back, his men dispersed,
And now is York in arms to second him.—
I pray thee, Buckingham, go and meet him,
And ask him, what's the reason of these arms.
Tell him, I'll send Duke Edmund to the Tower;—
And, Somerset, we will commit thee thither,
Until his army be dismissed from him.
Som. My lord,
I'll yield myself to prison willingly,
Or unto death, to do my country good.
K. Hen. In any case, be not too rough in terms,
For he is fierce, and cannot brook hard language.
Buck. I will, my lord; and doubt not so to deal,
As all things shall redound unto your good.
K. Hen. Come wife, let's in, and learn to govern better;
For yet may England curse my wretched reign. [*Exeunt*

SCENE X.—Kent. IDEN's Garden

Enter CADE

Cade. Fie on ambition! fie on myself, that have a sword, and yet am ready to famish! These five days have I hid me in these woods, and durst not peep out, for all the country is laid for me; but now am I so hungry, that if I might have a lease of my life for a thousand years, I could stay no longer. Wherefore, on a brick wall have I climbed into this garden, to see if I can eat grass, or pick a sallet another while, which is not amiss to cool a man's stomach this hot weather. And I think this word sallet was born to do me good: for many a time, but for a sallet, my brain-pan had been cleft with a brown bill; and many a time, when I have been dry and bravely marching, it hath served me instead of a quart-pot to drink in; and now the word sallet must serve me to feed on.

Enter IDEN, *with Servants, behind*

Iden. Lord! who would live turmoilèd in the court,
And may enjoy such quiet walks as these?
This small inheritance, my father left me,
Contenteth me, and worth a monarchy.
I seek not to wax great by others' waning;
Or gather wealth I care not with what envy:
Sufficeth that I have maintains my state,
And sends the poor well pleasèd from my gate.

Cade. Here's the lord of the soil come to seize me for a stray, for entering his fee-simple without leave. Ah, villain, thou wilt betray me, and get a thousand crowns of the king by carrying my head to him; but I'll make thee eat iron like an ostrich, and swallow my sword like a great pin, ere thou and I part.

Iden. Why, rude companion, whatsoe'er thou be,
I know thee not; why then should I betray thee?
Is't not enough, to break into my garden,
And like a thief to come to rob my grounds,
Climbing my walls in spite of me, the owner,
But thou wilt brave me with these saucy terms?

Cade. Brave thee? ay, by the best blood that ever was broached, and beard thee too. Look on me well: I have eat no meat these five days; yet, come thou and thy five men; and if I do not leave you all as dead as a door-nail, I pray God I may never eat grass more.

Iden. Nay, it shall ne'er be said, while England stands,
That Alexander Iden, an esquire of Kent,
Took odds to combat a poor famished man.

Oppose thy steadfast-gazing eyes to mine,
See if thou canst outface me with thy looks:
Set limb to limb, and thou art far the lesser;
Thy hand is but a finger to my fist;
Thy leg a stick, comparéd with this truncheon;
My foot shall fight with all the strength thou hast;
And if mine arm be heavéd in the air,
Thy grave is digged already in the earth.
As for words, whose greatness answers words,
Let this my sword report what speech forbears.

Cade. By my valour, the most complete champion that ever I heard.—Steel, if thou turn the edge, or cut not out the burly-boned clown in chines of beef ere thou sleep in thy sheath, I beseech Jove on my knees, thou mayest be turned to hobnails. [*They fight. Cade falls*] O! I am slain. Famine, and no other, hath slain me: let ten thousand devils come against me, and give me but the ten meals I have lost, and I'd defy them all. Wither, garden; and be henceforth a burying-place to all that do dwell in this house, because the unconquered soul of Cade is fled.

Iden. Is't Cade that I have slain, that monstrous traitor?
Sword, I will hallow thee for this thy deed,
And hang thee o'er my tomb, when I am dead:
Ne'er shall this blood be wipéd from thy point,
But thou shalt wear it as a herald's coat,
To emblaze the honour that thy master got.

Cade. Iden, farewell; and be proud of thy victory. Tell Kent from me, she hath lost her best man, and exhort all the world to be cowards; for I, that never feared any, am vanquished by famine, not by valour. [*Dies*

Iden. How much thou wrong'st me, Heaven be my judge.
Die, damnéd wretch, the curse of her that bare thee!
And as I thrust thy body in with my sword,
So wish I, I might thrust thy soul to hell.
Hence will I drag thee headlong by the heels
Unto a dunghill, which shall be thy grave,
And there cut off thy most ungracious head;
Which I will bear in triumph to the king,
Leaving thy trunk for crows to feed upon.

[*Exeunt Iden, dragging out the body, and Servants*

ACT FIVE

SCENE I.—The Same. Fields between Dartford and Blackheath

The King's Camp on one side. On the other, enter YORK *attended, with drum and colours; his Forces at some distance*

York. From Ireland thus comes York, to claim his right,
And pluck the crown from feeble Henry's head:
Ring, bells, aloud; burn, bonfires, clear and bright,
To entertain great England's lawful king.
Ah, *sancta majestas!* who would not buy thee dear?
Let them obey, that know not how to rule;
This hand was made to handle nought but gold:
I cannot give due action to my words,
Except a sword, or sceptre, balance it.
A sceptre shall it have, have I a soul,
On which I'll toss the flower-de-luce of France.

Enter BUCKINGHAM

Whom have we here? Buckingham, to disturb me?
The king hath sent him, sure: I must dissemble.
Buck. York, if thou meanest well, I greet thee well.
York. Humphrey of Buckingham, I accept thy greeting.
Art thou a messenger, or come of pleasure?
Buck. A messenger from Henry, our dread liege,
To know the reason of these arms in peace;
Or why thou,—being a subject as I am,—
Against thy oath and true allegiance sworn,
Shouldst raise so great a power without his leave,
Or dare to bring thy force so near the court.
York. [*Aside*] Scarce can I speak, my choler is so great.
O, I could hew up rocks, and fight with flint,
I am so angry at these abject terms;
And now, like Ajax Telamonius,
On sheep or oxen could I spend my fury.
I am far better born than is the king,
More like a king, more kingly in my thoughts;
But I must make fair weather yet awhile,
Till Henry be more weak, and I more strong—
O Buckingham, I pr'ythee, pardon me,
That I have given no answer all this while:
My mind was troubled with deep melancholy.
The cause why I have brought this army hither,
Is, to remove proud Somerset from the king,

Seditious to his grace, and to the state.
Buck. That is too much presumption on thy part;
But if thy arms be to no other end,
The king hath yielded unto thy demand:
The Duke of Somerset is in the Tower.
York. Upon thine honour, is he prisoner?
Buck. Upon mine honour, he is prisoner.
York. Then, Buckingham, I do dismiss my powers.—
Soldiers, I thank you all; disperse yourselves:
Meet me to-morrow in Saint George's field,
You shall have pay, and everything you wish.
And let my sovereign, virtuous Henry,
Command my eldest son,—nay, all my sons,
As pledges of my fealty and love;
I'll send them all, as willing as I live:
Lands, goods, horse, armour, anything I have
Is his to use, so Somerset may die.
Buck. York, I commend this kind submission:
We twain will go into his highness' tent.

Enter KING HENRY, *attended*

K. Hen. Buckingham, doth York intend no harm to us,
That thus he marcheth with thee arm in arm?
York. In all submission and humility,
York doth present himself unto your highness.
K. Hen. Then what intend these forces thou dost bring?
York. To heave the traitor Somerset from hence;
And fight against that monstrous rebel, Cade,
Who since I heard to be discomfited.

Enter IDEN, *with* CADE's *head*

Iden. If one so rude, and of so mean condition,
May pass into the presence of a king,
Lo, I present your grace a traitor's head,
The head of Cade, whom I in combat slew.
K. Hen. The head of Cade?—Great God, how just art Thou!—
O, let me view his visage being dead,
That living wrought me such exceeding trouble.
Tell me, my friend, art thou the man that slew him?
Iden. I was, an't like your majesty.
K. Hen. How art thou called and what is thy degree?
Iden. Alexander Iden, that's my name;
A poor esquire of Kent, that loves his king.
Buck. So please it you, my lord, 't were not amiss,
He were created knight for his good service.
K. Hen. Iden, kneel down. [*He kneels*] Rise up a knight.
We give thee for reward a thousand marks;
And will, that thou henceforth attend on us.

Iden. May Iden live to merit such a bounty,
And never live but true unto his liege.

K. Hen. See, Buckingham! Somerset comes with the queen:
Go, bid her hide him quickly from the duke.

Enter QUEEN MARGARET *and* SOMERSET

Q. Mar. For thousand Yorks he shall not hide his head,
But boldly stand, and front him to his face.

York. How now! is Somerset at liberty?
Then, York, unloose thy long-imprisoned thoughts,
And let thy tongue be equal with thy heart.
Shall I endure the sight of Somerset?—
False king, why hast thou broken faith with me,
Knowing how hardly I can brook abuse?
King did I call thee? no, thou art not king;
Not fit to govern and rule multitudes,
Which dar'st not, no, nor canst not rule a traitor.
That head of thine doth not become a crown;
Thy hand is made to grasp a palmer's staff,
And not to grace an awful princely sceptre.
That gold must round engirt these brows of mine;
Whose smile and frown, like to Achilles' spear,
Is able with the change to kill and cure.
Here is a hand to hold a sceptre up,
And with the same to act controlling laws.
Give place: by Heaven, thou shalt rule no more
O'er him whom Heaven created for thy ruler.

Som. O monstrous traitor!—I arrest thee, York,
Of capital treason 'gainst the king and crown.
Obey, audacious traitor: kneel for grace.

York. Wouldst have me kneel? first let me ask of these,
If they can brook I bow a knee to man?
Sirrah, call in my sons to be my bail; [*Exit an Attendant*
I know, ere they will have me go to ward,
They'll pawn their swords for my enfranchisement.

Q. Mar. Call hither Clifford; bid him come amain,
To say, if that the bastard boys of York
Shall be the surety for their traitor father. [*Exit Buckingham*

York. O blood-bespotted Neapolitan,
Outcast of Naples, England's bloody scourge,
The sons of York, thy betters in their birth,
Shall be their father's bail; and bane to those
That for my surety will refuse the boys.

Enter EDWARD *and* RICHARD PLANTAGENET, *with Forces, at one side; at the other, with Forces also, Old* CLIFFORD *and his Son*

See, where they come: I'll warrant they'll make it good.

Q. Mar. And here comes Clifford, to deny their bail.
Clif. Health and happiness to my lord the king! [*Kneels*
York. I thank thee, Clifford: say, what news with thee?
Nay, do not fright us with an angry look:
We are thy sovereign, Clifford, kneel again;
For thy mistaking so, we pardon thee.
Clif. This is my king, York: I do not mistake;
But thou mistak'st me much, to think I do.—
To Bedlam with him! is the man grown mad?
K. Hen. Ay, Clifford; a Bedlam and ambitious humour
Makes him oppose himself against his king.
Clif. He is a traitor: let him to the Tower,
And chop away that factious pate of his.
Q. Mar. He is arrested, but will not obey:
His sons, he says, shall give their words for him.
York. Will you not, sons?
Edw. Ay, noble father, if our words will serve.
Rich. And if words will not, then our weapons shall.
Clif. Why, what a brood of traitors have we here!
York. Look in a glass, and call thy image so;
I am thy king, and thou a false-heart traitor.—
Call hither to the stake my two brave bears,
That with the very shaking of their chains
They may astonish these fell-lurking curs:
Bid Salisbury, and Warwick, come to me.

Drums. Enter WARWICK *and* SALISBURY, *with Forces*

Clif. Are these thy bears? we'll bait thy bears to death,
And manacle the bear-ward in their chains,
If thou dar'st bring them to the baiting-place.
Rich. Oft have I seen a hot o'erweening cur
Run back and bite, because he was withheld;
Who, being suffered with the bear's fell paw,
Hath clapped his tail between his legs, and cried:
And such a piece of service will you do,
If you oppose yourselves to match Lord Warwick.
Clif. Hence, heap of wrath, foul indigested lump,
As crooked in thy manners as thy shape!
York. Nay, we shall heat you thoroughly anon.
Clif. Take heed, lest by your heat you burn yourselves.
K. Hen. Why, Warwick, hath thy knee forgot to bow?—
Old Salisbury,—shame to thy silver hair,
Thou mad misleader of thy brain-sick son!—
What, wilt thou on thy death-bed play the ruffian,
And seek for sorrow with thy spectacles?
O, where is faith? O, where is loyalty?
If it be banished from the frosty head,

Where shall it find a harbour in the earth?—
Wilt thou go dig a grave to find out war,
And shame thine honourable age with blood?
Why art thou old, and want'st experience?
Or wherefore dost abuse it, if thou hast it?
For shame! in duty bend thy knee to me,
That bows unto the grave with mickle age.

Sal. My lord, I have considered with myself
The title of this most renownéd duke;
And in my conscience do repute his grace
The rightful heir to England's royal seat.

K. Hen. Hast thou not sworn allegiance unto me?

Sal. I have.

K. Hen. Canst thou dispense with heaven for such an oath?

Sal. It is great sin to swear unto a sin,
But greater sin to keep a sinful oath.
Who can be bound by any solemn vow
To do a murderous deed, to rob a man,
To force a spotless virgin's chastity,
To reave the orphan of his patrimony,
To wring the widow from her customed right,
And have no other reason for this wrong,
But that he was bound by a solemn oath?

Q. Mar. A subtle traitor needs no sophister.

K. Hen. Call Buckingham, and bid him arm himself.

York. Call Buckingham, and all the friends thou hast,
I am resolved for death, or dignity.

Clif. The first I warrant thee, if dreams prove true.

War. You were best to go to bed, and dream again,
To keep thee from the tempest of the field.

Clif. I am resolved to bear a greater storm,
Than any thou canst conjure up to-day;
And that I'll write upon thy burgonet,
Might I but know thee by thy household badge.

War. Now, by my father's badge, old Nevil's crest,
The rampant bear chained to the ragged staff,
This day I'll wear aloft my burgonet,—
As on a mountain-top the cedar shows,
That keeps his leaves in spire of any storm,—
Even to affright thee with the view thereof.

Clif. And from thy burgonet I'll rend thy bear,
And tread it under foot with all contempt,
Despite the bear-ward that protects the bear.

Y. Clif. And so to arms, victorious father,
To quell the rebels, and their complices.

Rich. Fie! charity! for shame! speak not in spite,
For you shall sup with Jesu Christ to-night.

Y. Clif. Foul stigmatic, that's more than thou canst tell.

Rich. If not in heaven, you'll surely sup in hell.
[*Exeunt severally*

SCENE II.—Saint Albans

Alarums: Excursions. Enter WARWICK

War. Clifford of Cumberland, 't is Warwick calls:
And if thou dost not hide thee from the bear
Now, when the angry trumpet sounds alarm
And dead men's cries do fill the empty air,
Clifford, I say, come forth and fight with me!
Proud northern lord, Clifford of Cumberland,
Warwick is hoarse with calling thee to arms.

Enter YORK

How, now, my noble lord? what, all afoot?
York. The deadly-handed Clifford slew my steed;
But match to match I have encountered him,
And made a prey for carrion kites and crows
Even of the bonny beast he loved so well.

Enter CLIFFORD

War. Of one or both of us the time is come.
York. Hold, Warwick! seek thee out some other chase,
For I myself must hunt this deer to death.
War. Then, nobly, York; 't is for a crown thou fight'st.—
As I intend, Clifford, to thrive to-day,
It grieves my soul to leave thee unassailed. [*Exit*
Clif. What seest thou in me, York? why dost thou pause?
York. With thy brave bearing should I be in love,
But that thou art so fast mine enemy.
Clif. Nor should thy prowess want praise and esteem,
But that't is shown ignobly, and in treason.
York. So let it help me now against thy sword,
As I in justice and true right express it.
Clif. My soul and body on the action both!—
York. A dreadful lay! Address thee instantly.
Clif. *La fin couronne les œuvres.*
[*They fight, and Clifford falls and dies*
York. Thus war hath given thee peace, for thou art still.
Peace with his soul, Heaven, if it be thy will! [*Exit*

Enter Young CLIFFORD

Y. Clif. Shame and confusion! all is on the rout:
Fear frames disorder, and disorder wounds

Where it should guard. O war! thou son of hell,
Whom angry heavens do make their minister,
Throw in the frozen bosoms of our part
Hot coals of vengeance!—Let no soldier fly:
He that is truly dedicate to war
Hath no self-love; nor he that loves himself
Hath not essentially, but by circumstance,
The name of valour.—[*Seeing his father's body*]
O, let the vile world end,
And the premiséd flames of the last day
Knit earth and heaven together!
Now let the general trumpet blow his blast,
Particularities and petty sounds
To cease!—Wast thou ordained, dear father,
To lose thy youth in peace, and to achieve
The silver livery of adviséd age,
And, in thy reverence, and thy chair-days, thus
To die in ruffian battle?—Even at this sight,
My heart is turned to stone: and while't is mine,
It shall be stony. York not our old men spares;
No more will I their babes: tears virginal
Shall be to me even as the dew to fire;
And beauty, that the tyrant oft reclaims,
Shall to my flaming wrath be oil and flax.
Henceforth I will not have to do with pity:
Meet I an infant of the house of York,
Into as many gobbets will I cut it,
As wild Medea young Absyrtus did:
In cruelty will I seek out my fame.
Come, thou new ruin of old Clifford's house:
[*Taking up the body*
As did Æneas old Anchises bear,
So bear I thee upon my manly shoulders:
But then Æneas bare a living load,
Nothing so heavy as these woes of mine. [*Exit*

Enter RICHARD PLANTAGENET *and* SOMERSET *fighting.* SOMERSET *is killed*

Rich. So, lie thou there;—
For, underneath an ale-house' paltry sign,
The Castle in Saint Albans, Somerset
Hath made the wizard famous in his death.
Sword, hold thy temper; heart, be wrathful still:
Priests pray for enemies, but princes kill. [*Exit*

Alarums: Excursions. Enter KING HENRY, QUEEN MARGARET, *and others, retreating*

Q. Mar. Away, my lord! you are slow: for shame, away!

K. Hen. Can we outrun the heavens? good Margaret, stay.
Q. Mar. What are you made of? you'll nor fight, nor fly;
Now is it manhood, wisdom, and defence
To give the enemy way, and to secure us
By what we can, which can no more but fly.
[*Alarum afar off*
If you be ta'en, we then should see the bottom
Of all our fortunes: but if we haply scape
(As well we may, if not through your neglect),
We shall to London get, where you are loved,
And where this breach, now in our fortunes made,
May readily be stopped.

Enter Young CLIFFORD

Y. Clif. But that my heart's on future mischief set,
I would speak blasphemy ere bid you fly;
But fly you must: uncurable discomfit
Reigns in the hearts of all our present parts.
Away, for your relief! and we will live
To see their day, and them our fortune give.
Away, my lord, away! [*Exeunt*

SCENE III.—Fields near Saint Albans

Alarum: Retreat. Flourish; then enter YORK, RICHARD PLANTAGENET, WARWICK, *and Soldiers, with drum and colours*

York. Of Salisbury, who can report of him?
That winter lion, who in rage forgets
Agéd contusions and all brush of time,
And, like a gallant in the brow of youth,
Repairs him with occasion? This happy day
Is not itself, nor have we won one foot,
If Salisbury be lost.
Rich. My noble father,
Three times to-day I holp him to his horse,
Three times bestrid him; thrice I led him off,
Persuaded him from any further act:
But still, where danger was, still there I met him;
And like rich hangings in a homely house,
So was his will in his old feeble body.
But, noble as he is, look where he comes.

Enter SALISBURY

Sal. Now, by my sword, well hast thou fought to-day;
By the mass, so did we all.—I thank you, Richard:

God knows how long it is I have to live;
And it hath pleased Him, that three times to-day
You have defended me from imminent death.—
Well, lords, we have not got that which we have:
'T is not enough our foes are this time fled,
Being opposites of such repairing nature.
York. I know our safety is to follow them;
For, as I hear, the king is fled to London,
To call a present court of parliament:
Let us pursue him, ere the writs go forth.—
What says Lord Warwick? shall we after them?
War. After them? nay, before them, if we can.
Now, by my faith, lords, 't was a glorious day:
Saint Albans battle, won by famous York,
Shall be eternised in all age to come.—
Sound, drums and trumpets!—and to London all;
And more such days as these to us befall! [*Exeunt*

KING HENRY THE SIXTH

THIRD PART

DRAMATIS PERSONÆ

KING HENRY THE SIXTH
EDWARD, *Prince of Wales, his son*
LEWIS XI., *King of France*
DUKE OF SOMERSET, DUKE OF EXETER, EARL OF OXFORD, EARL OF NORTHUMBERLAND, EARL OF WESTMORELAND, LORD CLIFFORD — *on King Henry's side*
RICHARD PLANTAGENET, *Duke of York*
EDWARD, *Earl of March, afterwards King Edward IV.*, EDMUND, *Earl of Rutland*, GEORGE, *afterwards Duke of Clarence*, RICHARD, *afterwards Duke of Gloster* — *his sons*
DUKE OF NORFOLK, MARQUESS OF MONTAGUE, EARL OF WARWICK, EARL OF PEMBROKE, LORD HASTINGS, LORD STAFFORD — *of the Duke of York's party*
SIR JOHN MORTIMER, SIR HUGH MORTIMER — *uncles to the Duke of York*
HENRY, *Earl of Richmond, a youth*
LORD RIVERS, *brother to Lady Grey*
SIR WILLIAM STANLEY
SIR JOHN MONTGOMERY
SIR JOHN SOMERVILLE
Tutor to Rutland
Mayor of York
Lieutenant of the Tower
A nobleman
Two keepers
A huntsman
A son that has killed his father
A father that has killed his son

QUEEN MARGARET
LADY GREY, *afterwards Queen to Edward IV.*
BONA, *sister to the French queen*

Soldiers, and other Attendants on King Henry and King Edward, Messengers, Watchmen, etc.

SCENE—*England and France.*

THE THIRD PART OF

KING HENRY VI

ACT ONE

SCENE I.—London. The Parliament House

Drums. Some Soldiers of York's party break in. Then enter the DUKE OF YORK, EDWARD, RICHARD, NORFOLK, MONTAGUE, WARWICK, *and others, with White Roses in their hats*

War. I wonder how the king escaped our hands.
York. While we pursued the horsemen of the north,
He slily stole away, and left his men:
Whereat the great Lord of Northumberland,
Whose warlike ears could never brook retreat,
Cheered up the drooping army; and himself,
Lord Clifford, and Lord Stafford, all abreast,
Charged our main battle's front, and, breaking in,
Were by the swords of common soldiers slain.
Edw. Lord Stafford's father, Duke of Buckingham,
Is either slain or wounded dangerous:
I cleft his beaver with a downright blow;
That this is true, father, behold his blood.
[*Showing his bloody sword*
Mont. [*To York, showing his*] And, brother, here's the Earl of Wiltshire's blood,
Whom I encountered as the battles joined.
Rich. Speak thou for me, and tell them what I did.
[*Throwing down the Duke of Somerset's head*
York. Richard hath best deserved of all my sons.—
But, is your grace dead, my Lord of Somerset?
Norf. Such hope have all the line of John of Gaunt!
Rich. Thus do I hope to shake King Henry's head.
War. And so do I. Victorious Prince of York
Before I see thee seated in that throne,
Which now the house of Lancaster usurps,
I vow by Heaven these eyes shall never close.
This is the palace of the fearful king,
And this the regal seat: possess it, York;

For this is thine, and not King Henry's heirs'.
York. Assist me then, sweet Warwick, and I will;
For hither we have broken in by force.
Norf. We'll all assist you; he that flies shall die.
York. Thanks, gentle Norfolk.—Stay by me, my lords:—
And, soldiers, stay, and lodge by me this night.
War. And when the king comes, offer him no violence,
Unless he seek to thrust you out perforce.
[*The Soldiers retire*
York. The queen this day here holds her parliament,
But little thinks we shall be of her council.
By words or blows here let us win our right.
Rich. Armed as we are, let's stay within this house.
War. The bloody parliament shall this be called,
Unless Plantagenet, Duke of York, be king,
And bashful Henry be deposed, whose cowardice
Hath made us by-words to our enemies.
York. Then leave me not, my lords; be resolute;
I mean to take possession of my right.
War. Neither the king, nor he that loves him best,
The proudest he that holds up Lancaster,
Dare stir a wing, if Warwick shake his bells.
I'll plant Plantagenet, root him up who dares.—
Resolve thee, Richard: claim the English crown.
[*Warwick leads York to the throne, who seats himself*

Flourish. Enter KING HENRY, CLIFFORD, NORTHUMBERLAND, WESTMORELAND, EXETER, *and others, with Red Roses in their hats*

K. Hen. My lords, look where the sturdy rebel sits,
Even in the chair of state! belike, he means,
Backed by the power of Warwick, that false peer,
To aspire unto the crown, and reign as king.—
Earl of Northumberland, he slew thy father,—
And thine, Lord Clifford; and you both have vowed revenge
On him, his sons, his favourites, and his friends.
North. If I be not, heavens be revenged on me!
Clif. The hope thereof makes Clifford mourn in steel.
West. What! shall we suffer this? let's pluck him down:
My heart for anger burns, I cannot brook it.
K. Hen. Be patient, gentle Earl of Westmoreland.
Clif. Patience is for poltroons such as he:
He durst not sit there, had your father lived.
My gracious lord, here in the parliament
Let us assail the family of York.
North. Well hast thou spoken, cousin: be it so.
K. Hen. Ah! know you not, the city favours them,

And they have troops of soldiers at their beck?
Exe. But when the duke is slain, they'll quickly fly.
K. Hen. Far be the thought of this from Henry's heart,
To make a shambles of the parliament-house!
Cousin of Exeter, frowns, words, and threats,
Shall be the war that Henry means to use.
[*They advance to the Duke*
Thou factious Duke of York, descend my throne,
And kneel for grace and mercy at my feet:
I am thy sovereign.
York. I am thine.
Exe. For shame! come down. He made thee Duke of York.
York. 'T was my inheritance, as the earldom was.
Exe. Thy father was a traitor to the crown.
War. Exeter, thou art a traitor to the crown,
In following this usurping Henry.
Clif. Whom should he follow but his natural king?
War. True, Clifford; and that's Richard, Duke of York.
K. Hen. And shall I stand, and thou sit in my throne?
York. It must and shall be so. Content thyself.
War. Be Duke of Lancaster: let him be king.
West. He is both king and Duke of Lancaster;
And that the Lord of Westmoreland shall maintain.
War. And Warwick shall disprove it. You forget,
That we are those which chased you from the field,
And slew your father, and with colours spread
Marched through the city to the palace gates.
North. Yes, Warwick, I remember it to my grief;
And, by his soul, thou and thy house shall rue it.
West. Plantagenet, of thee, and these thy sons,
Thy kinsmen, and thy friends, I'll have more lives
Than drops of blood were in my father's veins.
Clif. Urge it no more; lest that, instead of words,
I send thee, Warwick, such a messenger,
As shall revenge his death before I stir.
War. Poor Clifford, how I scorn his worthless threats.
York. Will you we show our title to the crown?
If not, our swords shall plead it in the field.
K. Hen. What title hast thou, traitor, to the crown?
Thy father was, as thou art, Duke of York;
Thy grandfather, Roger Mortimer, Earl of March.
I am the son of Henry the Fifth,
Who made the Dauphin and the French to stoop,
And seized upon their towns and provinces.
War. Talk not of France, sith thou hast lost it all.
K. Hen. The lord Protector lost it, and not I:
When I was crowned, I was but nine months old.

Rich. You are old enough now, and yet, methinks, you lose.
Father, tear the crown from the usurper's head.
Edw. Sweet father, do so: set it on your head.
Mont. [*To York*] Good brother, as thou lov'st and honour'st arms,
Let's fight it out, and not stand cavilling thus.
Rich. Sound drums and trumpets, and the king will fly.
York. Sons, peace!
K. Hen. Peace thou, and give King Henry leave to speak.
War. Plantagenet shall speak first: hear him, lords;
And be you silent and attentive too,
For he that interrupts him shall not live.
K. Hen. Think'st thou, that I will leave my kingly throne,
Wherein my grandsire and my father sat?
No: first shall war unpeople this my realm;
Ay, and their colours—often borne in France,
And now in England, to our heart's great sorrow,—
Shall be my winding sheet.—Why faint you, lords?
My title's good, and better far than his.
War. Prove it, Henry, and thou shalt be king.
K. Hen. Henry the Fourth by conquest got the crown.
York. 'T was by rebellion against his king.
K. Hen. [*Aside*] I know not what to say: my title's weak.—
Tell me, may not a king adopt an heir?
York. What then?
K. Hen. An if he may, then am I lawful king;
For Richard, in the view of many lords,
Resigned the crown to Henry the Fourth,
Whose heir my father was, and I am his.
York. He rose against him, being his sovereign,
And made him to resign his crown perforce.
War. Suppose, my lords, he did it unconstrained,
Think you, 't were prejudicial to his crown?
Exe. No; for he could not so resign his crown,
But that the next heir should succeed and reign.
K. Hen. Art thou against us, Duke of Exeter?
Exe. His is the right, and therefore pardon me.
York. Why whisper you, my lords, and answer not?
Exe. My conscience tells me he is lawful king.
K. Hen. All will revolt from me, and turn to him.
North. Plantagenet, for all the claim thou lay'st,
Think not, that Henry shall be so deposed.
War. Deposed he shall be in despite of all.
North. Thou art deceived: 't is not thy southern power,
Of Essex, Norfolk, Suffolk, nor of Kent,—
Which makes thee thus presumptuous and proud,—

Can set the duke up in despite of me.
Clif. King Henry, be thy title right or wrong,
Lord Clifford vows to fight in thy defence:
May that ground gape, and swallow me alive,
Where I shall kneel to him that slew my father!
K. Hen. O Clifford, how thy words revive my heart!
York. Henry of Lancaster, resign thy crown.
What mutter you, or what conspire you, lords?
War. Do right unto this princely Duke of York,
Or I will fill the house with armèd men,
And o'er the chair of state where now he sits,
Write up his title with usurping blood.
[*He stamps with his foot, and the Soldiers show themselves*
K. Hen. My Lord of Warwick, hear me but one word.
Let me for this my life-time reign as king.
York. Confirm the crown to me, and to mine heirs,
And thou shalt reign in quiet while thou liv'st.
K. Hen. I am content: Richard Plantagenet,
Enjoy the kingdom after my decease.
Clif. What wrong is this unto the prince your son!
War. What good is this to England, and himself!
West. Base, fearful, and despairing Henry!
Clif. How hast thou injured both thyself and us!
West. I cannot stay to hear these articles.
North. Nor I.
Clif. Come, cousin, let us tell the queen these news.
West. Farewell, faint-hearted and degenerate king,
In whose cold blood no spark of honour bides.
North. Be thou a prey unto the house of York,
And die in bands for this unmanly deed!
Clif. In dreadful war may'st thou be overcome,
Or live in peace, abandoned, and despised!
[*Exeunt Northumberland, Clifford, and Westmoreland*
War. Turn this way, Henry, and regard them not.
Exe. They seek revenge, and therefore will not yield.
K. Hen. Ah, Exeter!
War. Why should you sigh, my lord?
K. Hen. Not for myself, Lord Warwick, but my son,
Whom I unnaturally shall disinherit.
But be it as it may, I here entail
The crown to thee, and to thine heirs for ever;
Conditionally, that here thou take an oath
To cease this civil war, and, whilst I live,
To honour me as thy king and sovereign;
And neither by treason, nor hostility,
To seek to put me down, and reign thyself.
York. This oath I willingly take, and will perform.
[*Coming from the throne*
War. Long live King Henry!—Plantagenet, embrace him.

K. Hen. And long live thou, and these thy forward sons!
York. Now York and Lancaster are reconciled.
Exe. Accursed be he that seeks to make them foes!
[*Sennet. The Lords come forward*
York. Farewell, my gracious lord: I'll to my castle.
War. And I'll keep London with my soldiers.
Norf. And I to Norfolk with my followers.
Mont. And I unto the sea from whence I came.
[*Exeunt York and his Sons, Warwick, Norfolk, Montague, Soldiers, and Attendants*
K. Hen. And I, with grief and sorrow, to the court.

Enter QUEEN MARGARET *and the* PRINCE OF WALES

Exe. Here comes the queen, whose looks bewray her anger:
I'll steal away.
K. Hen. Exeter, so will I.
Q. Mar. Nay, go not from me; I will follow thee.
K. Hen. Be patient, gentle queen, and I will stay.
Q. Mar. Who can be patient in such extremes?
Ah, wretched man! 'would I had died a maid,
And never seen thee, never borne thee son,
Seeing thou hast proved so unnatural a father!
Hath he deserved to lose his birthright thus?
Hadst thou but loved him half so well as I,
Or felt that pain which I did for him once,
Or nourished him, as I did with my blood,
Thou wouldst have left thy dearest heart-blood there,
Rather than have made that savage duke thine heir,
And disinherited thine only son.
Prince. Father, you cannot disinherit me.
If you be king, why should not I succeed?
K. Hen. Pardon me, Margaret;—pardon me, sweet son:—
The Earl of Warwick and the duke enforced me.
Q. Mar. Enforced thee! art thou king, and wilt be forced?
I shame to hear thee speak. Ah, timorous wretch!
Thou hast undone thyself, thy son, and me,
And given unto the house of York such head,
As thou shalt reign but by their sufferance.
To entail him and his heirs unto the crown,
What is it, but to make thy sepulchre,
And creep into it far before thy time?
Warwick is chancellor, and the Lord of Calais;
Stern Faulconbridge commands the narrow seas;
The duke is made Protector of the realm;
And yet shalt thou be safe? such safety finds
The trembling lamb, environéd with wolves.

Had I been there, which am a silly woman,
The soldiers should have tossed me on their pikes,
Before I would have granted to that act;
But thou preferr'st thy life before thine honour:
And seeing thou dost, I here divorce myself,
Both from thy table, Henry, and thy bed,
Until that act of parliament be repealed,
Whereby my son is disinherited.
The northern lords, that have forsworn thy colours,
Will follow mine, if once they see them spread;
And spread they shall be, to thy foul disgrace,
And utter ruin of the house of York.
Thus do I leave thee.—Come, son, let's away:
Our army is ready; come, we'll after them.

K. Hen. Stay, gentle Margaret, and hear me speak.

Q. Mar. Thou hast spoke too much already: get thee gone.

K. Hen. Gentle son Edward, thou wilt stay with me?

Q. Mar. Ay, to be murdered by his enemies.

Prince. When I return with victory from the field,
I'll see your grace; till then, I'll follow her.

Q. Mar. Come, son, away! we may not linger thus.
[*Exeunt Queen Margaret and the Prince*

K. Hen. Poor queen! how love to me, and to her son,
Hath made her break out into terms of rage!
Revenged may she be on that hateful duke,
Whose haughty spirit, wingèd with desire,
Will cost my crown, and, like an empty eagle,
Tire on the flesh of me and of my son!
The loss of those three lords torments my heart:
I'll write unto them, and entreat them fair.—
Come, cousin; you shall be the messenger.

Exe. And I, I hope, shall reconcile them all. [*Exeunt*

Scene II.—A Room in Sandal Castle, near Wakefield

Enter Edward, Richard, *and* Montague

Rich. Brother, though I be youngest, give me leave.

Edw. No, I can better play the orator.

Mont. But I have reasons strong and forcible.

Enter York

York. Why, how now, sons and brother, at a strife?
What is your quarrel? how began it first?

Edw. No quarrel, but a slight contention.

York. About what?

Rich. About that which concerns your grace, and us;

The crown of England, father, which is yours.
York. Mine, boy? not till King Henry be dead.
Rich. Your right depends not on his life, or death.
Edw. Now you are heir, therefore enjoy it now:
By giving the house of Lancaster leave to breathe,
It will outrun you, father, in the end.
York. I took an oath that he should quietly reign.
Edw. But for a kingdom any oath may be broken:
I'd break a thousand oaths to reign one year.
Rich. No; God forbid, your grace should be forsworn.
York. I shall be, if I claim by open war.
Rich. I'll prove the contrary, if you'll hear me speak.
York. Thou canst not, son: it is impossible.
Rich. An oath is of no moment, being not took
Before a true and lawful magistrate,
That hath authority over him that swears:
Henry had none, but did usurp the place;
Then, seeing't was he that made you to depose,
Your oath, my lord, is vain and frivolous.
Therefore, to arms. And, father, do but think,
How sweet a thing it is to wear a crown,
Within whose circuit is Elysium,
And all that poets feign of bliss and joy.
Why do we linger thus. I cannot rest,
Until the white rose that I wear be dyed
Even in the lukewarm blood of Henry's heart.
York. Richard, enough: I will be king, or die.—
Brother, thou shalt to London presently,
And whet on Warwick to this enterprise.—
Thou, Richard, shalt to the Duke of Norfolk
And tell him privily of our intent.—
You, Edward, shall unto my Lord Cobham,
With whom the Kentishmen will willingly rise:
In them I trust; for they are soldiers,
Witty, courteous, liberal, full of spirit.—
While you are thus employed, what resteth more
But that I seek occasion how to rise,
And yet the king not privy to my drift,
Nor any of the house of Lancaster?

Enter a Messenger

But, stay.—What news? Why com'st thou in such post?
Mess. The queen with all the northern earls and lords
Intend here to besiege you in your castle.
She is hard by with twenty thousand men,
And therefore fortify your hold, my lord.
York. Ay, with my sword. What! think'st thou, that we fear them?—

Edward and Richard, you shall stay with me;
My brother Montague shall post to London:
Let noble Warwick, Cobham, and the rest,
Whom we have left protectors of the king,
With powerful policy strengthen themselves,
And trust not simple Henry, nor his oaths.
Mont. Brother, I go; I'll win them, fear it not:
And thus most humbly I do take my leave. [*Exit*

Enter Sir John *and* Sir Hugh Mortimer

York. Sir John, and Sir Hugh Mortimer, mine uncles,
You are come to Sandal in a happy hour;
The army of the queen mean to besiege us.
Sir John. She shall not need, we'll meet her in the field.
York. What, with five thousand men?
Rich. Ay, with five hundred, father, for a need.
A woman's general; what should we fear?
[*A march afar off*
Edw. I hear their drums: let's set our men in order
And issue forth, and bid them battle straight.
York. Five men to twenty!—though the odds be great,
I doubt not, uncle, of our victory.
Many a battle have I won in France,
Whenas the enemy hath been ten to one:
Why should I not now have the like success?
[*Alarum. Exeunt*

Scene III.—Plains near Sandal Castle

Alarums; Excursions. Enter Rutland *and his Tutor*

Rut. Ah! whither shall I fly to 'scape their hands?
Ah, tutor! look, where bloody Clifford comes.

Enter Clifford *and Soldiers*

Clif. Chaplain, away: thy priesthood saves thy life.
As for the brat of this accursèd duke,
Whose father slew my father, he shall die.
Tut. And I, my lord, will bear him company.
Clif. Soldiers, away with him.
Tut. Ah, Clifford! murder not this innocent child,
Lest thou be hated both of God and man.
[*Exit, forced off by Soldiers*
Clif. How now! is he dead already? Or is it fear
That makes him close his eyes? I'll open them.
Rut. So looks the pent-up lion o'er the wretch
That trembles under his devouring paws;
And so he walks, insulting o'er his prey,

And so he comes to rend his limbs asunder.—
Ah, gentle Clifford! kill me with thy sword,
And not with such a cruel threatening look.
Sweet Clifford! hear me speak before I die:
I am too mean a subject for thy wrath;
Be thou revenged on men, and let me live.

Clif. In vain thou speak'st, poor boy: my father's blood
Hath stopped the passage where thy words should enter.

Rut. Then let my father's blood open it again:
He is a man, and, Clifford, cope with him.

Clif. Had I thy brethren here, their lives and thine
Were not revenge sufficient for me.
No, if I digged up thy forefathers' graves,
And hung their rotten coffins up in chains,
It could not slake mine ire, nor ease my heart.
The sight of any of the house of York
Is as a fury to torment my soul;
And till I root out their accursed line,
And leave not one alive, I live in hell.
Therefore—

Rut. O! let me pray before I take my death.—
To thee I pray: sweet Clifford, pity me!

Clif. Such pity as my rapier's point affords.

Rut. I never did thee harm: why wilt thou slay me?

Clif. Thy father hath.

Rut. But 't was ere I was born.
Thou hast one son, for his sake pity me,
Lest, in revenge thereof, sith God is just,
He be as miserably slain as I.
Ah, let me live in prison all my days;
And when I give occasion of offence,
Then let me die, for now thou hast no cause.

Clif. No cause?
Thy father slew my father: therefore, die. [*Stabs him*

Rut. *Di faciant laudis summa sit ista tuæ!* [*Dies*

Clif. Plantagenet! I come, Plantagenet!
And this thy son's blood, cleaving to my blade,
Shall rust upon my weapon till thy blood,
Congealed with this, do make me wipe off both. [*Exit*

Scene IV.—The Same

Alarum. Enter York

York. The army of the queen hath got the field:
My uncles both are slain in rescuing me;
And all my followers to the eager foe
Turn back, and fly like ships before the wind.

Or lambs pursued by hunger-starvéd wolves.
My sons—God knows, what hath bechancéd them:
But this I know, they have demeaned themselves
Like men born to renown, by life, or death.
Three times did Richard make a lane to me,
And thrice cried,—'Courage, father! fight it out!'
And full as oft came Edward to my side,
With purple foulchion, painted to the hilt
In blood of those that had encountered him:
And when the hardiest warriors did retire,
Richard cried,—'Charge! and give no foot of ground!'
And cried,—'A crown, or else a glorious tomb!
A sceptre, or an earthly sepulchre!'
With this, we charged again; but, out, alas!
We bodged again: as I have seen a swan
With bootless labour swim against the tide,
And spend her strength with over-matching waves.
[*A short alarum within*
Ah, hark! the fatal followers do pursue;
And I am faint, and cannot fly their fury;
And were I strong, I would not shun their fury.
The sands are numbered, that make up my life;
Here must I stay, and here my life must end.

Enter QUEEN MARGARET, CLIFFORD, NORTHUMBERLAND, *the young* PRINCE, *and Soldiers*

Come, bloody Clifford,—rough Northumberland,—
I dare your quenchless fury to more rage.
I am your butt, and I abide your shot.
North. Yield to our mercy, proud Plantagenet.
Clif. Ay, to such mercy, as his ruthless arm
With downright payment showed unto my father.
Now Phaëton hath tumbled from his car,
And made an evening at the noontide prick.
York. My ashes, as the phœnix, may bring forth
A bird that will revenge upon you all;
And in that hope I throw mine eyes to heaven,
Scorning whate'er you can afflict me with.
Why come you not?—what! multitudes, and fear?
Clif. So cowards fight, when they can fly no farther;
So doves do peck the falcon's piercing talons;
So desperate thieves, all hopeless of their lives,
Breathe out invectives 'gainst the officers.
York. O Clifford! but bethink thee once again,
And in thy thought o'errun my former time;
And, if thou canst for blushing, view this face,
And bite thy tongue that slanders him with cowardice
Whose frown hath made thee faint and fly ere this.
Clif. I will not bandy with thee word for word,

But buckle with thee blows, twice two for one. [*Draws*
Q. Mar. Hold, valiant Clifford! for a thousand causes
I would prolong awhile the traitor's life.—
Wrath makes him deaf: speak thou, Northumberland.
North. Hold, Clifford! do not honour him so much
To prick thy finger, though to wound his heart.
What valour were it, when a cur doth grin,
For one to thrust his hand between his teeth,
When he might spurn him with his foot away?
It is war's prize to take all vantages,
And ten to one is no impeach of valour.
[*They lay hands on York, who struggles*
Clif. Ay, ay: so strives the woodcock with the gin.
North. So doth the cony struggle in the net.
[*York is taken prisoner*
York. So triumph thieves upon their conquered booty;
So true men yield, with robbers so o'ermatched.
North. What would your grace have done unto him now?
Q. Mar. Brave warriors, Clifford and Northumberland,
Come, make him stand upon this molehill here,
That raught at mountains with outstretchéd arms,
Yet parted but the shadow with his hand.—
What! was it you, that would be England's king?
Was't you that revelled in our parliament,
And made a preachment of your high descent?
Where are your mess of sons to back you now?
The wanton Edward, and the lusty George?
And where's that valiant crook-back prodigy,
Dicky your boy, that, with his grumbling voice,
Was wont to cheer his dad in mutinies?
Or, with the rest, where is your darling Rutland?
Look York: I stained this napkin with the blood
That valiant Clifford with his rapier's point
Made issue from the bosom of the boy;
And if thine eyes can water for his death,
I give thee this to dry thy cheeks withal.
Alas, poor York! but that I hate thee deadly,
I should lament thy miserable state.
I pr'ythee, grieve, to make me merry, York:
What! hath thy fiery heart so parched thine entrails,
That not a tear can fall for Rutland's death?
Why art thou patient, man? thou shouldst be mad;
And I, to make thee mad, do mock thee thus.
Stamp, rave, and fret, that I may sing and dance.
Thou wouldst be fee'd, I see, to make me sport;
York cannot speak, unless he wear a crown.—
A crown for York!—and, lords, bow low to him.—
Hold you his hands, whilst I do set it on.—
[*Putting a paper crown on his head*

Ay, marry, sir, now looks he like a king.
Ay, this is he that took King Henry's chair,
And this is he was his adopted heir.—
But how is it, that great Plantagenet
Is crowned so soon, and broke his solemn oath?
As I bethink me, you should not be king,
Till our King Henry had shook hands with death.
And will you pale your head in Henry's glory,
And rob his temples of the diadem,
Now in his life, against your holy oath?
O! 't is a fault too too unpardonable.—
Off with the crown; and, with the crown, his head!
And, whilst we breathe, take time to do him dead.

Clif. That is my office, for my father's sake.

Q. Mar. Nay, stay; let's hear the orisons he makes.

York. She-wolf of France, but worse than wolves of France;
Whose tongue more poisons than the adder's tooth!
How ill-beseeming is it in thy sex
To triumph, like an Amazonian trull,
Upon their woes whom fortune captivates!
But that thy face is, visor-like, unchanging,
Made impudent with use of evil deeds,
I would assay, proud queen, to make thee blush:
To tell thee whence thou cam'st, of whom derived,
Were shame enough to shame thee, wert thou not shameless.
Thy father bears the type of King of Naples,
Of both the Sicils, and Jerusalem,
Yet not so wealthy as an English yeoman.
Hath that poor monarch taught thee to insult?
It needs not, nor it boots thee not, proud queen;
Unless the adage must be verified,
That beggars, mounted, run their horse to death.
'T is beauty that doth oft make women proud;
But God he knows thy share thereof is small.
'T is virtue that doth make them most admired;
The contrary doth make thee wondered at.
'T is government that makes them seem divine;
The want thereof makes thee abominable.
Thou art as opposite to every good,
As the Antipodes are unto us,
Or as the south to the septentrion.
O tiger's heart, wrapped in a woman's hide!
How couldst thou drain the life-blood of the child,
To bid the father wipe his eyes withal;
And yet be seen to bear a woman's face?
Women are soft, mild, pitiful, and flexible;
Thou stern, obdurate, flinty, rough, remorseless.
Bidd'st thou me rage? why, now thou hast thy wish:
Wouldst have me weep? why, now thou hast thy will.

For raging wind blows up incessant showers,
And when the rage allays, the rain begins.
These tears are my sweet Rutland's obsequies,
And every drop cries vengeance for his death,
'Gainst thee, fell Clifford, and thee, false Frenchwoman.

North. Beshrew me, but his passions move me so,
That hardly can I check my eyes from tears.

York. That face of his the hungry cannibals
Would not have touched, would not have stained with blood;
But you are more inhuman, more inexorable,
O, ten times more, than tigers of Hyrcania,
See, ruthless queen, a hapless father's tears!
This cloth thou dipp'dst in blood of my sweet boy,
And I with tears do wash the blood away.
Keep thou the napkin, and go boast of this;
And if thou tell'st the heavy story right,
Upon my soul, the hearers will shed tears;
Yea, even my foes will shed fast-falling tears,
And say,—'Alas! it was a piteous deed.'—
There, take the crown, and with the crown my curse,
And in thy need such comfort come to thee,
As now I reap at thy too cruel hand!—
Hard-hearted Clifford, take me from the world;
My soul to heaven, my blood upon your heads!

North. Had he been slaughter-man to all my kin,
I should not, for my life, but weep with him,
To see how inly sorrow gripes his soul.

Q. Mar. What! weeping-ripe, my Lord Northumberland?
Think but upon the wrong he did us all,
And that will quickly dry thy melting tears.

Clif. Here's for my oath; here's for my father's death. [*Stabbing him*

Q. Mar. And here's to right our gentle-hearted king. [*Stabbing him*

York. Open thy gate of mercy, gracious God!
My soul flies through these wounds to seek out thee. [*Dies*

Q. Mar. Off with his head, and set it on York gates:
So York may overlook the town of York.

[*Flourish. Exeunt*

ACT TWO

Scene I.—A Plain near Mortimer's Cross in Herefordshire

A March. Enter Edward *and* Richard, *with their Power*

Edw. I wonder, how our princely father 'scaped;
Or whether he be 'scaped away, or no,
From Clifford's and Northumberland's pursuit.
Had he been ta'en, we should have heard the news;
Had he been slain, we should have heard the news;
Or had he 'scaped, methinks we should have heard
The happy tidings of his good escape.—
How fares my brother? why is he so sad?
Rich. I cannot joy, until I be resolved
Where our right valiant father is become.
I saw him in the battle range about,
And watched him how he singled Clifford forth.
Methought, he bore him in the thickest troop,
As doth a lion in a herd of neat:
Or as a bear, encompassed round with dogs;
Who having pinched a few, and made them cry,
The rest stand all aloof, and bark at him.
So fared our father with his enemies;
So fled his enemies my warlike father:
Methinks, 't is prize enough to be his son.
See, how the morning opes her golden gates,
And takes her farewell of the glorious sun:
How well resembles it the prime of youth,
Trimmed like a younker, prancing to his love!
Edw. Dazzle mine eyes, or do I see three suns?
Rich. Three glorious suns, each one a perfect sun,
Not separated with the racking clouds,
But severed in a pale clear-shining sky.
See, see! they join, embrace, and seem to kiss,
As if they vowed some league inviolable:
Now are they but one lamp, one light, one sun!
In this the heaven figures some event.
Edw. 'T is wondrous strange, the like yet never heard of,
I think, it cites us, brother, to the field,
That we, the sons of brave Plantagenet,
Each one already blazing by our meeds,
Should, notwithstanding, join our lights together,
And over-shine the earth, as this the world.
Whate'er it bodes, henceforward will I bear
Upon my target three fair-shining suns.
Rich. Nay, bear three daughters: by your leave I speak it,

You love the breeder better than the male.

Enter a Messenger

But what art thou, whose heavy looks foretell
Some dreadful story hanging on thy tongue?
Mess. Ah, one that was a woful looker-on,
Whenas the noble Duke of York was slain,
Your princely father, and my loving lord.
Edw. O, speak no more! for I have heard too much.
Rich. Say, how he died, for I will hear it all.
Mess. Environéd he was with many foes;
And stood against them, as the hope of Troy
Against the Greeks, that would have entered Troy.
But Hercules himself must yield to odds;
And many strokes, though with a little axe,
Hew down and fell the hardest-timbered oak.
By many hands your father was subdued;
But only slaughtered by the ireful arm
Of unrelenting Clifford, and the queen,
Who crowned the gracious duke in high despite;
Laughed in his face; and, when with grief he wept,
The ruthless queen gave him, to dry his cheeks,
A napkin steepéd in the harmless blood
Of sweet young Rutland, by rough Clifford slain:
And, after many scorns, many foul taunts,
They took his head, and on the gates of York
They set the same; and there it doth remain,
The saddest spectacle that e'er I viewed.
Edw. Sweet Duke of York! our prop to lean upon,
Now thou art gone, we have no staff, no stay.
O Clifford! boisterous Clifford! thou hast slain
The flower of Europe for his chivalry;
And treacherously hast thou vanquished him,
For, hand to hand, he would have vanquished thee.
Now, my soul's palace is become a prison:
Ah, would she break from hence, that this my body
Might in the ground be closéd up in rest!
For never henceforth shall I joy again,
Never, O, never, shall I see more joy.
Rich. I cannot weep, for all my body's moisture
Scarce serves to quench my furnace-burning heart:
Nor can my tongue unload my heart's great burden;
For selfsame wind, that I should speak withal,
Is kindling coals that fire all my breast,
And burn me up with flames that tears would quench.
To weep is to make less the depth of grief:
Tears, then, for babes; blows and revenge for me!—
Richard, I bear thy name, I'll venge thy death,
Or die renownéd by attempting it.

Edw. His name that valiant duke hath left with thee;
His dukedom and his chair with me is left.
Rich. Nay, if thou be that princely eagle's bird,
Show thy descent by gazing 'gainst the sun:
For chair and dukedom, throne and kingdom say;
Either that is thine, or else thou wert not his.

March. Enter WARWICK *and* MONTAGUE, *with their Army*

War. How now, fair lords? What fare? what news abroad?
Rich. Great Lord of Warwick, if we should recount
Our baleful news, and at each word's deliverance
Stab poniards in our flesh till all were told,
The words would add more anguish than the wounds.
O valiant lord! the Duke of York is slain.
Edw. O Warwick! Warwick! that Plantagenet,
Which held thee dearly as his soul's redemption,
Is by the stern Lord Clifford done to death.
War. Ten days ago I drowned these news in tears,
And now, to add more measure to your woes,
I come to tell you things sith then befallen.
After the bloody fray at Wakefield fought,
Where your brave father breathed his latest gasp,
Tidings, as swiftly as the posts could run,
Were brought me of your loss, and his depart.
I, then in London, keeper of the king,
Mustered my soldiers, gathered flocks of friends,
And very well appointed, as I thought,
Marched towards Saint Albans to intercept the queen,
Bearing the king in my behalf along;
For by my scouts I was advértiséd,
That she was coming with a full intent
To dash our late decree in parliament,
Touching King Henry's oath and your succession.
Short tale to make,—we at Saint Albans met,
Our battles joined and both sides fiercely fought;
But, whether 't was the coldness of the king,
Who looked full gently on his warlike queen,
That robbed my soldiers of their heated spleen,
Or whether 't was report of her success,
Or more than common fear of Clifford's rigour,
Who thunders to his captives blood and death,
I cannot judge: but, to conclude with truth,
Their weapons like to lightning came and went;
Our soldiers—like the night-owl's lazy flight,
Or like an idle thresher with a flail,—
Fell gently down, as if they struck their friends.
I cheered them up with justice of our cause,
With promise of high pay and great rewards:

But all in vain; they had no heart to fight,
And we, in them, no hope to win the day;
So that we fled: the king unto the queen;
Lord George your brother, Norfolk, and myself,
In haste, post-haste, are come to join with you;
For in the marches here, we heard, you were
Making another head to fight again.
Edw. Where is the Duke of Norfolk, gentle Warwick?
And when came George from Burgundy to England?
War. Some six miles off the duke is with the soldiers;
And for your brother, he was lately sent
From your kind aunt, Duchess of Burgundy,
With aid of soldiers to this needful war.
Rich. 'T was odds, belike, when valiant Warwick fled:
Oft have I heard his praises in pursuit,
But ne'er, till now, his scandal of retire.
War. Nor now my scandal, Richard, dost thou hear;
For thou shalt know, this strong right hand of mine,
Can pluck the diadem from faint Henry's head,
And wring the awful sceptre from his fist,
Were he as famous, and as bold in war,
As he is famed for mildness, peace, and prayer.
Rich. I know it well, Lord Warwick; blame me not:
'T is love I bear thy glories makes me speak.
But in this troublous time, what's to be done?
Shall we go throw away our coats of steel,
And wrap our bodies in black mourning gowns
Numbering our Ave-Maries with our beads?
Or shall we on the helmets of our foes
Tell our devotion with revengeful arms?
If for the last, say—'Ay, and to it, lords.'
War. Why, therefore Warwick came to seek you out,
And therefore comes my brother Montague.
Attend me, lords. The proud insulting queen,
With Clifford, and the haught Northumberland,
And of their feather many more proud birds,
Have wrought the easy-melting king like wax.
He swore consent to your succession,
His oath enrollèd in the parliament;
And now to London all the crew are gone,
To frustrate both his oath, and what beside
May make against the house of Lancaster:
Their power, I think, is thirty thousand strong.
Now, if the help of Norfolk, and myself,
With all the friends that thou, brave Earl of March,
Amongst the loving Welshmen canst procure,
Will but amount to five-and-twenty thousand,
Why, *Via!* to London will we march amain,
And once again bestride our foaming steeds,
And once again cry—'Charge! upon our foes!'

But never once again turn back, and fly.
Rich. Ay, now, methinks, I hear great Warwick speak.
Ne'er may he live to see a sunshine day,
That cries—'Retire,' if Warwick bid him stay.
Edw. Lord Warwick, on thy shoulder will I lean;
And when thou fail'st,—as God forbid the hour!—
Must Edward fall, which peril Heaven forfend!
War. No longer Earl of March, but Duke of York;
The next degree is England's royal throne;
For King of England shalt thou be proclaimed
In every borough as we pass along;
And he that throws not up his cap for joy,
Shall for the fault make forfeit of his head.
King Edward,—valiant Richard,—Montague,—
Stay we no longer dreaming of renown,
But sound the trumpets, and about our task.
Rich. Then, Clifford, were thy heart as hard as steel,
As thou hast shown it flinty by thy deeds,
I come to pierce it, or to give thee mine.
Edw. Then strike up, drums!—God and Saint George for us!

Enter a Messenger

War. How now? what news?
Mess. The Duke of Norfolk sends you word by me,
The queen is coming with a puissant host;
And craves your company for speedy counsel.
War. Why then it sorts: brave warriors, let's away.
[*Exeunt*

Scene II.—Before York

Flourish. Enter King Henry, Queen Margaret, *the* Prince of Wales, Clifford, *and* Northumberland, *with drums and trumpets.*

Q. Mar. Welcome, my lord, to this brave town of York.
Yonder's the head of that arch-enemy,
That sought to be encompassed with your crown:
Doth not the object cheer your heart, my lord?
K. Hen. Ay, as the rocks cheer them that fear their wrack:
To see this sight, it irks my very soul.—
Withhold revenge, dear God! 't is not my fault,
Nor wittingly have I infringed my vow.
Clif. My gracious liege, this too much lenity,
And harmful pity, must be laid aside.
To whom do lions cast their gentle looks?
Not to the beasts that would usurp their den.
Whose hand is that the forest bear doth lick?

Not his that spoils her young before her face.
Who 'scapes the lurking serpent's mortal sting?
Not he that sets his foot upon her back.
The smallest worm will turn, being trodden on;
And doves will peck in safeguard of their brood.
Ambitious York did level at thy crown;
Thou smiling, while he knit his angry brows;
He, but a duke, would have his son a king,
And raise his issue like a loving sire;
Thou, being a king, blessed with a goodly son,
Didst yield consent to disinherit him,
Which argued thee a most unloving father.
Unreasonable creatures feed their young;
And though man's face be fearful to their eyes,
Yet, in protection of their tender ones,
Who hath not seen them, even with those wings
Which sometime they have used in fearful flight,
Make war with him that climbed unto their nest,
Offering their own lives in their young's defence?
For shame, my liege! make them your precedent.
Were it not pity, that this goodly boy
Should lose his birthright by his father's fault,
And long hereafter say unto his child,—
'What my great-grandfather and grandsire got,
My careless father fondly gave away.'
Ah! what a shame were this! Look on the boy;
And let his manly face, which promiseth
Successful fortune, steel thy melting heart
To hold thine own, and leave thine own with him.
K. Hen. Full well hath Clifford played the orator,
Inferring arguments of mighty force.
But, Clifford, tell me, didst thou never hear,
That things ill got had ever bad success?
And happy always was it for that son
Whose father for his hoarding went to hell?
I'll leave my son my virtuous deeds behind;
And would my father had left me no more;
For all the rest is held at such a rate
As brings a thousand-fold more care to keep,
Than in possession any jot of pleasure.
Ah, cousin York! would thy best friends did know
How it doth grieve me that thy head is here!
Q. Mar. My lord, cheer up your spirits: our foes are nigh,
And this soft courage makes your followers faint.
You promised knighthood to our forward son;
Unsheathe your sword, and dub him presently.—
Edward, kneel down.
K. Hen. Edward Plantagenet, arise a knight;
And learn this lesson,—Draw thy sword in right.

Prince. My gracious father, by your kingly leave,
I'll draw it as apparent to the crown,
And in that quarrel use it the death.
Clif. Why, that is spoken like a toward prince.

Enter a Messenger

Mess. Royal commanders, be in readiness:
For, with a band of thirty thousand men,
Comes Warwick, backing of the Duke of York;
And in the towns, as they do march along,
Proclaims him king, and many fly to him.
Darraign your battle, for they are at hand.
Clif. I would, your highness would depart the field:
The queen hath best success when you are absent.
Q. Mar. Ay, good my lord, and leave us to our fortune.
K. Hen. Why, that's my fortune too; therefore I'll stay.
North. Be it with resolution then to fight.
Prince. My royal father, cheer these noble lords,
And hearten those that fight in your defence.
Unsheathe your sword, good father: cry, 'Saint George!'

March. Enter EDWARD, GEORGE, RICHARD, WARWICK, NORFOLK, MONTAGUE, *and Soldiers*

Edw. Now, perjured Henry, wilt thou kneel for grace,
And set thy diadem upon my head,
Or bide the mortal fortune of the field?
Q. Mar. Go, rate thy minions, proud insulting boy!
Becomes it thee to be thus bold in terms,
Before thy sovereign, and thy lawful king?
Edw. I am his king, and he should bow his knee;
I was adopted heir by his consent;
Since when, his oath is broke: for, as I hear,
You, that are king, though he do wear the crown,
Have caused him, by new act of parliament,
To blot out me, and put his own son in.
Clif. And reason too:
Who should succeed the father but the son?
Rich. Are you there, butcher?—O! I cannot speak.
Clif. Ay, crook-back; here I stand, to answer thee,
Or any he the proudest of thy sort.
Rich. 'T was you that killed young Rutland, was it not?
Clif. Ay, and old York, and yet not satisfied.
Rich. For God's sake, lords, give signal to the fight.
War. What say'st thou, Henry, wilt thou yield the crown?
Q. Mar. Why, how now, long-tongued Warwick! dare you speak?

When you and I met at Saint Albans last,
Your legs did better service than your hands.
War. Then 't was my turn to fly, now it is thine.
Clif. You said so much before, and yet you fled.
War. 'T was not your valour, Clifford, drove me thence.
North. No, nor your manhood, that durst make you stay.
Rich. Northumberland, I hold thee reverently.
Break off the parley; scarce I can refrain
The execution of my big-swoln heart
Upon that Clifford, that cruel child-killer.
Clif. I slew thy father: call'st thou him a child?
Rich. Ay, like a dastard, and a treacherous coward,
As thou didst kill our tender brother Rutland;
But ere sunset I'll make thee curse the deed.
K. Hen. Have done with words, my lords, and hear me speak.
Q. Mar. Defy them then, or else hold close thy lips.
K. Hen. I pr'ythee, give no limits to my tongue:
I am a king, and privileged to speak.
Clif. My liege, the wound that bred this meeting here
Cannot be cured by words; therefore be still.
Rich. Then, executioner, unsheathe thy sword.
By Him that made us all, I am resolved
That Clifford's manhood lies upon his tongue.
Edw. Say, Henry, shall I have my right, or no?
A thousand men have broke their fasts to-day,
That ne'er shall dine, unless thou yield the crown.
War. If thou deny, their blood upon thy head;
For York in justice puts his armour on.
Prince. If that be right which Warwick says is right,
There is no wrong but everything is right.
Rich. Whoever got thee, there thy mother stands;
For, well I wot, thou hast thy mother's tongue.
Q. Mar. But thou art neither like thy sire, nor dam;
But like a foul misshapen stigmatic,
Marked by the destinies to be avoided,
As venom toads, or lizards' dreadful stings.
Rich. Iron of Naples, hid with English gilt,
Whose father bears the title of a king,—
As if a channel should be called the sea,—
Sham'st thou not, knowing whence thou art extraught,
To let thy tongue detect thy base-born heart?
Edw. A wisp of straw were worth a thousand crowns,
To make this shameless callat know herself.
Helen of Greece was fairer far than thou,
Although thy husband may be Menelaus;
And ne'er was Agamemnon's brother wronged
By that false woman, as this king by thee.
His father revelled in the heart of France,

And tamed the king, and made the Dauphin stoop;
And had he matched according to his state,
He might have kept that glory to this day;
But when he took a beggar to his bed,
And graced thy poor sire with his bridal-day,
Even then that sunshine brewed a shower for him,
That washed his father's fortunes forth of France,
And heaped sedition on his crown at home.
For what hath broached this tumult, but thy pride?
Hadst thou been meek, our title still had slept,
And we, in pity of the gentle king,
Had slipped our claim until another age.

Geo. But when we saw our sunshine made thy spring,
And that thy summer bred us no increase,
We set the axe to thy usurping root:
And though the edge hath something hit ourselves,
Yet, know thou, since we have begun to strike,
We'll never leave, till we have hewn thee down,
Or bathed thy growing with our heated bloods.

Edw. And in this resolution I defy thee;
Not willing any longer conference,
Since thou deniest the gentle king to speak.—
Sound trumpets!—let our bloody colours wave!
And either victory, or else a grave.

Q. Mar. Stay, Edward.

Edw. No, wrangling woman; we'll no longer stay:
These words will cost ten thousand lives this day. [*Exeunt*

Scene III.—A Field of Battle near Towton

Alarums: Excursions. Enter Warwick

War. Forspent with toil, as runners with a race,
I lay me down a little while to breathe;
For strokes received, and many blows repaid,
Have robbed my strong-knit sinews of their strength,
And, spite of spite, needs must I rest awhile.

Enter Edward, *running*

Edw. Smile, gentle Heaven, or strike, ungentle death!
For this world frowns, and Edward's sun is clouded.

War. How now, my lord? what hap? what hope of good?

Enter George

Geo. Our hap is lost, our hope but sad despair:
Our ranks are broke, and ruin follows us.
What counsel give you? whither shall we fly?

Edw. Bootless is flight: they follow us with wings;
And weak we are, and cannot shun pursuit.

Enter Richard

Rich. Ah, Warwick! why hast thou withdrawn thyself?
Thy brother's blood the thirsty earth hath drunk,
Broached with the steely point of Clifford's lance;
And in the very pangs of death he cried,
Like to a dismal clangor heard from far,
'Warwick, revenge! brother, revenge my death!'
So, underneath the belly of their steeds,
That stained their fetlocks in his smoking blood,
The noble gentleman gave up the ghost.
War. Then let the earth be drunken with our blood:
I'll kill my horse, because I will not fly.
Why stand we like soft-hearted women here,
Wailing our losses, whilst the foe doth rage;
And look upon, as if the tragedy
Were played in jest by counterfeiting actors?
Here on my knee I vow to God above,
I'll never pause again, never stand still,
Till either death hath closed these eyes of mine,
Or fortune given me measure of revenge.
Edw. O Warwick! I do bend my knee with thine;
And, in this vow, do chain my soul to thine.—
And, ere my knee rise from the earth's cold face,
I throw my hands, mine eyes, my heart to thee,
Thou setter-up and plucker-down of kings,
Beseeching thee,—if with thy will it stands
That to my foes this body must be prey,—
Yet that thy brazen gates of heaven may ope,
And give sweet passage to my sinful soul.—
Now, lords, take leave until we meet again,
Where'er it be, in heaven, or in earth.
Rich. Brother, give me thy hand;—and, gentle Warwick,
Let me embrace thee in my weary arms.
I, that did never weep, nor melt with woe,
That winter should cut off our spring-time so.
War. Away, away! Once more, sweet lords, farewell.
Geo. Yet let us all together to our troops,
And give them leave to fly that will not stay,
And call them pillars that will stand to us;
And if we thrive promise them such rewards
As victors wear at the Olympian games.
This may plant courage in their quailing breasts;
For yet is hope of life, and victory.—
Forslow no longer; make we hence amain. [*Exeunt*

SCENE IV.—The Same. Another Part of the Field

Excursions. Enter RICHARD *and* CLIFFORD

Rich. Now, Clifford, I have singled thee alone.
Suppose, this arm is for the Duke of York,
And this for Rutland; both bound to revenge,
Wert thou environed with a brazen wall.
Clif. Now, Richard, I am with thee here alone.
This is the hand that stabbed thy father York,
And this the hand that slew thy brother Rutland;
And there's the heart that triumphs in their death,
And cheers these hands, that slew thy sire and brother,
And so, have at thee!
[*They fight. Warwick comes; Clifford flies*
Rich. Nay, Warwick, single out some other chase;
For I myself will hunt this wolf to death. [*Exeunt*

SCENE V.—Another Part of the Field

Alarum. Enter KING HENRY

K. Hen. This battle fares like to the morning's war,
When dying clouds contend with growing light;
What time the shepherd, blowing of his nails,
Can neither call it perfect day, nor night.
Now sways it this way, like a mighty sea,
Forced by the tide to combat with the wind:
Now sways it that way, like the selfsame sea,
Forced to retire by the fury of the wind:
Sometime, the flood prevails; and then, the wind;
Now, one the better, then, another best;
Both tugging to be victors, breast to breast,
Yet neither conqueror, nor conqueréd:
So is the equal poise of this fell war.
Here, on this molehill, will I sit me down.
To whom God will, there be the victory;
For Margaret my queen, and Clifford too,
Have chid me from the battle; swearing both,
They prosper best of all when I am thence.
'Would I were dead! if God's good will were so;
For what is in this world but grief and woe?
O God! methinks, it were a happy life,
To be no better than a homely swain;
To sit upon a hill, as I do now,
To carve out dials quaintly, point by point,

Thereby to see the minutes how they run,
How many make the hour full complete;
How many hours bring about the day;
How many days will finish up the year;
How many years a mortal man may live.
When this is known, then to divide the times:
So many hours must I tend my flock;
So many hours must I take my rest;
So many hours must I contemplate;
So many hours must I sport myself;
So many days my ewes have been with young;
So many weeks ere the poor fools will ean;
So many years ere I shall shear the fleece:
So minutes, hours, days, months, and years,
Passed over to the end they were created,
Would bring white hairs unto a quiet grave.
Ah, what a life were this! how sweet! how lovely!
Gives not the hawthorn-bush a sweeter shade
To shepherds looking on their silly sheep,
Than doth a rich-embroidered canopy
To kings that fear their subjects' treachery?
O, yes, it doth; a thousand-fold it doth.
And to conclude,—the shepherd's homely curds,
His cold thin drink out of his leather bottle,
His wonted sleep under a fresh tree's shade,
All which secure and sweetly he enjoys,
Is far beyond a prince's delicates,
His viands sparkling in a golden cup,
His body couchéd in a curious bed,
When care, mistrust, and treason waits on him.

Alarum. Enter a Son that hath killed his Father, with the dead body

Son. Ill blows the wind that profits nobody.
This man, whom hand to hand I slew in fight,
May be possesséd with some store of crowns:
And I, that haply take them from him now,
May yet ere night yield both my life and them
To some man else, as this dead man doth me.
Who's this?—O God! it is my father's face,
Whom in this conflict I unawares have killed.
O heavy times, begetting such events!
From London by the king was I pressed forth:
My father, being the Earl of Warwick's man,
Came on the part of York, pressed by his master;
And I, who at his hands received my life,
Have by my hands of life bereavéd him.—
Pardon me, God, I knew not what I did;—
And pardon, father, for I knew not thee.—

My tears shall wipe away these bloody marks:
And no more words, till they have flowed their fill.
K. Hen. O piteous spectacle! O bloody times!
While lions war and battle for their dens,
Poor harmless lambs abide their enmity.
Weep, wretched man, I'll aid thee, tear for tear;
And let our hearts, and eyes, like civil war,
Be blind with tears, and break o'ercharged with grief.

Enter a Father, who has killed his Son, with the body in his arms

Fath. Thou that so stoutly hast resisted me,
Give me thy gold, if thou hast any gold,
For I have bought it with an hundred blows.—
But let me see:—is this our foeman's face?
Ah, no, no, no! it is mine only son!—
Ah, boy! if any life be left in thee,
Throw up thine eye; see, see, what showers arise,
Blown with the windy tempest of my heart,
Upon thy wounds, that kill mine eye and heart!—
O, pity, God, this miserable age!
What stratagems, how fell, how butcherly,
Erroneous, mutinous, and unnatural,
This deadly quarrel daily doth beget!—
O boy! thy father gave thee life too soon,
And hath bereft thee of thy life too late.
K. Hen. Woe above woe! grief more than common grief!
O, that my death would stay these ruthful deeds!
O, pity, pity! gentle Heaven, pity!—
The red rose and the white are on his face,
The fatal colours of our striving houses:
The one his purple blood right well resembles;
The other his pale cheeks, methinks, presenteth;
Wither one rose, and let the other flourish!
If you contend, a thousand lives must wither.
Son. How will my mother, for a father's death,
Take on with me, and ne'er be satisfied!
Fath. How will my wife for slaughter of my son,
Shed seas of tears, and ne'er be satisfied!
K. Hen. How will the country, for these woful chances,
Misthink the king, and not be satisfied!
Son. Was ever son so rued a father's death?
Fath. Was ever father so bemoaned his son?
K. Hen. Was ever king so grieved for subjects' woe?
Much is your sorrow; mine, ten times so much.
Son. I'll bear thee hence, where I may weep my fill.
[*Exit, with the body*

Fath. These arms of mine shall be thy winding-sheet;
My heart, sweet boy, shall be thy sepulchre,
For from my heart thine image ne'er shall go.
My sighing breast shall be thy funeral bell;
And so obsequious will thy father be,
Son, for the loss of thee, having no more,
As Priam was for all his valiant sons.
I'll bear thee hence; and let them fight that will,
For I have murdered where I should not kill.
[*Exit, with the body*

K. Hen. Sad-hearted men, much overgone with care,
Here sits a king more woful than you are.

Alarum: Excursions. Enter QUEEN MARGARET, PRINCE OF WALES, *and* EXETER

Prince. Fly, father, fly! for all your friends are fled,
And Warwick rages like a chafèd bull.
Away! for death doth hold us in pursuit.

Q. Mar. Mount you, my lord: towards Berwick post amain.
Edward and Richard, like a brace of greyhounds
Having the fearful flying hare in sight,
With fiery eyes, sparkling for very wrath,
And bloody steel grasped in their ireful hands,
Are at our backs; and therefore hence amain.

Exe. Away! for vengeance comes along with them.
Nay, stay not to expostulate; make speed,
Or else come after: I'll away before.

K. Hen. Nay, take me with thee, good sweet Exeter:
Not that I fear to stay, but love to go
Whither the queen intends. Forward! away! [*Exeunt*

SCENE VI.—The Same

A loud Alarum. Enter CLIFFORD, *wounded*

Clif. Here burns my candle out; ay, here it dies,
Which, while it lasted, gave King Henry light.
O, Lancaster, I fear thy overthrow,
More than my body's parting with my soul.
My love and fear glued many friends to thee;
And now I fall thy tough commixture melts,
Impairing Henry, strengthening misproud York;
And whither fly the gnats, but to the sun?
And who shines now but Henry's enemies?
O Phœbus! hadst thou never given consent
That Phaëthon should check thy fiery steeds,

Thy burning car never had scorched the earth;
And, Henry, hadst thou swayed as kings should do,
Or as thy father, and his father, did,
Giving no ground unto the house of York,
They never then had sprung like summer-flies;
I and ten thousand in this luckless realm
Had left no mourning widows for our death,
And thou this day hadst kept thy chair in peace.
For what doth cherish weeds but gentle air?
And what makes robbers bold but too much lenity?
Bootless are plaints, and cureless are my wounds;
No way to fly, nor strength to hold out flight:
The foe is merciless, and will not pity;
For at their hands I have deserved no pity.
The air hath got into my deadly wounds,
And much effuse of blood doth make me faint.—
Come, York, and Richard, Warwick, and the rest;
I stabbed your fathers' bosoms, split my breast. [*He faints*

Alarum and Retreat. Enter EDWARD, GEORGE, RICHARD, MONTAGUE, WARWICK, *and Soldiers*

Edw. Now breathe we, lords: good fortune bids us pause,
And smooth the frowns of war with peaceful looks.—
Some troops pursue the bloody-minded queen,
That led calm Henry, though he were a king,
As doth a sail, filled with a fretting gust,
Command an argosy to stem the waves.
But thank you, lords, that Clifford fled with them?
War. No, 't is impossible he should escape;
For, though before his face I speak the words,
Your brother Richard marked him for the grave;
And wheresoe'er he is, he's surely dead.
[*Clifford groans and dies*
Edw. Whose soul is that which takes her heavy leave?
Rich. A deadly groan, like life and death's departing.
Edw. See who it is: and, now the battle's ended,
If friend, or foe, let him be gently used.
Rich. Revoke that doom of mercy, for 't is Clifford;
Who not contented that he lopped the branch
In hewing Rutland when his leaves put forth,
But set his murdering knife unto the root
From whence that tender spray did sweetly spring,—
I mean, our princely father, Duke of York.
War. From off the gates of York fetch down the head,
Your father's head, which Clifford placèd there;
Instead whereof, let this supply the room:
Measure for measure must be answerèd.
Edw. Bring forth that fatal screech-owl to our house

That nothing sung but death to us and ours:
Now death shall stop his dismal threatening sound,
And his ill-boding tongue no more shall speak.
[*Attendants bring the body forward*
War.—I think, his understanding is bereft.—
Speak, Clifford, dost thou know who speaks to thee?—
Dark cloudy death o'ershades his beams of life,
And he nor sees, nor hears us what we say.
Rich. O, would he did! and so, perhaps, he doth:
'T is but his policy to counterfeit,
Because he would avoid such bitter taunts
Which in the time of death he gave our father.
Geo. If so you think'st, vex him with eager words.
Rich. Clifford! ask mercy, and obtain no grace.
Edw. Clifford! repent in bootless penitence.
War. Clifford! devise excuses for thy faults.
Geo. While we devise fell tortures for thy faults.
Rich. Thou didst love York, and I am son to York.
Edw. Thou pitiedst Rutland, I will pity thee.
Geo. Where's Captain Margaret, to fence you now?
War. They mock thee, Clifford: swear as thou wast wont.
Rich. What! not an oath? nay, then the world goes hard,
When Clifford cannot spare his friends an oath.—
I know by that, he's dead; and, by my soul,
If this right hand would buy two hours' life
That I in all despite might rail at him,
This hand should chop it off; and with the issuing blood
Stifle the villain, whose unstaunchéd thirst
York and young Rutland could not satisfy.
War. Ay, but he's dead. Off with the traitor's head,
And rear it in the place your father's stands.
And now to London with triumphant march,
There to be crownéd England's royal king.
From whence shall Warwick cut the sea to France,
And ask the Lady Bona for thy queen.
So shalt thou sinew both these lands together;
And, having France thy friend, thou shalt not dread
The scattered foe that hopes to rise again;
For though they cannot greatly sting to hurt,
Yet look to have them buz, to offend thine ears.
First will I see the coronation,
And then to Brittany I'll cross the sea,
To effect this marriage, so it please my lord.
Edw. Even as thou wilt, sweet Warwick, let it be;
For in thy shoulder do I build my seat,
And never will I undertake the thing,
Wherein thy counsel and consent is wanting.—
Richard, I will create thee Duke of Gloster;—

And George, of Clarence;—Warwick, as ourself,
Shall do, and undo, as him pleaseth best.
Rich. Let me be Duke of Clarence, George of Gloster,
For Gloster's dukedom is too ominous.
War. Tut! that's a foolish observation:
Richard, be Duke of Gloster. Now to London,
To see these honours in possession. [*Exeunt*

ACT THREE

Scene I.—A Chase in the North of England

Enter two Keepers, with cross-bows in their hands

First Keep. Under this thick-grown brake we'll shroud ourselves;
For through this laund anon the deer will come;
And in this covert will we make our stand,
Culling the principal of all the deer.
Sec. Keep. I'll stay above the hill, so both may shoot.
First Keep. That cannot be; the noise of thy cross-bow
Will scare the herd, and so my shoot is lost.
Here stand we both, and aim we at the best:
And, for the time shall not seem tedious,
I'll tell thee what befell me on a day,
In this self place where now we mean to stand.
Sec. Keep. Here comes a man, let's stay till he be past.

Enter King Henry, *disguised, with a prayer-book*

K. Hen. From Scotland am I stol'n, even of pure love,
To greet mine own land with my wishful sight.
No, Harry, Harry, 't is no land of thine;
Thy place is filled, thy sceptre wrung from thee,
Thy balm washed off wherewith thou wast anointed:
No bending knee will call thee Cæsar now,
No humble suitors press to speak for right,
No, not a man comes for redress of thee,
For how can I help them, and not myself?
First Keep. Ay, here's a deer whose skin's a keeper's fee;
This is the *quondam* king; let's seize upon him.
K. Hen. Let me embrace the sour adversities;
For wise men say, it is the wisest course.
Sec. Keep. Why linger we? let us lay hands upon him.
First Keep. Forbear awhile: we'll hear a little more.

K. Hen. My queen and son are gone to France for aid;
And, as I hear, the great commanding Warwick
Is thither gone, to crave the French king's sister
To wife for Edward. If this news be true,
Poor queen and son, your labour is but lost:
For Warwick is a subtle orator,
And Lewis a prince soon won with moving words.
By this account then, Margaret may win him,
For she's a woman to be pitied much:
Her sighs will make a battery in his breast,
Her tears will pierce into a marble heart;
The tiger will be mild whiles she doth mourn,
And Nero will be tainted with remorse
To hear and see her plaints, her brinish tears.
Ay, but she's come to beg; Warwick to give:
She on his left side craving aid for Henry,
He on his right asking a wife for Edward.
She weeps, and says—her Henry is deposed;
He smiles, and says—his Edward is installed;
That she, poor wretch, for grief can speak no more:
Whiles Warwick tells his title, smooths the wrong,
Inferreth arguments of mighty strength,
And, in conclusion wins the king from her,
With promise of his sister, and what else,
To strengthen and support King Edward's place.
O Margaret! thus 't will be; and thou, poor soul,
Art then forsaken, as thou went'st forlorn.

Sec. Keep. Say, what art thou that talk'st of kings and queens?

K. Hen. More than I seem, and less than I was born to:
A man at least, for less I should not be;
And men may talk of kings, and why not I?

Sec. Keep. Ay, but thou talk'st as if thou wert a king.

K. Hen. Why, so I am, in mind; and that's enough.

Sec. Keep. But, if thou be a king, where is thy crown?

K. Hen. My crown is in my heart, not on my head;
Not decked with diamonds, and Indian stones,
Nor to be seen: my crown is called, content;
A crown it is, that seldom kings enjoy.

Sec. Keep. Well, if you be a king crowned with content,
Your crown content, and you, must be contented
To go along with us; for, as we think,
You are the king King Edward hath deposed;
And we his subjects, sworn in all allegiance,
Will apprehend you as his enemy.

K. Hen. But did you never swear, and break an oath?

Sec. Keep. No, never such an oath; nor will not now.

K. Hen. Where did you dwell, when I was King of England?

Sec. Keep. Here in this country, where we now remain.

K. Hen. I was anointed king at nine months old;
My father and my grandfather were kings;
And you were sworn true subjects unto me:
And tell me then, have you not broke your oaths?
First Keep. No:
For we were subjects but while you were king.
K. Hen. Why, am I dead? do I not breathe a man?
Ah, simple men! you know not what you swear.
Look, as I blow this feather from my face,
And as the air blows it to me again,
Obeying with my wind when I do blow,
And yielding to another when it blows,
Commanded always by the greater gust:
Such is the lightness of you common men
But do not break your oaths; for of that sin
My mild entreaty shall not make you guilty.
Go where you will, the king shall be commanded;
And be you kings: command, and I'll obey.
First Keep. We are true subjects to the king, King Edward.
K. Hen. So would you be again to Henry,
If he were seated as King Edward is.
First Keep. We charge you, in God's name, and the king's,
To go with us unto the officers.
K. Hen. In God's name, lead; your king's name be obeyed:
And what God will, that let your king perform;
And what he will, I humbly yield unto. [*Exeunt*

Scene II.—London. A Room in the Palace

Enter King Edward, Gloster, Clarence, *and* Lady Grey

K. Edw. Brother of Gloster, at Saint Albans field
This lady's husband, Sir Richard Grey, was slain,
His lands then seized on by the conqueror:
Her suit is now, to repossess those lands;
Which we in justice cannot well deny,
Because in quarrel of the house of York
The worthy gentleman did lose his life.
Glo. Your highness shall do well to grant her suit;
It were dishonour to deny it her.
K. Edw. It were no less; but yet I'll make a pause.
Glo. [*Aside to Clarence*] Yea; is it so?
I see the lady hath a thing to grant,
Before the king will grant her humble suit.
Clar. [*Aside to Gloster*] He knows the game: how true he keeps the wind!

Glo. [*Aside to Clarence*] Silence!
K. Edw. Widow, we will consider of your suit,
And come some other time to know our mind.
L. Grey. Right gracious lord, I cannot brook delay:
May it please your highness to resolve me now,
And what your pleasure is shall satisfy me.
Glo. [*Aside to Clarence*] Ay, widow? then I'll warrant you all your lands,
An if what pleases him shall pleasure you.
Fight closer, or, good faith, you'll catch a blow.
Clar. [*Aside to Gloster*] I fear her not, unless she chance to fall.
Glo. [*Aside to Clarence*] God forbid that, for he'll take vantages.
K. Edw. How many children hast thou, widow? tell me.
Clar. [*Aside to Gloster*] I think, he means to beg a child of her.
Glo. [*Aside to Clarence*] Nay, whip me then; he'll rather give her two.
L. Grey. Three, my most gracious lord.
Glo. [*Aside to Clarence*] You shall have four, if you'll be ruled by him.
K. Edw. 'T were pity, they should lose their father's lands.
L. Grey. Be pitiful, dread lord, and grant it then.
K. Edw. Lords, give us leave: I'll try this widow's wit.
Glo. [*Aside to Clarence*] Ay, good leave have you; for you will have leave,
Till youth take leave, and leave you to the crutch.
[*Gloster and Clarence stand apart*
K. Edw. Now, tell me, madam, do you love your children?
L. Grey. Ay, full as dearly as I love myself.
K. Edw. And would you not do much, to do them good?
L. Grey. To do them good I would sustain some harm.
K. Edw. Then get your husband's lands, to do them good.
L. Grey. Therefore I came unto your majesty.
K. Edw. I'll tell you how these lands are to be got.
L. Grey. So shall you bind me to your highness' service.
K. Edw. What service wilt thou do me, if I give them?
L. Grey. What you command, that rests in me to do.
K. Edw. But you will take exceptions to my boon
L. Grey. No, gracious lord, except I cannot do it.
K. Edw. Ay, but thou canst do what I mean to ask.
L. Grey. Why then, I will do what your grace commands.
Glo. [*Aside to Clarence*] He plies her hard; and much rain wears the marble.
Clar. [*Aside to Gloster*] As red as fire! nay, then her wax must melt.

L. Grey. Why stops my lord? shall I not hear my task?
K. Edw. An easy task: 't is but to love a king.
L. Grey. That 's soon performed, because I am a subject.
K. Edw. Why then, thy husband's lands I free give thee.
L. Grey. I take my leave with many thousand thanks.
Glo. [*Aside to Clarence*] The match is made: she seals it with a curtsy.
K. Edw. But stay thee; 't is the fruits of love I mean.
L. Grey. The fruits of love I mean, my loving liege.
K. Edw. Ay, but, I fear me, in another sense.
What love think'st thou I sue so much to get?
L. Grey. My love till death, my humble thanks, my prayers:
That love which virtue begs, and virtue grants.
K. Edw. No, by my troth, I did not mean such love.
L. Grey. Why, then you mean not as I thought you did.
K. Edw. But now you partly may perceive my mind.
L. Grey. My mind will never grant what I perceive
Your highness aims at, if I aim aright.
K. Edw. To tell thee plain, I aim to lie with thee.
L. Grey. To tell you plain, I had rather lie in prison.
K. Edw. Why, then thou shalt not have thy husband's lands.
L. Grey. Why, then mine honesty shall be my dower;
For by that loss I will not purchase them.
K. Edw. Therein thou wrong'st thy children mightily.
L. Grey. Herein your highness wrongs both them and me.
But, mighty lord, this merry inclination
Accords not with the sadness of my suit;
Please you dismiss me, either with ay, or no.
K. Edw. Ay, if thou wilt say ay to my request;
No, if thou dost say no to my demand.
L. Grey. Then, no, my lord. My suit is at an end.
Glo. [*Aside to Clarence*] The widow likes him not, she knits her brows.
Clar. [*Aside to Gloster*] He is the bluntest wooer in Christendom.
K. Edw. [*Aside*] Her looks do argue her replete with modesty;
Her words do show her wit incomparable;
All her perfections challenge sovereignty;
One way, or other, she is for a king,
And she shall be my love, or else my queen.—
Say, that King Edward take thee for his queen?
L. Grey. 'T is better said than done, my gracious lord:
I am a subject fit to jest withal,
But far unfit to be a sovereign.

K. Edw. Sweet widow, by my state, I swear to thee,
I speak no more than what my soul intends;
And that is, to enjoy thee for my love.
L. Grey. And that is more than I will yield unto.
I know, I am too mean to be your queen,
And yet too good to be your concubine.
K. Edw. You cavil, widow: I did mean, my queen.
L. Grey. 'T will grieve your grace, my sons should call you father.
K. Edw. No more than when my daughters call thee mother.
Thou art a widow, and thou hast some children;
And, by God's mother, I, being but a bachelor,
Have other some: why, 't is a happy thing
To be the father unto many sons.
Answer no more, for thou shalt be my queen.
Glo. [*Aside to Clarence*] The ghostly father now hath done his shrift.
Clar. [*Aside to Gloster*] When he was made a shriver 't was for shift.
K. Edw. Brothers, you muse what chat we two have had.
Glo. The widow likes it not, for she looks very sad.
K. Edw. You'd think it strange if I should marry her.
Clar. To whom, my lord?
K. Edw. Why, Clarence, to myself.
Glo. That would be ten days' wonder at the least.
Clar. That's a day longer than a wonder lasts.
Glo. By so much is the wonder in extremes.
K. Edw. Well, jest on, brothers: I can tell you both,
Her suit is granted for her husband's lands.

Enter a Nobleman

Nob. My gracious lord, Henry your foe is taken,
And brought your prisoner to your palace gate.
K. Edw. See that he be conveyed unto the Tower:—
And go we, brothers, to the man that took him,
To question of his apprehension.—
Widow, go you along.—Lords, use her honourably.
[*Exeunt all but Gloster*
Glo. Ay, Edward will use women honourably.
Would he were wasted, marrow, bones, and all,
That from his loins no hopeful branch may spring,
To cross me from the golden time I look for!
And yet, between my soul's desire, and me,—
The lustful Edward's title buried,—
Is Clarence, Henry, and his son young Edward,
And all the unlooked for issue of their bodies,
To take their rooms, ere I can place myself:
A cold premeditation for my purpose!

Why then, I do but dream on sovereignty;
Like one that stands upon a promontory,
And spies a far-off shore where he would tread,
Wishing his foot were equal with his eye;
And chides the sea that sunders him from thence,
Saying—he'll lade it dry to have his way:
So do I wish the crown, being so far off,
And so I chide the means that keep me from it;
And so I say—I'll cut the causes off,
Flattering me with impossibilities.—
My eye's too quick, my heart o'erweens too much,
Unless my hand and strength could equal them.
Well, say there is no kingdom then for Richard,
What other pleasure can the world afford?
I'll make my heaven in a lady's lap,
And deck my body in gay ornaments,
And witch sweet ladies with my words and looks.
O miserable thought! and more unlikely,
Than to accomplish twenty golden crowns.
Why, love forswore me in my mother's womb:
And, for I should not deal in her soft laws,
She did corrupt frail nature with some bribe,
To shrink mine arm up like a withered shrub:
To make an envious mountain on my back,
Where sits deformity to mock my body;
To shape my legs of an unequal size;
To disproportion me in every part;
Like to a chaos, or an unlicked bear-whelp,
That carries no impression like the dam.
And am I then a man to be beloved!
O monstrous fault, to harbour such a thought!
Then, since this earth affords no joy to me
But to command, to check, to o'erbear such
As are of better person than myself,
I'll make my heaven to dream upon the crown;
And, whiles I live, to account this world but hell,
Until my misshaped trunk, that bears this head,
Be round impalèd with a glorious crown.
And yet I know not how to get the crown,
For many lives stand between me and home:
And I,—like one lost in a thorny wood,
That rends the thorns, and is rent with the thorns,
Seeking a way, and straying from the way,
Not knowing how to find the open air,
But toiling desperately to find it out,—
Torment myself to catch the English crown:
And from that torment I will free myself,
Or hew my way out with a bloody axe.
Why, I can smile, and murder while I smile,
And cry, content, to that which grieves my heart.

And wet my cheeks with artificial tears,
And frame my face to all occasions.
I'll drown more sailors than the mermaid shall,
I'll slay more gazers than the basilisk;
I'll play the orator as well as Nestor,
Deceive more slily than Ulysses could,
And, like a Sinon, take another Troy.
I can add colours to the chameleon,
Change shapes with Proteus, for advantages,
And set the murderous Machiavel to school.
Can I do this, and cannot get a crown?
Tut! were it further off, I'll pluck it down. [*Exit*

Scene III.—France. A Room in the Palace

Flourish. Enter Lewis *the French King, and* Lady Bona, *attended: the* King *takes his state. Then enter* Queen Margaret, Prince Edward, *and the* Earl of Oxford

K. Lew. [*Rising*] Fair Queen of England, worthy Margaret,
Sit down with us: it ill befits thy state
And birth, that thou shouldst stand, while Lewis doth sit
Q. Mar. No, mighty king of France; now Margaret
Must strike her sail, and learn awhile to serve,
Where kings command. I was, I must confess,
Great Albion's queen in former golden days;
But now mischance hath trod my title down,
And with dishonour laid me on the ground
Where I must take like seat unto my fortune,
And to my humble seat conform myself.
K. Lew. Why, say, fair queen, whence springs this deep despair?
Q. Mar. From such a cause as fills mine eyes with tears,
And stops my tongue, while heart is drowned in cares.
K. Lew. Whate'er it be, be thou still like thyself,
And sit thee by our side: [*seats her by him*] yield not thy neck
To fortune's yoke, but let thy dauntless mind
Still ride in triumph over all mischance.
Be plain, Queen Margaret, and tell thy grief;
It shall be eased, if France can yield relief.
Q. Mar. Those gracious words revive my drooping thoughts,
And give my tongue-tied sorrows leave to speak.
Now, therefore, be it known to noble Lewis,
That Henry, sole possessor of my love,
Is of a king become a banished man,

And forced to live in Scotland, a forlorn;
While proud ambitious Edward, Duke of York,
Usurps the regal title, and the seat
Of England's true-anointed lawful king.
This is the cause, that I, poor Margaret,
With this my son, Prince Edward, Henry's heir,
Am come to crave thy just and lawful aid;
And if thou fail us, all our hope is done.
Scotland hath will to help, but cannot help;
Our people and our peers are both misled,
Our treasure seized, our soldiers put to flight,
And, as thou seest, ourselves in heavy plight.
K. Lew. Renownèd queen, with patience calm the storm,
While we bethink a means to break it off.
Q. Mar. The more we stay, the stronger grows our foe.
K. Lew. The more I stay, the more I'll succour thee.
Q. Mar. O, but impatience waiteth on true sorrow:
And see where comes the breeder of my sorrow.

Enter WARWICK, *attended*

K. Lew. What's he, approacheth boldly to our presence?
Q. Mar. Our Earl of Warwick. Edward's greatest friend.
K. Lew. Welcome, brave Warwick, What brings thee to France?
[*Descending from his state. Queen Margaret rises*
Q. Mar. Ay, now begins a second storm to rise;
For this is he that moves both wind and tide.
War. From worthy Edward, King of Albion,
My lord and sovereign, and thy vowèd friend,
I come, in kindness, and unfeignèd love,
First, to do greetings to thy royal person:
And then, to crave a league of amity;
And lastly, to confirm that amity
With nuptial knot, if thou vouchsafe to grant
That virtuous Lady Bona, thy fair sister,
To England's king in lawful marriage.
Q. Mar. If that go forward, Henry's hope is done.
War. [*To Bona*] And, gracious madam, in our king's behalf,
I am commanded, with your leave and favour.
Humbly to kiss your hand, and with my tongue
To tell the passion of my sovereign's heart;
Where fame, late entering at his heedful ears,
Hath placed thy beauty's image, and thy virtue.
Q. Mar. King Lewis, and Lady Bona, hear me speak,
Before you answer Warwick. His demand

Springs not from Edward's well-meant honest love,
But from deceit, bred by necessity;
For how can tyrants safely govern home,
Unless abroad they purchase great alliance?
To prove him tyrant, this reason may suffice,
That Henry liveth still; but were he dead,
Yet here Prince Edward stands, King Henry's son.
Look, therefore, Lewis, that by this league and marriage
Thou draw not on thy danger and dishonour;
For though usurpers sway the rule awhile,
Yet heavens are just, and time suppresseth wrongs.

War. Injurious Margaret!

Prince. And why not queen?

War. Because thy father Henry did usurp,
And thou no more art prince than she is queen.

Oxf. Then Warwick disannuls great John of Gaunt,
Which did subdue the greatest part of Spain;
And, after John of Gaunt, Henry the Fourth,
Whose wisdom was a mirror to the wisest;
And after that wise prince, Henry the Fifth,
Who by his prowess conqueréd all France:
From these our Henry lineally descends.

War. Oxford, how haps it in this smooth discourse,
You told not, how Henry the Sixth hath lost
All that which Henry the Fifth had gotten?
Methinks, these peers of France should smile at that.
But for the rest,—you tell a pedigree
Of threescore and two years; a silly time
To make prescription for a kingdom's worth.

Oxf. Why, Warwick, canst thou speak against thy liege,
Whom thou obeyedst thirty and six years,
And not bewray thy treason with a blush?

War. Can Oxford, that did ever fence the right,
Now buckler falsehood with a pedigree?
For shame! leave Henry, and call Edward king.

Oxf. Call him my king, by whose injurious doom
My elder brother, the Lord Aubrey Vere,
Was done to death? and more than so, my father,
Even in the downfall of his mellowed years,
When nature brought him to the door of death?
No, Warwick, no; while life upholds this arm,
This arm upholds the house of Lancaster.

War. And I the house of York.

K. Lew. Queen Margaret, Prince Edward, and Oxford,
Vouchsafe at our request to stand aside,
While I use further conference with Warwick.

Q. Mar. Heavens grant, that Warwick's words bewitch him not! [*Retiring with the Prince and Oxford*

K. Lew. Now, Warwick, tell me, even upon thy conscience,

Is Edward your true king? for I were loth
To link with him that were not lawful chosen.
War. Thereon I pawn my credit, and mine honour.
K. Lew. But is he gracious in the people's eye?
War. The more, that Henry was unfortunate.
K. Lew. Then further, all dissembling set aside,
Tell me for truth the measure of his love
Unto our sister Bona.
War. Such it seems,
As may beseem a monarch like himself.
Myself have often heard him say, and swear,
That this his love was an eternal plant,
Whereof the root was fixed in virtue's ground,
The leaves and fruit maintained with beauty's sun,
Exempt from envy, but not from disdain,
Unless the Lady Bona quit his pain.
K. Lew. Now, sister, let us hear your firm resolve.
Bona. Your grant, or your denial, shall be mine.—
[*To Warwick*] Yet I confess, that often ere this day,
When I have heard your king's desert recounted,
Mine ear hath tempted judgment to desire.
K. Lew. Then, Warwick, thus:—our sister shall be Edward's;
And now forthwith shall articles be drawn
Touching the jointure that your king must make,
Which with her dowry shall be counterpoised.—
Draw near, Queen Margaret, and be a witness,
That Bona shall be wife to the English king.
Prince. To Edward, but not to the English king.
Q. Mar. Deceitful Warwick! it was thy device,
By this alliance to make void my suit:
Before thy coming, Lewis was Henry's friend.
K. Lew. And still is friend to him and Margaret:
But if your title to the crown be weak,
As may appear by Edward's good success,
Then 't is but reason, that I be released
From giving aid which late I promiséd.
Yet shall you have all kindness at my hand,
That your estate requires, and mine can yield.
War. Henry now lives in Scotland, at his ease,
Where having nothing, nothing can he lose.
And as for you yourself, our *quondam* queen,
You have a father able to maintain you,
And better 't were you troubled him than France.
Q. Mar. Peace! impudent and shameless Warwick, peace,
Proud setter-up and puller-down of kings:
I will not hence, till with my talk and tears,
Both full of truth, I make King Lewis behold
Thy sly conveyance, and thy lord's false love;

For both of you are birds of selfsame feather.
[*A horn sounded within*
K. Lew. Warwick, this is some post to us, or thee.

Enter a Messenger

Mess. My lord ambassador, these letters are for you,
Sent from your brother, Marquess Montague;—
These from our king unto your majesty;—
And, madam, these for you; from whom, I know not.
[*They all read their letters*
Oxf. I like it well, that our fair queen and mistress
Smiles at her news, while Warwick frowns at his.
Prince. Nay, mark how Lewis stamps as he were nettled:
I hope all's for the best.
K. Lew. Warwick, what are thy news? and yours, fair queen?
Q. Mar. Mine, such as fill my heart with unhoped joys.
War. Mine, full of sorrow and heart's discontent.
K. Lew. What! has your king married the Lady Grey,
And now, to soothe your forgery and his,
Sends me a paper to persuade me patience?
Is this the alliance that he seeks with France?
Dares he presume to scorn us in this manner?
Q. Mar. I told your majesty as much before:
This proveth Edward's love, and Warwick's honesty.
War. King Lewis, I here protest, in sight of heaven,
And by the hope I have of heavenly bliss,
That I am clear from this misdeed of Edward's;
No more my king, for he dishonours me,
But most himself, if he could see his shame.
Did I forget, that by the house of York
My father came untimely to his death?
Did I let pass the abuse done to my niece?
Did I impale him with the regal crown?
Did I put Henry from his native right?
And am I guerdoned at the last with shame?
Shame on himself, for my desert is honour:
And to repair my honour lost for him,
I here renounce him, and return to Henry,
My noble queen, let former grudges pass,
And henceforth I am thy true servitor.
I will revenge his wrong to Lady Bona,
And replant Henry in his former state.
Q. Mar. Warwick, these words have turned my hate to love;
And I forgive and quite forget old faults,
And joy that thou becom'st King Henry's friend.

War. So much his friend, ay, his unfeignéd friend,
That if King Lewis vouchsafe to furnish us
With some few bands of chosen soldiers,
I'll undertake to land them on our coast,
And force the tyrant from his seat by war.
'T is not his new-made bride shall succour him:
And as for Clarence, as my letters tell me,
He's very likely now to fall from him,
For matching more for wanton lust than honour,
Or than for strength and safety of our country.
Bona. Dear brother, how shall Bona be revenged,
But by thy help to this distresséd queen?
Q. Mar. Renownéd prince, how shall poor Henry live,
Unless thou rescue him from foul despair?
Bona. My quarrel, and this English queen's, are one.
War. And mine, fair Lady Bona, joins with yours.
K. Lew. And mine, with hers, and thine, and Margaret's.
Therefore, at last, I firmly am resolved,
You shall have aid.
Q. Mar. Let me give humble thanks for all at once.
K. Lew. Then, England's messenger, return in post;
And tell false Edward, thy supposéd king,
That Lewis of France is sending over masquers,
To revel it with him and his new bride.
Thou seest what's passed; go fear thy king withal.
Bona. Tell him, in hope he'll prove a widower shortly,
I'll wear the willow garland for his sake.
Q. Mar. Tell him, my mourning weeds are laid aside,
And I am ready to put armour on.
War. Tell him from me, that he hath done me wrong,
And therefore I'll uncrown him ere 't be long.
There's thy reward: be gone. [*Exit Messenger*
K. Lew. But, Warwick, thou,
And Oxford, with five thousand men,
Shall cross the seas, and bid false Edward battle:
And, as occasion serves, this noble Queen
And Prince shall follow with a fresh supply.
Yet, ere thou go, but answer me one doubt:
What pledge have we of thy firm loyalty?
War. This shall assure my constant loyalty:—
That if our Queen and this young Prince agree,
I'll join mine eldest daughter, and my joy,
To him forthwith in holy wedlock bands.
Q. Mar. Yes, I agree, and thank you for your motion.
Son Edward, she is fair and virtuous,
Therefore delay not, give thy hand to Warwick;
And with thy hand thy faith irrevocable,
That only Warwick's daughter shall be thine.

Prince. Yes, I accept her, for she well deserves it;
And here, to pledge my vow, I give my hand.
[*He gives his hand to Warwick*

K. Lew. Why stay we now? These soldiers shall be levied,
And thou, Lord Bourbon, our high admiral,
Shall waft them over with our royal fleet.—
I long till Edward fall by war's mischance,
For mocking marriage with a dame of France.
[*Exeunt all but Warwick*

War. I came from Edward as ambassador,
But I return his sworn and mortal foe:
Matter of marriage was the charge he gave me,
But dreadful war shall answer his demand.
Had he none else to make a stale but me?
Then none but I shall turn his jest to sorrow.
I was the chief that raised him to the crown,
And I 'll be chief to bring him down again:
Not that I pity Henry's misery,
But seek revenge on Edward's mockery. [*Exit*

ACT FOUR

Scene I.—London. A Room in the Palace

Enter Gloster, Clarence, Somerset, *and* Montague

Glo. Now tell me, brother Clarence, what think you
Of this new marriage with the Lady Grey?
Hath not our brother made a worthy choice?

Clar. Alas! you know, 't is far from hence to France:
How could he stay till Warwick made return?

Som. My lords, forbear this talk: here comes the king.

Glo. And his well-chosen bride.

Clar. I mind to tell him plainly what I think.

Flourish. Enter King Edward, *attended;* Lady Grey, *as Queen;* Pembroke, Stafford, *and* Hastings

K. Edw. Now, brother of Clarence, how like you our choice,
That you stand pensive as half malcontent?

Clar. As well as Lewis of France, or the Earl of Warwick;
Which are so weak of courage, and in judgment,
That they'll take no offence at our abuse.

K. Edw. Suppose they take offence without a cause,

They are but Lewis and Warwick: I am Edward,
Your king and Warwick's, and must have my will.
Glo. And you shall have your will, because our king;
Yet hasty marriage seldom proveth well.
K. Edw. Yea, brother Richard, are you offended too?
Glo. Not I:
No, God forbid, that I should wish them severed
Whom God hath joined together; ay, and 't were pity,
To sunder them that yoke so well together.
K. Edw. Setting your scorns, and your mislike, aside,
Tell me some reason why the Lady Grey
Should not become my wife, and England's queen.—
And you, too, Somerset, and Montague,
Speak freely what you think.
Clar. Then this is mine opinion,—That King Lewis
Becomes your enemy, for mocking him
About the marriage of the Lady Bona.
Glo. And Warwick, doing what you gave in charge,
Is now dishonourèd by this new marriage.
K. Edw. What, if both Lewis and Warwick be appeased
By such invention as I can devise?
Mont. Yet to have joined with France in such alliance,
Would more have strengthened this our commonwealth
'Gainst foreign storms, than any home-bred marriage.
Hast. Why, knows not Montague, that of itself
England is safe, if true within itself?
Mont. Yes; but the safer, when 't is backed with France.
Hast. 'Tis better using France, than trusting France.
Let us be backed with God, and with the seas,
Which he hath given for fence impregnable,
And with their helps only defend ourselves:
In them and in ourselves our safety lies.
Clar. For this one speech Lord Hastings well deserves
To have the heir of the Lord Hungerford.
K. Edw. Ay, what of that? it was my will, and grant;
And for this once my will shall stand for law.
Glo. And yet, methinks your grace hath not done well,
To give the heir and daughter of Lord Scales
Unto the brother of your loving bride:
She better would have fitted me, or Clarence;
But in your bride you bury brotherhood.
Clar. Or else you would not have bestowed the heir
Of the Lord Bonville on your new wife's son,
And leave your brothers to go speed elsewhere.
K. Edw. Alas, poor Clarence, is it for a wife,
That thou malcontent? I will provide thee.
Clar. In choosing for yourself you showed your judgment;
Which being shallow, you shall give me leave

To play the broker in mine own behalf;
And to that end I shortly mind to leave you.
K. Edw. Leave me, or tarry, Edward will be king,
And not be tied unto his brother's will.
Q. Eliz. My lords, before it pleased his majesty
To raise my state to title of a queen,
Do me but right, and you must all confess
That I was not ignoble of descent:
And meaner than myself have had like fortune.
But as this title honours me and mine,
So your dislikes, to whom I would be pleasing,
Do cloud my joys with danger and with sorrow.
K. Edw. My love, forbear to fawn upon their frowns.
What danger, or what sorrow can befall thee,
So long as Edward is thy constant friend,
And their true sovereign, whom they must obey?
Nay, whom they shall obey, and love thee too,
Unless they seek for hatred at my hands;
Which if they do, yet will I keep thee safe,
And they shall feel the vengeance of my wrath.
Glo. [*Aside*] I hear, yet say not much, but think the more.

Enter a Messenger

K. Edw. Now, messenger, what letters, or what news,
From France?
Mess. My sovereign liege, no letters, and few words;
But such as I, without your special pardon,
Dare not relate.
K. Edw. Go to, we pardon thee: therefore, in brief,
Tell me their words as near as thou canst guess them.
What answer makes King Lewis unto our letters?
Mess. At my depart these were his very words:—
'Go tell false Edward, thy supposéd king,
That Lewis of France is sending over masquers,
To revel it with him and his new bride.'
K. Edw. Is Lewis so brave? belike, he thinks me Henry.
But what said Lady Bona to my marriage?
Mess. These were her words, uttered with mild disdain:
'Tell him, in hope he'll prove a widower shortly,
I'll wear the willow garland for his sake.'
K. Edw. I blame not her, she could say little less;
She had the wrong: but what said Henry's queen?
For I have heard that she was there in place.
Mess. 'Tell him,' quoth she, 'my mourning weeds are done,
And I am ready to put armour on.'
K. Edw. Belike, she minds to play the Amazon.
But what said Warwick to these injuries?

Mess. He, more incensed against your majesty
Than all the rest, discharged me with these words:—
'Tell him from me, that he hath done me wrong,
And therefore I'll uncrown him ere 't be long.'
K. Edw. Ha! durst the traitor breathe out so proud words?
Well, I will arm me, being thus forewarned:
They shall have wars, and pay for their presumption.
But say, is Warwick friends with Margaret?
Mess. Ay, gracious sovereign: they're so linked in friendship,
That young Prince Edward marries Warwick's daughter.
Clar. Belike, the elder; Clarence will have the younger.
Now, brother king, farewell, and sit you fast,
For I will hence to Warwick's other daughter;
That, though I want a kingdom, yet in marriage
I may not prove inferior to yourself.—
You, that love me and Warwick, follow me.
[*Exit Clarence, and Somerset follow*
Glo. [*Aside*] Not I:
My thoughts aim at a further matter; I
Stay, not for the love of Edward, but the crown.
K. Edw. Clarence and Somerset both gone to Warwick!
Yet am I armed against the worst can happen,
And haste is needful in this desperate case.—
Pembroke, and Staffold, you in our behalf
Go levy men, and make prepare for war;
They are already, or quickly will be landed:
Myself in person will straight follow you.
[*Exeunt Pembroke and Stafford*
But, ere I go, Hastings, and Montague,
Resolve my doubt. You twain, of all the rest,
Are near to Warwick by blood, and by alliance:
Tell me if you love Warwick more than me?
If it be so, then both depart to him:
I rather wish you foes than hollow friends;
But, if you mind to hold your true obedience,
Give me assurance with some friendly vow,
That I may never have you in suspect.
Mont. So God help Montague, as he proves true!
Hast. And Hastings, as he favours Edward's cause!
K. Edw. Now, brother Richard, will you stand by us?
Glo. Ay, in despite of all that shall withstand you.
K. Edw. Why so; then am I sure of victory.
Now therefore let us hence; and lose no hour,
Till we meet Warwick with his foreign power. [*Exeunt*

SCENE II.—A Plain in Warwickshire

Enter WARWICK *and* OXFORD *with French and other Forces*

War. Trust me, my lord, all hitherto goes well:
The common people by numbers swarm to us.

Enter CLARENCE *and* SOMERSET

But see, where Somerset and Clarence come!
Speak suddenly, my lords, are we all friends?
Clar. Fear not that, my lord.
War. Then, gentle Clarence, welcome unto Warwick:
And welcome, Somerset.—I hold it cowardice,
To rest mistrustful where a noble heart
Hath pawned an open hand in sign of love;
Else might I think, that Clarence, Edward's brother,
Were but a feignéd friend to our proceedings:
But welcome, sweet Clarence; my daughter shall be thine.
And now what rests, but in night's coverture,
Thy brother being carelessly encamped,
His soldiers lurking in the towns about,
And but attended by a simple guard,
We may surprise and take him at out pleasure?
Our scouts have found the adventure very easy:
That as Ulysses and stout Diomede
With sleight and manhood stole to Rheusus' tents,
And brought from thence the Thracian fatal steeds;
So we, well covered with the night's black mantle,
At unawares may beat down Edward's guard,
And seize himself; I say not, slaughter him,
For I intend but only to surprise him.—
You, that will follow me to this attempt,
Applaud the name of Henry with your leader.
[*They all cry* 'HENRY!'
Why, then, let's on our way in silent sort:
For Warwick and his friends, God and Saint George!
[*Exeunt*

SCENE III.—Edward's Camp near Warwick

Enter certain Watchmen to guard the King's Tent

First Watch. Come on, my masters each man take his stand:
The king by this is set him down to sleep.
Sec. Watch. What, will he not to bed?

First Watch. Why, no; for he hath made a solemn vow,
Never to lie and take his natural rest,
Till Warwick or himself be quite suppressed.
Sec. Watch. To-morrow then, belike, shall be the day,
If Warwick be so near as men report.
Third Watch. But say, I pray, what nobleman is that,
That with the king here resteth in his tent?
First Watch 'T is the Lord Hastings, the king's chiefest friend.
Third Watch. O, is it so? But why commands the king,
That his chief followers lodge in towns about him,
While he himself keeps in the cold field?
Sec. Watch. 'T is the more honour, because more dangerous.
Third Watch. Ay, but give me worship and quietness;
I like it better than a dangerous honour.
If Warwick knew in what estate he stands,
'T is to be doubted, he would waken him.
First Watch. Unless our halberds did shut up his passage.
Sec. Watch. Ay; wherefore else guard we his royal tent,
But to defend his person from night-foes?

Enter WARWICK, CLARENCE, OXFORD, SOMERSET *and Forces*

War. This is his tent; and see, where stand his guard.
Courage, my masters; honour now, or never!
But follow me, and Edward shall be ours.
First Watch. Who goes there?
Sec. Watch. Stay, or thou diest.
[*Warwick, and the rest, cry all*—'WARWICK! WARWICK!' *and set upon the Guard; who fly, crying*—'ARM! ARM!' *Warwick, and the rest, following them*

Drums beating, and trumpets sounding, re-enter WARWICK, *and the rest, bringing the* KING *out in his gown, sitting in a chair:* GLOSTER *and* HASTINGS *fly over the stage*

Som. What are they that fly there?
War. Richard and Hastings: let them go; here's the duke.
K. Edw. The duke! why, Warwick, when we parted last,
Thou call'dst me king!
War. Ay, but the case is altered:
When you disgraced me in my embassade,
Then I degraded you from being king,
And come now to create you Duke of York.
Alas! how should you govern any kingdom,
That know not how to use ambassadors,

Nor how to be contented with one wife,
Nor how to use your brothers brotherly,
Nor how to study for the people's welfare,
Nor how to shroud yourself from enemies?
K. Edw. Yea, brother of Clarence, art thou here too?
Nay, then I see that Edward needs must down.—
Yet, Warwick, in despite of all mischance,
Of thee thyself, and thy complices,
Edward will always bear himself as king:
Though fortune's malice overthrow my state,
My mind exceeds the compass of her wheel.
War. Then, for his mind, be Edward England's king:
[*Takes off his crown*
But Henry now shall wear the English crown,
And be true king indeed; thou but the shadow.—
My Lord of Somerset, at my request,
See that forthwith Duke Edward be conveyed
Unto my brother, Archbishop of York.
When I have fought with Pembroke and his fellows,
I'll follow you, and tell what answer
Lewis, and the Lady Bona, send to him:—
Now, for a while, farewell, good Duke of York.
K. Edw. What fates impose, that men must needs abide:
It boots not to resist both wind and tide.
[*Exit King Edward led out; Somerset with him*
Oxf. What now remains, my lords, for us to do,
But march to London with our soldiers?
War. Ay, that's the first thing we have to do;
To free King Henry from imprisonment,
And see him seated in the regal throne. [*Exeunt*

Scene IV.—London. A Room in the Palace

Enter Queen Elizabeth *and* Rivers

Riv. Madam, what makes you in this sudden change?
Q. Eliz. Why, brother Rivers, are you yet to learn,
What late misfortune is befall'n King Edward?
Riv. What, loss of some pitched battle against Warwick?
Q. Eliz. No, but the loss of his own royal person.
Riv. Then is my sovereign slain?
Q. Eliz. Ay, almost slain, for he is taken prisoner;
Either betrayed by falsehood of his guard,
Or by his foe surprised at unawares:
And, as I further have to understand,
Is new committed to the Bishop of York,
Fell Warwick's brother, and by that our foe.

Riv. These news, I must confess, are full of grief;
Yet, gracious madam, bear it as you may:
Warwick may lose, that now hath won the day.
Q. Eliz. Till then, fair hope must hinder life's decay;
And I the rather wean me from despair,
For love of Edward's offspring in my womb:
This is it that makes me bridle passion,
And bear with mildness my misfortune's cross;
Ay, ay, for this I draw in many a tear,
And stop the rising of blood-sucking sighs,
Lest with my sighs or tears I blast or drown
King Edward's fruit, true heir to the English crown.
Riv. But, madam, where is Warwick then become?
Q. Eliz. I am informed, that he comes towards London,
To set the crown once more on Henry's head.
Guess thou the rest; King Edward's friends must down:
But to prevent the tyrant's violence,
(For trust not him that hath once broken faith,)
I'll hence forthwith unto the sanctuary,
To save at least the heir of Edward's right:
There shall I rest secure from force, and fraud.
Come, therefore; let us fly while we may fly:
If Warwick take us, we are sure to die. [*Exeunt*

SCENE V.—A Park near Middleham Castle in Yorkshire

Enter GLOSTER, HASTINGS, SIR WILLIAM STANLEY, *and others*

Glo. Now, my Lord Hastings, and Sir William Stanley,
Leave off to wonder why I drew you hither,
Into this chiefest thicket of the park.
Thus stands the case. You know, our king, my brother,
Is prisoner to the bishop here, at whose hands
He hath good usage and great liberty,
And often, but attended with weak guard,
Comes hunting this way to disport himself.
I have advértised him by secret means,
That if about this hour he makes this way,
Under the colour of his usual game,
He shall here find his friends, with horse and men,
To set him free from his captivity.

Enter KING EDWARD *and a Huntsman*

Hunt. This way, my lord, for this way lies the game.
K. Edw. Nay, this way, man: see, where the huntsmen stand.—

Now, brother of Gloster, Lord Hastings, and the rest,
Stand you thus close, to steal the bishop's deer?
Glo. Brother, the time and case requireth haste.
Your horse stands ready at the park-corner.
K. Edw. But whither shall we then?
Hast. To Lynn, my lord; and ship from thence to Flanders.
Glo. Well guessed, believe me; for that was my meaning.
K. Edw. Stanley, I will requite thy forwardness.
Glo. But wherefore stay we? 't is no time to talk.
K. Edw. Huntsman, what say'st thou? wilt thou go along?
Hunt. Better do so, than tarry and be hanged.
Glo. Come then; away! let's have no more ado.
K. Edw. Bishop, farewell: shield thee from Warwick's frown,
And pray that I may repossess the crown. [*Exeunt*

Scene VI.—A Room in the Tower

Enter King Henry, Clarence, Warwick, Somerset, *young* Richmond, Oxford, Montague, *Lieutenant of the Tower, and Attendants*

K. Hen. Master lieutenant, now that God and friends
Have shaken Edward from the regal seat,
And turned my captive state to liberty,
My fear to hope, my sorrows unto joys,
At our enlargement what are they due fees?
Lieu. Subjects may challenge nothing of their sovereigns;
But if an humble prayer may prevail,
I then crave pardon of your majesty.
K. Hen. For what, lieutenant? for well using me?
Nay, be thou sure, I'll well requite thy kindness,
For that it made my imprisonment a pleasure:
Ay, such a pleasure as incagéd birds
Conceive, when, after many moody thoughts,
At last by notes of household harmony
They quite forget their loss of liberty.—
But, Warwick, after God, thou set'st me free,
And chiefly therefore I thank God, and thee;
He was the author, thou the instrument.
Therefore, that I may conquer fortune's spite,
By living low, where fortune cannot hurt me,
And that the people of this blesséd land
May not be punished with my thwarting stars,
Warwick, although my head still wear the crown,

I here resign my government to thee,
For thou art fortunate in all thy deeds.
War. Your grace hath still been famed for virtuous,
And now may seem as wise as virtuous,
By spying and avoiding fortune's malice;
For few men rightly temper with the stars:
Yet in this one thing let me blame your grace,
For choosing me when Clarence is in place.
Clar. No, Warwick, thou art worthy of the sway,
To whom the heavens in thy nativity
Adjudged an olive branch, and laurel crown,
As likely to be blest in peace, and war;
And, therefore, I yield thee my free consent.
War. And I choose Clarence only for protector.
K. Hen. Warwick, and Clarence, give me both your hands.
Now join your hands, and with your hands your hearts,
That no dissension hinder government:
I make you both protectors of this land.
While I myself will lead a private life,
And in devotion spend my latter days,
To sin's rebuke, and my Creator's praise.
War. What answers Clarence to his sovereign's will?
Clar. That he consents, if Warwick yield consent;
For on thy fortune I repose myself.
War. Why then, though loth, yet must I be content.
We'll yoke together, like a double shadow
To Henry's body, and supply his place;
I mean, in bearing weight of government,
While he enjoys the honour, and his ease.
And, Clarence, now then it is more than needful
Forthwith that Edward be pronounced a traitor,
And all his lands and goods be confiscate.
Clar. What else? and that succession be determined.
War. Ay, therein Clarence shall not want his part.
K. Hen. But, with the first of all your chief affairs,
Let me entreat (for I command no more),
That Margaret your queen, and my son Edward,
Be sent for to return from France with speed:
For, till I see them here, by doubtful fear
My joy of liberty is half eclipsed.
Clar. It shall be done, my sovereign, with all speed.
K. Hen. My Lord of Somerset! what youth is that,
Of whom you seem to have so tender care?
Som. My liege, it is young Henry, Earl of Richmond.
K. Hen. Come hither, England's hope. [*Lays his hand on his head*] If secret powers
Suggest but truth to my divining thoughts,
This pretty lad will prove our country's bliss.
His looks are full of peaceful majesty;

His head by nature framed to wear a crown,
His hand to wield a sceptre, and himself
Likely in time to bless a regal throne.
Make much of him, my lords; for this is he
Must help you more than you are hurt by me.

Enter a Messenger

War. What news, my friend?
Mess. That Edward is escapéd from your brother,
And fled, as he hears since, to Burgundy.
War. Unsavoury news! but how made he escape?
Mess. He was conveyed by Richard Duke of Gloster,
And the Lord Hastings, who attended him
In secret ambush on the forest side,
And from the bishop's huntsmen rescued him;
For hunting was his daily exercise.
War. My brother was too careless of his charge.—
But let us hence, my sovereign, to provide
A salve for any sore that may betide.
[*Exeunt all but Somerset, Richmond, and Oxford*
Som. My lord, I like not of this flight of Edward's;
For, doubtless, Burgundy will yield him help,
And we shall have more wars before 't be long.
As Henry's late presaging prophecy
Did glad my heart with hope of this young Richmond,
So doth my heart misgive me, in these conflicts
What may befall him to his harm and ours:
Therefore, Lord Oxford, to prevent the worst,
Forthwith we'll send him hence to Brittany,
Till storms be past of civil enmity.
Oxf. Ay, for if Edward repossess the crown,
'T is like that Richmond with the rest shall down.
Som. It shall be so; he shall to Brittany.
Come therefore; let's about it speedily. [*Exeunt*

Scene VII.—Before York

Enter King Edward, Gloster, Hastings, *and Forces*

K. Edw. Now, brother Richard, Lord Hastings, and the rest,
Yet thus far fortune maketh us amends,
And says that once more I shall interchange
My wanéd state for Henry's regal crown.
Well have we passed, and now repassed the seas,
And brought desiréd help from Burgundy:
What then remains, we being thus arrived

From Ravenspurg haven before the gates of York,
But that we enter, as into our dukedom?
Glo. The gates made fast!—Brother, I like not this;
For many men, that stumble at the threshold,
Are well foretold that danger lurks within.
K. Edw. Tush, man! abodements must not now affright us:
By fair or foul means we must enter in,
For hither will our friends repair to us.
Hast. My liege, I'll knock once more to summon them.

Enter, on the walls, the MAYOR OF YORK, *and his Brethren*

May. My lords, we were forewarnèd of your coming,
And shut the gates for safety of ourselves;
For now we owe allegiance unto Henry.
K. Edw. But, master mayor, if Henry be young king,
Yet Edward, at the least, is Duke of York.
May. True, my good lord; I know you for no less.
K. Edw. Why, and I challenge nothing but my dukedom,
As being well content with that alone.
Glo. [*Aside*] But when the fox hath once got in his nose,
He'll soon find means to make the body follow.
Hast. Why, master mayor, why stand you in a doubt?
Open the gates: we are King Henry's friends.
May. Ay, say you so? the gates shall then be opened.
[*Exeunt from above*
Glo. A wise stout captain, and soon persuaded!
Hast. The good old man would fain that all were well,
So 't were not 'long of him; but, being entered,
I doubt not, I, but we shall soon persuade
Both him and all his brothers unto reason.

Re-enter the MAYOR, *and two Aldermen, below*

K. Edw. So, master mayor; these gates must not be shut,
But in the night, or in the time of war.
What, fear not, man, but yield me up the keys,
[*Takes his keys*
For Edward will defend the town, and thee,
And all those friends that deign to follow me.

March. Enter MONTGOMERY *and Forces*

Glo. Brother, this is Sir John Montgomery,
Our trusty friend, unless I be deceived.

K. Edw. Welcome, Sir John; but why come you in arms?
Mont. To help King Edward in his time of storm,
As every loyal subject ought to do.
K. Edw. Thanks, good Montgomery; but we now forgot
Our title to the crown, and only claim
Our dukedom, till God please to send the rest.
Mont. Then fare you well, for I will hence again:
I came to serve a king, and not a duke.—
Drummer, strike up, and let us march away.
[*A march begun*
K. Edw. Nay, stay, Sir John, awhile; and we'll debate,
By what safe means the crown may be recovered.
Mont. What talk you of debating? in few words,
If you'll not here proclaim yourself our king,
I'll leave you to your fortune, and be gone
To keep them back that come to succour you.
Why shall we fight, if you pretend no title?
Glo. Why, brother, wherefore stand you on nice points?
K. Edw. When we grow stronger, then we'll make our claim.
Till then, 't is wisdom to conceal our meaning.
Hast. Away with scrupulous wit! now arms must rule.
Glo. And fearless minds climb soonest unto crowns.
Brother, we will proclaim you out of hand:
The bruit thereof will bring you many friends.
K. Edw. Then be it as you will; for 't is my right,
And Henry but usurps the diadem.
Mont. Ay, now my sovereign speaketh like himself,
And now will I be Edward's champion.
Hast. Sound, trumpet! Edward shall be here proclaimed.—
Come, fellow-soldier, make thou proclamation.
[*Gives him a paper. Flourish*
Sold. [*Reads*] 'Edward the Fourth, by the grace of God, King of England and France, and Lord of Ireland, etc.'
Mont. And whosoe'er gainsays King Edward's right,
By this I challenge him to single fight.
[*Throws down his gauntlet*
All. Love live Edward the Fourth!
King Edw. Thanks, brave Montgomery, and thanks unto you all:
If fortune serve me, I'll requite this kindness.
Now, for this night, let's harbour here in York,
And when the morning sun shall raise his car
Above the border of this horizon,
We'll forward towards Warwick and his mates;
For, well I wot that Henry is no soldier.—

Ah, froward Clarence! how evil it beseems thee,
To flatter Henry, and forsake thy brother!
Yet, as we may, we'll meet both thee and Warwick.—
Come on, brave soldiers: doubt not of the day;
And, that once gotten, doubt not of large pay. [*Exeunt*

Scene VIII.—London. A Room in the Palace

Flourish. Enter King Henry, Warwick, Clarence, Montague, Exeter, *and* Oxford

War. What counsel, lords? Edward from Belgia.
With hasty Germans, and blunt Hollanders,
Hath passed in safety through the narrow seas,
And with his troops doth march amain to London:
And many giddy people flock to him.
K. Hen. Let's levy men, and beat him back again.
Clar. A little fire is quickly trodden out,
Which, being suffered, rivers cannot quench.
War. In Warwickshire I have true-hearted friends,
Not mutinous in peace, yet bold in war;
Those will I muster up:—and thou, son Clarence,
Shalt stir up in Suffolk, Norfolk, and in Kent,
The knights and gentlemen to come with thee:—
Thou, brother Montague, in Buckingham,
Northampton, and in Leicestershire, shalt find
Men well inclined to hear what thou command'st—
And thou, brave Oxford, wondrous well beloved
In Oxfordshire, shalt muster up thy friends.—
My sovereign, with the loving citizens,
Like to his island girt in with the ocean,
Or modest Dian circles with her nymphs,
Shall rest in London, till we come to him.—
Fair lords, take leave, and stand not to reply.—
Farewell my sovereign.
K. Hen. Farewell, my Hector, and my Troy's true hope.
Clar. In sign of truth, I kiss your highness' hand.
K. Hen. Well-minded Clarence, be thou fortunate.
Mont. Comfort, my lord;—and so I take my leave.
Oxf. [*Kissing Henry's hand*] And thus I seal my truth, and bid adieu.
K. Hen. Sweet Oxford, and my loving Montague,
And all at once, once more a happy farewell.
War. Farewell, sweet lords: let's meet at Coventry.
[*Exeunt Warwick, Clarence, Oxford, and Montague*
K. Hen. Here at the palace will I rest awhile.
Cousin of Exeter, what thinks your lordship?

Methinks the power, that Edward hath in field,
Should not be able to encounter mine.
Exe. The doubt is, that he will seduce the rest.
K. Hen. That's not my fear; my meed hath got me fame,
I have not stopped mine ears to their demands,
Nor posted off their suits with slow delays;
My pity hath been balm to heal their wounds;
My mildness hath allayed their swelling griefs,
My mercy dried their water-flowing tears;
I have not been desirous of their wealth,
Nor much oppressed them with great subsidies,
Nor forward of revenge, though they much erred.
Then, why should they love Edward more than me?
No, Exeter, these graces challenge grace:
And, when the lion fawns upon the lamb,
The lamb will never cease to follow him.
[*Shout within:* 'A LANCASTER! A LANCASTER!'
Exe. Hark, hark, my lord! what shouts are these?

Enter KING EDWARD, GLOSTER, *and Soldiers*

K. Edw. Seize on the shame-faced Henry! bear him hence,
And once again proclaim us King of England.—
You are the fount that makes small brooks to flow:
Now stops thy spring; my sea shall suck them dry,
And swell so much the higher by their ebb.
Hence with him to the Tower! let him not speak.
[*Exeunt some with King Henry*
And, lords, towards Coventry bend we our course,
Where peremptory Warwick now remains.
The sun shines hot, and, if we use delay,
Cold biting winter mars our hoped-for hay.
Glo. Away betimes, before his forces join,
And take the great-grown traitor unawares:
Brave warriors, march amain towards Coventry. [*Exeunt*

ACT FIVE

SCENE I.—Coventry

Enter, upon the walls, WARWICK, *the* MAYOR OF COVENTRY, *two Messengers, and others*

War. Where is the post that came from valiant Oxford?
How far hence is thy lord, mine honest fellow?

First Mess. By this at Dunsmore, marching hitherward.
War. How far off is our brother Montague?—
Where is the post that came from Montague?
Sec. Mess. By this at Daintry, with a puissant troop.

Enter SIR JOHN SOMERVILLE

War. Say, Somerville, what says my loving son?
And, by thy guess, how nigh is Clarence now?
Som. At Southam I did leave him with his forces,
And do expect him here some two hours hence.
[*Drum heard*
War. Then Clarence is at hand, I hear his drum.
Som. It is not his, my lord; here Southam lies:
The drum your honour hears marcheth from Warwick.
War. Who should that be? belike, unlooked-for friends.
Som. They are at hand, and you shall quickly know.

March. Flourish. Enter KING EDWARD, GLOSTER, *and Forces*

K. Edw. Go, trumpet, to the walls, and sound a parle.
Glo. See how the surly Warwick mans the wall.
War. O unbid spite! is sportful Edward come?
Where slept out scouts, or how are they seduced,
That we could hear no news of his repair?
K. Edw. Now, Warwick, wilt thou ope the city gates?
Speak gentle words, and humbly bend thy knee,
Call Edward king, and at his hands beg mercy,
And he shall pardon thee these outrages.
War. Nay, rather, wilt thou draw thy forces hence,
Confess who set thee up and plucked thee down?
Call Warwick patron, and be penitent,
And thou shalt still remain the Duke of York.
Glo. I thought, at least, he would have said—the king,
Or did he make the jest against his will?
War. Is not a dukedom, sir, a goodly gift?
Glo. Ay, by my faith, for a poor earl to give:
I'll do thee service for so good a gift.
War. 'T was I, that gave the kingdom to thy brother.
K. Edw. Why then, 't is mine, if but by Warwick's gift.
War. Thou art no Atlas for so great a weight:
And, weakling, Warwick, takes his gift again;
And Henry is my king, Warwick his subject.
K. Edw. But Warwick's king is Edward's prisoner;
And, gallant Warwick, do but answer this:
What is the body, when the head is off?
Glo. Alas! that Warwick had no more forecast,
But, whiles he thought to steal the single ten,
The king was slily fingered from the deck!

You left poor Henry at the Bishop's palace,
And, ten to one, you'll meet him in the Tower.
K. Edw. 'T is even so: yet you are Warwick still.
Glo. Come, Warwick, take the time; kneel down, kneel down.
Nay, when? Strike now, or else the iron cools.
War. I had rather chop this hand off at a blow,
And with the other fling it at thy face,
Than bear so low a sail to strike to thee.
K. Edw. Sail how thou canst, have wind and tide thy friend,
This hand, fast wound about thy coal-black hair,
Shall, whiles thy head is warm, and new cut off,
Write in the dust this sentence with thy blood,—
'Wind-changing Warwick now can change no more.

Enter OXFORD, *with drum and colours*

War. O cheerful colours! see, where Oxford comes.
Oxf. Oxford, Oxford, for Lancaster!
[*Oxford and his forces enter the city*
Glo. The gates are open, let us enter too.
K. Edw. So other foes may set upon our backs.
Stand we in good array; for they, no doubt,
Will issue out again, and bid us battle:
If not, the city being but of small defence,
We'll quickly rouse the traitors in the same.
War. O, welcome, Oxford, for we want thy help.

Enter MONTAGUE, *with drum and colours*

Mont. Montague, Montague, for Lancaster!
[*He and his forces enter the city*
Glo. Thou and thy brother both shall buy this treason,
Even with the dearest blood your bodies bear.
K. Edw. The harder matched, the greater victory:
My mind presageth happy gain, and conquest.

Enter SOMERSET, *with drum and colours*

Som. Somerset, Somerset, for Lancaster!
[*He and his forces enter the city*
Glo. Two of thy name, both Dukes of Somerset,
Have sold their lives unto the house of York;
And thou shalt be the third, if this sword hold.

Enter CLARENCE, *with drum and colours*

War. And lo! where George of Clarence sweeps along,
Of force enough to bid his brother battle;
With whom an upright zeal to right prevails,

More than the nature of a brother's love.—
[*Gloster and Clarence whisper*
Come, Clarence, come; thou wilt, if Warwick calls.
Clar. Father of Warwick, know you what this means?
[*Taking the red rose out of his hat*
Look here, I throw my infamy at thee:
I will not ruinate my father's house,
Who gave his blood to lime the stones together
And set up Lancaster. Why, trow'st thou, Warwick
That Clarence is so harsh, so blunt-unnatural,
To bend the fatal instruments of war
Against his brother, and his lawful king?
Perhaps, thou will object my holy oath:
To keep that oath, were more impiety
Than Jephtha's, when he sacrificed his daughter.
I am so sorry for my trespass made,
That to deserve well at my brother's hands,
I here proclaim myself thy mortal foe;
With resolution, wheresoe'er I meet thee,—
As I will meet thee, if thou stir abroad,—
To plague thee for thy foul misleading me.
And so, proud-hearted Warwick, I defy thee,
And to my brother turn my blushing cheeks.—
Pardon me, Edward, I will make amends;
And, Richard, do not frown upon my faults,
For I will henceforth be no more unconstant.
K. Edw. Now welcome more, and ten times more beloved,
Than if thou never hadst deserved our hate.
Glo. Welcome, good Clarence: this is brother-like.
War. O passing traitor, perjured, and unjust!
K. Edw. What, Warwick, wilt thou leave the town, and fight,
Or shall we beat the stones about thine ears?
War. Alas! I am not cooped here for defence:
I will away towards Barnet presently,
And bid thee battle, Edward, if thou dar'st.
K. Edw. Yes, Warwick, Edward dares, and leads the way.—
Lords, to the field! Saint George, and victory!
[*March. Exeunt*

SCENE II.—A Field of Battle near Barnet

Alarums and Excursions. Enter KING EDWARD, *bringing in* WARWICK *wounded*

K. Edw. So, lie thou there: die thou, and die our fear;
For Warwick was a bug that feared us all.—

Now Montague, sit fast: I seek for thee,
That Warwick's bones may keep thine company. [*Exit*

War. Ah! who is nigh? come to me, friend or foe,
And tell me, who is victor, York, or Warwick?
Why ask I that? my mangled body shows,
My blood, my want of strength, my sick heart shows,
That I must yield my body to the earth,
And, by my fall, the conquest to my foe.
Thus yields the cedar to the axe's edge,
Whose arms gave shelter to the princely eagle,
Under whose shade the ramping lion slept;
Whose top-branch overpeered Jove's spreading tree,
And kept low shrubs from winter's powerful wind.
These eyes, that now are dimmed with death's black veil,
Have been as piercing as the midday sun,
To search the secret treasons of the world:
The wrinkles in my brows, now filled with blood,
Were likened oft to kingly sepulchres;
For who lived king, but I could dig his grave?
And who durst smile when Warwick bent his brow?
Lo, now my glory smeared in dust and blood!
My parks, my walks, my manors that I had,
Even now forsake me; and, of all my lands
Is nothing left me but my body's length.
Why, what is pomp, rule, reign, but earth and dust?
And, live we how we can, yet die we must.

Enter OXFORD *and* SOMERSET

Som. Ah, Warwick, Warwick! wert thou as we are,
We might recover all our loss again.
The queen from France hath brought a puissant power;
Even now we heard the news. Ah, couldst thou fly!

War. Why, then I would not fly.—Ah, Montague!
If thou be there, sweet brother, take my hand,
And with thy lips keep in my soul awhile.
Thou lov'st me not; for, brother, if thou didst,
Thy tears would wash this cold congealéd blood,
That glues my lips, and will not let me speak.
Come quickly, Montague, or I am dead.

Som. Ah, Warwick, Montague hath breathed his last;
And to the latest gasp cried out for Warwick,
And said—'Commend me to my valiant brother.
And more he would have said; and more he spoke,
Which sounded like a cannon in a vault,
That might not be distinguished: but, at last,
I well might hear, delivered with a groan,—
'O farewell, Warwick!'

War. Sweet rest his soul!—Fly, lords, and save yourselves;

For Warwick bids you all farewell, to meet in heaven.
[*Dies*

Oxf. Away, away, to meet the queen's great power!
[*Exeunt, bearing off Warwick's body*

Scene III.—Another Part of the Field

Flourish. Enter King Edward *in triumph; with* Clarence, Gloster, *and the rest*

K. Edw. Thus far our fortune keeps an upward course,
And we are graced with wreaths of victory.
But, in the midst of this bright-shining day,
I spy a black, suspicious, threat'ning cloud,
That will encounter with our glorious sun,
Ere he attain his easeful western bed:
I mean, my lords, those powers, that the queen
Hath raised in Gallia, have arrived our coast,
And, as we hear, march on to fight with us.

Clar. A little gale will soon disperse that cloud,
And blow it to the source from whence it came:
Thy very beams will dry those vapours up,
For every cloud engenders not a storm.

Glo. The queen is valued thirty thousand strong,
And Somerset, with Oxford, fled to her;
If she have time to breathe, be well-assured,
Her faction will be full as strong as ours.

K. Edw. We are advértised by our loving friends,
That they do hold their course toward Tewksbury.
We having now the best at Barnet field,
Will thither straight, for willingness rids way;
And, as we march, our strength will be augmented
In every county as we go along.—
Strike up the drum! cry—Courage! and away.
[*Flourish. Exeunt*

Scene IV.—Plains near Tewksbury

March. Enter Queen Margaret, Prince Edward, Somerset, Oxford, *and Soldiers*

Q. Mar. Great lords, wise men ne'er sit and wail their loss,
But cheerly seek how to redress their harms.
What though the mast be now blown overboard,
The cable broke, the holding-anchor lost,

And half our sailors swallowed in the flood;
Yet lives our pilot still: is't meet that he
Should leave the helm, and, like a fearful lad,
With tearful eyes add water to the sea,
And give more strength to that which hath too much,
Whiles in his moan the ship splits on the rock,
Which industry and courage might have saved?
Ah, what a shame! ah, what a shame were this!
Say, Warwick was our anchor; what of that?
And Montague our topmast; what of him?
Our slaughtered friends the tackles; what of these?
Why, is not Oxford here another anchor,
And Somerset another goodly mast?
The friends of France our shrouds and tacklings?
And, though unskilled, why not Ned and I
For once allowed the skilful pilot's charge?
We will not from the helm, to sit and weep,
But keep our course, though the rough wind say no,
From shelves and rocks that threaten us with wrack.
As good to chide the waves, as speak them fair.
And what is Edward but a ruthless sea?
What Clarence but a quicksand of deceit,
And Richard but a ragged fatal rock?
All these the enemies to our poor bark.
Say, you can swim; alas! 't is but a while:
Tread on the sand; why, there you quickly sink:
Bestride the rock; the tide will wash you off,
Or else you famish; that's a threefold death.
This speak, I, lords, to let you understand,
In case some one of you would fly from us,
That there's no hoped-for mercy with the brothers,
More than with ruthless waves, with sands, and rocks.
Why, courage, then! what cannot be avoided,
'T were childish weakness to lament, or fear.
Prince. Methinks, a woman of this valiant spirit
Should, if a coward heard her speak these words,
Infuse his breast with magnanimity,
And make him, naked, foil a man at arms.
I speak not this as doubting any here;
For, did I but suspect a fearful man,
He should have leave to go away betimes,
Lest, in our need, he might infect another,
And make him of like spirit to himself.
If any such be here,—as God forbid!—
Let him depart before we need his help.
Oxf. Women and children of so high a courage,
And warriors faint! why, 't were perpetual shame.—
O brave young prince! thy famous grandfather,
Doth live again in thee: long may'st thou live,
To bear his image, and renew his glories!

Som. And he that will not fight for such a hope,
Go home to bed, and, like the owl by day,
If he arise, be mocked and wondered at.
Q. Mar. Thanks, gentle Somerset:—sweet Oxford, thanks.
Prince. And take his thanks, that yet hath nothing else.

Enter a Messenger

Mess. Prepare you, lords, for Edward is at hand,
Ready to fight: therefore, be resolute.
Oxf. I thought no less: it is his policy
To haste thus fast, to find us unprovided.
Som. But he's deceived: we are in readiness.
Q. Mar. This cheers my heart to see your forwardness.
Oxf. Here pitch our battle; hence we will not budge.

Flourish and March. Enter KING EDWARD, CLARENCE GLOSTER, *and Forces*

K. Edw. Brave followers, yonder stands the thorny wood,
Which, by the heavens' assistance and your strength,
Must by the roots be hewn up yet ere night.
I need not add more fuel to your fire,
For, well I wot, ye blaze to burn them out.
Give signal to the fight, and to it, lords!
Q. Mar. Lords, knights, and gentlemen, what I should say,
My tears gainsay; for every word I speak,
Ye see, I drink the water of mine eyes.
Therefore, no more but this:—Henry, your sovereign
Is prisoner to the foe; his state usurped,
His realm a slaughter-house, his subjects slain,
His statues cancelled, and his treasure spent;
And yonder is the wolf that makes this spoil.
You fight in justice: then, in God's name, lords,
Be valiant and give signal to the fight.
[*Exeunt both Armies*

SCENE V.—Another Part of the Field

Alarums: Excursions: and afterwards a Retreat. Then enter KING EDWARD, CLARENCE, GLOSTER, *and forces; with* QUEEN MARGARET, OXFORD, *and* SOMERSET, *prisoners*

K. Edw. Now, here a period of tumultuous broils.
Away with Oxford to Ham's Castle straight:

For Somerset, off with his guilty head.
Go bear them hence: I will not hear them speak.
Oxf. For my part, I'll not trouble thee with words.
Som. Nor I; but stoop with patience to my fortune.
[*Exeunt Oxford and Somerset, guarded*
Q. Mar. So part we sadly in this troublous world,
To meet with joy in sweet Jerusalem.
K. Edw. Is proclamation made, that who finds Edward
Shall have a high reward, and he his life?
Glo. It is: and lo, where youthful Edward comes!

Enter Soldiers, with Prince Edward

K. Edw. Bring forth the gallant: let us hear him speak.
What! can so young a thorn begin to prick?
Edward, what satisfaction can'st thou make,
For bearing arms, for stirring up my subjects,
And all the trouble thou hast turned me to?
Prince. Speak like a subject, proud ambitious York.
Suppose, that I am now my father's mouth:
Resign thy chair, and where I stand kneel thou,
Whilst I propose the selfsame words to thee
Which, traitor, thou wouldst have me answer to.
Q. Mar. Ah, that thy father had been so resolved!
Glo. That you might still have worn the petticoat,
And ne'er have stol'n the breech from Lancaster.
Prince. Let Æsop fable in a winter's night;
His currish riddles sort not with this place.
Glo. By Heaven, brat, I'll plague you for that word.
Q. Mar. Ay, thou wast born to be a plague to men.
Glo. For God's sake, take away this captive scold.
Prince. Nay, take away this scolding crookback, rather.
K. Edw. Peace, wilful boy, or I will charm your tongue.
Clar. Untutored lad, thou art too malapert.
Prince. I know my duty: you are all undutiful.
Lascivious Edward,—and thou perjured George,—
And thou misshapen Dick,—I tell ye all,
I am your better, traitors as ye are;
And thou usurp'st my father's right and mine.
K. Edw. Take that, the likeness of this railer here.
[*Stabs him*
Glo. Sprawl'st thou? take that, to end thy agony.
[*Stabs him*
Clar. And there's for twitting me with perjury.
[*Stabs him*
Q. Mar. O, kill me too!
Glo. Marry, and shall. [*Offers to kill her*
K. Edw. Hold, Richard, hold! for we have done too much.
Glo. Why should she live, to fill the world with words?

K. Edw. What! doth she swoon? use means for her recovery.
Glo. Clarence, excuse me to the king, my brother.
I'll hence to London on a serious matter:
Ere ye come there, be sure to hear some news.
Clar. What? what?
Glo. The Tower! the Tower! [*Exit*
Q. Mar. O Ned! sweet Ned! speak to thy mother, boy:
Canst thou not speak?—O traitors! murderers!
They that stabbed Cæsar shed no blood at all,
Did not offend, nor were not worthy blame,
If this foul deed were by to equal it:
He was a man; this, in respect, a child;
And men ne'er spend their fury on a child.
What's worse than murderer, that I may name it?
No, no; my heart will burst, an if I speak;
And I will speak, that so my heart may burst.—
Butchers and villains! bloody cannibals!
How sweet a plant have you untimely cropped!
You have no children, butchers! if you had,
The thought of them would have stirred up remorse:
But, if you ever chance to have a child,
Look in his youth to have him so cut off,
As, deathsmen, you have rid this sweet young prince!
K. Edw. Away with her! go, bear her hence perforce.
Q. Mar. Nay, never bear me hence, despatch me here:
Here sheathe thy sword, I'll pardon thee my death.
What! wilt thou not?—then, Clarence, do it thou.
Clar. By Heaven, I will not do thee so much ease.
Q. Mar. Good Clarence, do; sweet Clarence, do thou do it.
Clar. Didst thou not hear me swear I would not do it?
Q. Mar. Ay, but thou usest to forswear thyself:
'T was sin before, but now 't is charity.
What! wilt thou not? Where is that devil's butcher,
Hard-favoured Richard? Richard, where art thou?
Thou art not here: murder is thy alms-deed:
Petitioners for blood thou ne'er putt'st back.
K. Edw. Away, I say! I charge ye, bear her hence.
Q. Mar. So come to you, and yours, as to this prince! [*Exit*
K. Edw. Where's Richard gone?
Clar. To London all in post; and, as I guess,
To make a bloody supper in the Tower.
K. Edw. He's sudden, if a thing comes in his head.
Now march we hence: discharge the common sort
With pay and thanks, and let's away to London,
And see out gentle queen how well she fares:
By this, I hope, she hath a son for me. [*Exeunt*

SCENE VI.—London. A Room in the Tower

KING HENRY *is discovered sitting with a book in his hand, the Lieutenant attending. Enter* GLOSTER

Glo. Good day, my lord. What, at your book so hard?
K. Hen. Ay, my good lord: my lord, I should say rather:
'T is sin to flatter; good was little better:
Good Gloster, and good devil, were alike,
And both preposterous; therefore, not good lord.
Glo. Sirrah, leave us to ourselves: we must confer.
[*Exit Lieutenant*
K. Hen. So flies the reckless shepherd from the wolf:
So first the harmless sheep doth yield his fleece,
And next his throat unto the butcher's knife.—
What scene of death hath Roscius now to act?
Glo. Suspicion always haunts the guilty mind:
The thief doth fear each bush an officer.
K. Hen. The bird, that hath been limèd in a bush,
With trembling wings, misdoubteth every bush;
And I, the hapless male to one sweet bird,
Have now the fatal object in my eye,
Where my poor young was limed, was caught, and killed.
Glo. Why, what a peevish fool was that of Crete,
That taught his son the office of a fowl?
And yet, for all his wings, the fool was drowned.
K. Hen. I, Dædalus; my poor boy, Icarus;
Thy father, Minos, that denied our course;
The sun, that seared the wings of my sweet boy,
Thy brother Edward; and thyself, the sea,
Whose envious gulf did swallow up his life,
Ah, kill me with thy weapon, not with words.
My breast can better brook thy dagger's point
Than can my ears that tragic history.
But wherefore dost thou come? is't for my life?
Glo. Think'st thou I am an executioner?
K. Hen. A persecutor, I am sure, thou art:
If murdering innocents be executing,
Why, then thou art an executioner.
Glo. Thy son I killed for his presumption.
K. Hen. Hadst thou been killed, when first thou didst presume,
Thou hadst not lived to kill a son of mine.
And thus I prophesy,—that many a thousand,
Which now mistrust no parcel of my fear,
And many an old man's sigh, and many a widow's,
And many an orphan's water-standing eye,—
Men for their sons', wives for their husbands',

Orphans for their parents' timeless death,—
Shall rue the hour that ever thou wast born.
The owl shrieked at thy birth, an evil sign;
The night-crow cried, aboding luckless time;
Dogs howled, and hideous tempest shook down trees;
The raven rooked her on the chimney's top,
And chattering pies in dismal discords sung.
Thy mother felt more than a mother's pain,
And yet brought forth less than a mother's hope;
To wit, an indigest and deformed lump,
Not like the fruit of such a goodly tree.
Teeth hadst thou in thy head, when thou wast born,
To signify, thou cam'st to bite the world:
And, if the rest be true which I have heard,
Thou cam'st—

Glo. I'll hear no more;—die, prophet, in thy speech: [*Stabs him*
For this, amongst the rest, was I ordained.

K. Hen. Ay, and for much more slaughter after this.
O! God forgive my sins, and pardon thee. [*Dies*

Glo. What! will the aspiring blood of Lancaster
Sink in the ground? I thought it would have mounted.
See, how my sword weeps for the poor king's death!
O, may such purple tears be always shed
From those that wish the downfall of our house!—
If any spark of life be yet remaining,
Down, down to hell; and say I sent thee thither: [*Stabs him again*
I, that have neither pity, love, nor fear.
Indeed, 't is true, that Henry told me of;
For I have often heard my mother say,
I came into the world with my legs forward.
Had I not reason, think ye, to make haste,
And seek their ruin that usurped our right?
The midwife wondered; and the women cried,
'O, Jesus bless us, he is born with teeth!'
And so I was; which plainly signified
That I should snarl, and bite, and play the dog.
Then, since the heavens have shaped my body so,
Let hell make crook'd my mind to answer it.
I have no brother, I am like no brother;
And this word Love, which greybeards call divine,
Be resident in men like one another,
And not in me:—I am myself alone.—
Clarence, beware: thou keep'st me from the light;
But I will sort a pitchy day for thee:
For I will buz abroad such prophecies,
That Edward shall be fearful of his life;
And then, to purge his fear, I'll be thy death.
King Henry, and the prince his son, are gone:

Clarence, thy turn is next, and then the rest;
Counting myself but bad, till I be best.—
I'll throw thy body in another room,
And triumph, Henry, in thy day of doom.
[*Exit, with the body*

SCENE VII.—London. A Room in the Palace

KING EDWARD *is discovered sitting on his throne;* QUEEN ELIZABETH *with the infant Prince,* CLARENCE, GLOSTER HASTINGS, *and others, near him*

K. Edw. Once more we sit in England's royal throne,
Re-purchased with the blood of enemies.
What valiant foemen, like to autumn's corn,
Have we mowed down, in tops of all their pride!
Three Dukes of Somerset, threefold renowned
For hardy and undoubted champions;
Two Cliffords, as the father and the son;
And two Northumberlands: two braver men
Ne'er spurred their coursers at the trumpet's sound;
With them, the two brave bears, Warwick and Montague,
That in their chains fettered the kingly lion,
And made the forest tremble when they roared.
Thus have we swept suspicion from our seat,
And made our footstool of security.—
Come hither, Bess, and let me kiss my boy.—
Young Ned, for thee, thine uncles and myself
Have in our armours watched the winter's night,
Went all a-foot in summer's scalding heat,
That thou might'st repossess the crown in peace;
And of our labours thou shalt reap the gain.
Glo. [*Aside*] I'll blast his harvest, if your head were laid;
For yet I am not looked on in the world.
This shoulder was ordained so thick, to heave;
And heave it shall some weight, or break my back.—
Work thou the way, and thou shalt execute.
K. Edw. Clarence, and Gloster, love my lovely queen,
And kiss your princely nephew, brothers both.
Clar. The duty that I owe unto your majesty,
I seal upon the lips of this sweet babe.
Q. Eliz. Thanks, noble Clarence, worthy brother, thanks.
Glo. And, that I love the tree from whence thou sprang'st,
Witness the loving kiss I give the fruit.—
[*Aside*] To say the truth, so Judas kissed his master,
And cried All hail! whenas he meant All harm.

K. Edw. Now am I seated as my soul delights,
Having my country's peace and brothers' loves.
Clar. What will your grace have done with Margaret?
Reignier, her father, to the King of France
Hath pawned the Sicils and Jerusalem,
And hither have they sent it for her ransom.
K. Edw. Away with her, and waft her hence to France.—
And now what rests, but that we spend the time
With stately triumphs, mirthful comic shows,
Such as befits the pleasure of the court?
Sound, drums and trumpets!—farewell, sour annoy!
For here, I hope, begins our lasting joy. [*Exeunt*

THE FAMOUS HISTORY OF THE LIFE
OF
KING HENRY THE EIGHTH

DRAMATIS PERSONÆ

King Henry the Eighth
Cardinal Wolsey
Cardinal Campeius
Capucius, *Ambassador from Charles V.*
Cranmer, *Archbishop of Canterbury*
Duke of Norfolk
Duke of Suffolk
Duke of Buckingham
Earl of Surrey
Lord Chamberlain
Lord Chancellor
Gardiner, *Bishop of Winchester*
Bishop of Lincoln
Lord Abergavenny
Lord Sands
Sir Henry Guildford
Sir Thomas Lovell
Sir Anthony Denny
Sir Nicholas Vaux
Secretaries to Wolsey
Cromwell, *servant to Wolsey*
Griffith, *gentleman-usher to Queen Katharine*
Three other gentlemen
Garter King-at-arms
Doctor Butts, *physician to the King*
Surveyor to the Duke of Buckingham
Brandon, *and a Serjeant-at-arms*
Door-keeper of the Council-chamber
Porter, and his man
Page to Gardiner. A crier

Queen Katharine, *wife to King Henry*
Anne Bullen, *her Maid of Honour*
An old lady, friend to Anne Bullen
Patience, *woman to Queen Katharine*

Several Lords and Ladies in the Dumb-shows; Women attending upon the Queen; Spirits, which appear to her; Scribes, Officers, Guards, and other attendants

Scene—*Chiefly in London and Westminster; once, at Kimbolton*

THE FAMOUS HISTORY OF THE LIFE OF

KING HENRY THE EIGHTH

PROLOGUE

I COME no more to make you laugh: things now
That bear a weighty and a serious brow,
Sad, high, and working, full of state and woe,
Such noble scenes as draw the eye to flow,
We now present. Those that can pity, here
May, if they think it well, let fall a tear;
The subject will deserve it. Such as give
Their money out of hope they may believe,
May here find Truth too. Those that come to see
Only a show or two, and so agree
The play may pass, if they be still and willing,
I'll undertake, may see away their shilling
Richly in two short hours. Only they
That come to hear a merry, bawdy play,
A noise of targets, or to see a fellow
In a long motley coat, guarded with yellow,
Will be deceived; for, gentle hearers, know,
To rank our chosen truth with such a show
As fool and fight is, beside forfeiting
Our own brains, and the opinion that we bring
To make that only true we now intend,
Will leave us never an understanding friend.
Therefore, for goodness' sake, and as you are known
The first and happiest hearers of the town,
Be sad, as we would make ye: think, ye see
The very persons of our noble story,
As they were living; think, you see them great,
And followed with the general throng and sweat
Of thousand friends; then, in a moment, see
How soon this mightiness metes misery:
And if you can be merry then, I'll say
A man may weep upon his wedding-day.

ACT ONE

SCENE I.—London. An Ante-chamber in the Palace

Enter the DUKE OF NORFOLK, *at one door; at the other, the* DUKE OF BUCKINGHAM, *and the* LORD ABERGAVENNY

Buck. Good morrow, and well met. How have ye done
Since last we saw in France?
Nor. I thank your grace,
Healthful; and ever since a fresh admirer
Of what I saw there.
Buck. An untimely ague
Stayed me a prisoner in my chamber when
Those suns of glory, those two lights of men,
Met in the vale of Andren.
Nor. 'Twixt Guynes and Arde;
I was then present, saw them salute on horseback;
Beheld them, when they lighted, how they clung
In their embracement as they grew together,
Which had they, what four throned ones could have weighed
Such a compounded one?
Buck. All the whole time
I was my chamber's prisoner.
Nor. Then you lost
The view of earthly glory: men might say,
Till this time Pomp was single, but now married
To one above itself. Each following day
Became the next day's master, till the last
Made former wonders its. To-day the French
All clinquant, all in gold, like heathen gods,
Shone down the English; and to-morrow they
Made Britain, India: every man that stood
Showed like a mine. Their dwarfish pages were
As cherubins, all gilt; the madams too,
Not used to toil, did almost sweat to bear
The pride upon them, that their very labour
Was to them as a painting. Now this masque
Was cried incomparable; and the ensuing night
Made it a fool and beggar. The two Kings,
Equal in lustre, were now best, now worst,
As presence did present them, him in eye,
Still him in praise; and, being present both,
'T was said, they saw but one, and no discerner
Durst wag his tongue in censure. When these suns
(For so they phrase them) by their heralds challenged
The noble spirits to arms, they did perform
Beyond thought's compass; that former fabulous story,

Being now seen possible enough, got credit,—
That Bevis was believed.
Buck. O, you go far.
Nor. As I belong to worship, and affect
In honour honesty, the tract of everything
Would by a good discourser lose some life
Which action's self was tongue to. All was royal;
To the disposing of it nought rebelled;
Order gave each thing view, the office did
Distinctly his full function.
Buck. Who did guide,
I mean, who set the body and the limbs
Of this great sport together?
Nor. As you guess;
One, certes, that promises no element
In such a business.
Buck. I pray you, who, my lord?
Nor. All this was ordered by the good discretion
Of the right reverend Cardinal of York.
Buck. The devil speed him! No man's pie is freed
From his ambitious finger. What had he
To do in these fierce vanities? I wonder,
That such a keech can with his very bulk
Take up the rays o' the beneficial sun,
And keep it from the earth.
Nor. Surely, sir,
There's in him stuff that puts him to these ends.
For, being not propped by ancestry, whose grace
Chalks successors their way; nor called upon
For high feats done to the Crown; neither allied
To eminent assistants; spider-like,
Out of his self-drawing web,—give us note,—
The force of his own merit makes his way,
A gift that Heaven gives for him, which buys
A place next to the king.
Aber. I cannot tell
What Heaven hath given him; let some graver eye
Pierce into that; but I can see his pride
Peep through each part of him: whence has he that?
If not from hell, the devil is a niggard,
Or has given all before, and he begins
A new hell in himself.
Buck. Why the devil,
Upon this French going-out, took he upon him,
Without the privity o' the King, t' appoint
Who should attend on him? He makes up the file
Of all the gentry; for the most part such
To whom as great a charge as little honour
He meant to lay upon: and his own letter,
The honourable Board of Council out,

Must fetch him in the papers.
Aber. I do know
Kinsmen of mine, three at the least, that have
By this so sickened their estates, that never
They shall abound as formerly.
Buck. O, many
Have broke their backs with laying manors on them
For this great journey. What did this vanity,
But minister communication of
A most poor issue?
Nor. Grievingly I think
The peace between the French and us not values
The cost that did conclude it.
Buck. Every man
After the hideous storm that followed, was
A thing inspired, and, not consulting, broke
Into a general prophecy,—that this tempest,
Dashing the garment of this peace, aboded
The sudden breach on 't.
Nor. Which is budded out;
For France hath flawed the league, and hath attached
Our merchants' goods at Bordeaux.
Aber. Is it therefore
The ambassador is silenced?
Nor. Marry, is 't.
Aber. A proper title of a peace and purchased
At a superfluous rate.
Buck. Why, all this business
Our reverend Cardinal carried.
Nor. Like it your grace,
The State takes notice of the private difference
Betwixt you and the Cardinal I advise you,—
And take it from a heart that wishes towards you
Honour and plenteous safety—that you read
The Cardinal's malice and his potency
Together; to consider further, that
What his high hatred would effect wants not
A minister in his power. You know his nature,
That he's revengeful; and I know his sword
Hath a sharp edge; it's long, and 't may be said,
It reaches far; and where 't will not extend,
Thither he darts it. Bosom up my counsel,
You'll find it wholesome. Lo, where comes that rock,
That I advise your shunning.

Enter CARDINAL WOLSEY, *the purse borne before him, certain of the Guard, and two Secretaries with papers. The* CARDINAL *in his passage fixeth his eye on* BUCKINGHAM, *and* BUCKINGHAM *on him, both full of disdain*

Wol. The Duke of Buckingham's surveyor? ha!
Where's his examination?
First Secr. Here, so please you.
Wol. Is he in person ready?
First Secr. Ay, please your grace.
Wol. Well, we shall then know more; and Buckingham
Shall lessen this big look. [*Exeunt Cardinal and his Train*
Buck. This butcher's cur is venom-mouthed, and I
Have not the power to muzzle him; therefore best
Not wake him in his slumber. A beggar's look
Outworths a noble's blood.
Nor. What, are you chafed?
Ask God for temperance; that's the appliance only
Which your disease requires.
Buck. I read in's looks
Matter against me; and his eye reviled
Me, as his abject object: at this instant
He bores me with some trick. He's gone to the King;
I'll follow, and outstare him.
Nor. Stay, my lord,
And let your reason with your choler question
What't is you go about. To climb steep hills
Requires slow pace at first: anger is like
A full-hot horse, who being allowed his way,
Self-mettle tires him. Not a man in England
Can advise me like you: be to yourself
As you would to your friend.
Buck. I'll to the King;
And from a mouth of honour quite cry down
This Ipswich fellow's insolence, or proclaim
There's difference in no persons.
Nor. Be advised;
Heat not a furnace for your foe so hot
That it do singe yourself. We may outrun
By violent swiftness that which we run at,
And lose by over-running. Know you not,
The fire that mounts the liquor till 't run o'er,
In seeming to augment it, wastes it? Be advised:
I say again, there is no English soul
More stronger to direct you than yourself,
If with the sap of reason you would quench,
Or but allay, the fire of passion.
Buck. Sir,
I am thankful to you, and I'll go along

By your prescription; but this top-proud fellow,—
Whom from the flow of gall I name not, but
From sincere motions—by intelligence,
And proofs as clear as founts in July when
We see each grain of gravel, I do know
To be corrupt and treasonous.

Nor. Say not, treasonous.

Buck. To the King I'll say't; and make my vouch as strong
As shore of rock. Attend. This holy fox,
Or wolf, or both—for he is equal ravenous,
As he is subtle, and as prone to mischief
As able to perform 't, his mind and place
Infecting one another, yea, reciprocally—
Only to show his pomp as well in France
As here at home, suggests the King, our master,
To this last costly treaty, the interview,
That swallowed so much treasure, and like a glass
Did break i' the rinsing.

Nor. 'Faith, and so it did.

Buck. Pray, give me favour, sir. This cunning Cardinal
The articles o' the combination drew
As himself pleased; and they were ratified,
As he cried, 'Thus let be:' to as much end
As give a crutch to the dead. But our Count-Cardinal
Has done this, and 't is well; for worthy Wolsey,
Who cannot err, he did it. Now this follows,
Which, as I take it, is a kind of puppy
To the old dam, treason: Charles the Emperor,
Under pretence to see the Queen, his aunt—
For 't was, indeed, his colour; but he came
To whisper Wolsey—here makes visitation.
His fears were, that the interview betwixt
England and France might, through their amity,
Breed him some prejudice; for from this league
Peeped harms that menaced him: he privily
Deals with our Cardinal, and, as I trow—
Which I do well; for, I am sure, the Emperor
Paid ere he promised, whereby his suit was granted
Ere it was asked—but when the way was made,
And paved with gold, the Emperor thus desired:
That he would please to alter the King's course,
And break the foresaid peace. Let the King know—
As soon he shall, by me—that thus the Cardinal
Does buy and sell his honour as he pleases,
And for his own advantage.

Nor. I am sorry
To hear this of him; and could wish he were
Something mistaken in 't.

Buck. No, not a syllable.

I do pronounce him in that very shape
He shall appear in proof.

Enter BRANDON; *a Serjeant-at-Arms before him, and two or three of the Guard*

Bran. Your office, serjeant; execute it.
Serj. Sir,
My lord the Duke of Buckingham, and Earl
Of Hereford, Stafford, and Northampton, I
Arrest thee of high treason in the name
Of our most sovereign King.
Buck. Lo you, my lord,
The net has fallen upon me! I shall perish
Under device and practice.
Bran. I am sorry
To see you ta'en from liberty, to look on
The business present. 'T is his highness' pleasure,
You shall to the Tower.
Buck. It will help me nothing
To plead mine innocence; for that dye is on me
Which makes my whit'st part black. The will of Heaven
Be done, in this and all things.—I obey.—
O, my Lord Aberga'ny, fare you well!
Bran. Nay, he must bear you company.—[*To Abergavenny*] The King
Is pleased you shall to the Tower, till you know
How he determines further.
Aber. As the Duke said,
The will of Heaven be done, and the King's pleasure
By me obeyed.
Bran. Here is a warrant from
The King to attach Lord Montacute; and the bodies
Of the Duke's confessor, John de la Car,
One Gilbert Peck, his chancellor.—
Buck. So, so;
These are the limbs o' the plot. No more, I hope.
Bran. A monk o' the Chartreux.
Buck. O, Nicholas Hopkins?
Bran. He.
Buck. My surveyor is false: the o'er-great Cardinal
Hath showed him gold. My life is spanned already:
I am the shadow of poor Buckingham,
Whose figure even this instant cloud puts on,
By darkening my clear sun.—My lord, farewell. [*Exeunt*

SCENE II.—The Council-chamber

Cornets. Enter KING HENRY, *leaning on the* CARDINAL'S *shoulder, the Nobles, and* SIR THOMAS LOVELL: *the* CARDINAL *places himself under the* KING'S *feet on his right side*

K. Hen. My life itself, and the best heart of it,
Thanks you for this great care: I stood i' the level
Of a full charged confederacy, and gave thanks
To you that choked it.—Let be called before us
That gentleman of Buckingham's: in person
I'll hear him his confessions justify;
And point by point the treasons of his master
He shall again relate.

A noise within, crying, 'ROOM FOR THE QUEEN!' *Enter the* QUEEN, *ushered by the* DUKES OF NORFOLK *and* SUFFOLK: *she kneels. The* KING *rises from his state, takes her up, kisses, and placeth her by him*

Q. Kath. Nay, we must longer kneel: I am a suitor.
K. Hen. Arise, and take place by us:—half your suit
Never name to us: you have half our power:
The other moiety, ere you ask, is given;
Repeat your will, and take it.
Q. Kath. Thank your majesty.
That you would love yourself, and in that love
Not unconsidered leave your honour, nor
The dignity of your office, is the point
Of my petition.
K. Hen. Lady mine, proceed.
Q. Kath. I am solicited, not by a few,
And those of true condition, that your subjects
Are in great grievance. There have been commissions
Sent down among 'em, which hath flawed the heart
Of all their loyalties: wherein, although,
My good lord Cardinal, they vent reproaches
Most bitterly on you, as putter-on
Of these exactions, yet the King our master,—
Whose honour Heaven shield from soil!—even he escapes not
Language unmannerly; yea, such which breaks
The sides of loyalty, and almost appears
In loud rebellion.
Nor. Not 'almost appears,'—
It doth appear; for upon these taxations,
The clothiers all, not able to maintain
The many to them longing, have put off

The spinsters, carders, fullers, weavers; who,
Unfit for other life, compelled by hunger
And lack of other means, in desperate manner
Daring the event to the teeth, are all in uproar,
And Danger serves among them.

K. Hen. Taxation!
Wherein? and what taxation?—My lord Cardinal,
You that are blamed for it alike with us,
Know you of this taxation?

Wol. Please you, sir,
I know but of a single part, in aught
Pertains to the state; and front but in that file
Where others tell steps with me.

Q. Kath. No, my lord,
You know no more than others: but you frame
Things, that are known alike, which are not wholesome
To those which would not know them, and yet must
Perforce be their acquaintance. These exactions
Whereof my sovereign would have note, they are
Most pestilent to the hearing; and to bear 'em,
The back is sacrificed to the load. They say
They are devised by you; or else you suffer
Too hard an exclamation.

K. Hen. Still exaction!
The nature of it? In what kind, let's know,
Is this exaction?

Q. Kath. I am much too venturous
In tempting of your patience; but am boldened
Under your promised pardon. The subjects' grief
Comes through commissions, which compel from each
The sixth part of his substance, to be levied
Without delay; and the pretence for this
Is named: your wars in France. This makes bold mouths:
Tongues spit their duties out, and cold hearts freeze
Allegiance in them: their curses now
Live where their prayers did; and it's come to pass
That tractable obedience is a slave
To each incensèd will. I would, your highness
Would give it quick consideration; for
There is no primer business.

K. Hen. By my life,
This is against our pleasure.

Wol. And for me,
I have no further gone in this, than by
A single voice, and that not passed me but
By learned approbation of the judges. If I am
Traduced by ignorant tongues, which neither know
My faculties nor person yet will be
The chronicles of my doing, let me say
'T is but the fate of place and the rough brake

That virtue must go through. We must not stint
Our necessary actions in the fear
To cope malicious censurers, which ever,
As ravenous fishes, do a vessel follow
That is new-trimmed, but benefit no further
Than vainly longing. What we oft do best,
By sick interpreters, once weak ones, is
Not ours, or not allowed; what worst, as oft,
Hitting a grosser quality, is cried up
For our best action. If we shall stand still,
In fear our motion will be mocked or carped at,
We should take root here where we sit, or sit
State-statues only.

K. Hen. Things done well,
And with a care, exempt themselves from fear;
Things done without example, in their issue
Are to be feared. Have you a precedent
Of this commission? I believe, not any.
We must not rend our subjects from our laws,
And stick them in our will. Sixth part of each?
A trembling contribution! Why, we take
From every tree, lop, bark, and part o' the timber;
And, though we leave it with a root, thus hacked,
The air will drink the sap. To every county,
Where this is questioned, send our letters, with
Free pardon to each man that has denied
The force of this commission. Pray, look to 't;
I put it to your care.

Wol. [*To the Secretary*] A word with you.
Let there be letters writ to every shire,
Of the King's grace and pardon. The grieved commons
Hardly conceive of me; let it be noised,
That through our intercession this revokement
And pardon comes. I shall anon advise you
Further in the proceeding. [*Exit Secretary*

Enter Surveyor

Q. Kath. I am sorry that the Duke of Buckingham
Is run in your displeasure.

K. Hen. It grieves many:
The gentleman is learned, and a most rare speaker;
To nature none more bound, his training such
That he may furnish and instruct great teachers,
And never seek for aid out of himself.
Yet see,
When these so noble benefits shall prove
Not well disposed, the mind growing once corrupt,
They turn to vicious forms, ten times more ugly
Than ever they were fair. This man so cómplete,

Who was enrolled 'mongst wonders, and when we,
Almost with ravished listening, could not find
His hour of speech a minute; he, my lady,
Hath into monstrous habits put the graces
That once were his, and is become as black
As if besmeared in hell. Sit by us; you shall hear—
This was his gentleman in trust—of him
Things to strike honour sad.—Bid him recount
The fore-recited practices; whereof
We cannot feel too little, hear too much.

Wol. Stand forth, and with bold spirit relate what you,
Most like a careful subject, have collected
Out of the Duke of Buckingham.

K. Hen. Speak freely.

Surv. First, it was usual with him, every day
It would infect his speech, that if the King
Should without issue die, he'll carry 't so
To make the sceptre his. These very words
I've heard him utter to his son-in-law,
Lord Aberga'ny, to whom by oath he menaced
Revenge upon the Cardinal.

Wol. Please your highness, note
This dangerous conception in this point.
Not friended by his wish, to your high person
His will is most malignant; and it stretches
Beyond you, to your friends.

Q. Kath. My learned lord Cardinal,
Deliver all with charity.

K. Hen. Speak on.
How grounded he his title to the crown
Upon our fail? to this point hast thou heard him
At any time speak aught?

Surv. He was brought to this
By a vain prophecy of Nicholas Henton.

K. Hen. What was that Henton?

Surv. Sir, a Chartreux friar,
His confessor: who fed him every minute
With words of sovereignty.

K. Hen. How know'st thou this?

Surv. Not long before your highness sped to France,
The Duke being at the Rose, within the parish
Saint Lawrence Poultney, did of me demand
What was the speech among the Londoners
Concerning the French journey? I replied,
Men feared the French would prove perfidious,
To the King's danger. Presently the Duke
Said, 't was the fear, indeed; and that he doubted
'T would prove the verity of certain words
Spoke by a holy monk, 'that oft,' says he,
'Hath sent to me, wishing me to permit

John de la Car, my chaplain, a choice hour
To hear from him a matter of some moment:
Whom after, under the confession's seal,
He solemnly had sworn that what he spoke
My chaplain to no creature but to me
Should utter, with demure confidence.
This pausingly ensued—"Neither the King nor 's heirs,
Tell you the Duke, shall prosper: bid him strive
To gain the love of the commonalty: the Duke
Shall govern England."'

Q. Kath. If I know you well,
You were the Duke's surveyor, and lost your office
On the complaint o' the tenants: take good heed
You charge not in your spleen a noble person,
And spoil your nobler soul. I say, take heed;
Yes, heartily beseech you.

K. Hen. Let him on.—
Go forward.

Surv. On my soul, I'll speak but truth.
I told my lord the Duke, by the devil's illusions
The monk might be deceived; and that 't was dangerous for him
To ruminate on this so far until
It forged him some design, which, being believed,
It was much like to do. He answered, 'Tush!
It can do me no damage;' adding further,
That had the King in his last sickness failed,
The Cardinal's and Sir Thomas Lovell's heads
Should have gone off.

K. Hen. Ha! what, so rank? Ah ha!
There's mischief in this man.—Canst thou say further?

Surv. I can, my liege.

K. Hen. Proceed.

Surv. Being at Greenwich,
After your highness had reproved the Duke
About Sir William Blomer,—

K. Hen. I remember
Of such a time: being my sworn servant,
The Duke retained him his.—But on: what hence?

Surv. 'If,' quoth he, 'I for this had been committed,
As, to the Tower, I thought—I would have played
The part my father meant to act upon
The usurper Richard; who, being at Salisbury,
Made suit to come in 's presence; which if granted,
As he made semblance of his duty, would
Have put his knife into him.'

K. Hen. A giant traitor!

Wol. Now, madam, may his highness live in freedom,
And this man out of prison?

Q. Kath. God mend all!

K. Hen. There's something more would out of thee: what say'st?
Surv. After 'the Duke his father,' with 'the knife,'
He stretched him, and, with one hand on his dagger,
Another spread on his breast, mounting his eyes,
He did discharge a horrible oath; whose tenor
Was—were he evil used, he would outgo
His father, by as much as a performance
Does an irresolute purpose.
K. Hen. There's his period,
To sheathe his knife in us. He is attached;
Call him to present trial: if he may
Find mercy in the law, 't is his; if none,
Let him not seek 't of us. By day and night,
He 's traitor to the height. [*Exeunt*

Scene III.—A Room in the Palace

Enter the Lord Chamberlain *and* Lord Sands

Cham. Is 't possible the spells of France should juggle
Men into such strange mysteries?
Sands. New customs,
Though they be never so ridiculous,
Nay, let 'em be unmanly, yet are followed.
Cham. As far as I see, all the good our English
Have got by the late voyage is but merely
A fit or two o' the face; but they are shrewd ones,
For when they hold 'em, you would swear directly
Their very noses had been counsellors
To Pepin or Clotharius, they keep state so.
Sands. They have all new legs, and lame ones; one would take it,
That never saw 'em pace before, the spavin
And springhalt reigned among 'em.
Cham. Death! my lord,
Their clothes are after such a pagan cut too,
That, sure, they've worn out Christendom.

Enter Sir Thomas Lovell

How now?
What news, Sir Thomas Lovell?
Lov. 'Faith, my lord,
I hear of none, but the new proclamation
That's clapped upon the court-gate.
Cham. What is 't for?
Lov. The reformation of our travelled gallants,
That fill the court with quarrels, talk, and tailors.

Cham. I am glad 't is there: now, I would pray our monsieurs
To think an English courtier may be wise,
And never see the Louvre.
Lov. They must either—
For so run the conditions—leave those remnants
Of fool, and feather, that they got in France,
With all their honourable points of ignorance
Pertaining thereunto, as fights and fireworks;
Abusing better men than they can be,
Out of a foreign wisdom: renouncing clean
The faith they have in tennis and tall stockings,
Short blistered breeches, and those types of travel,
And understand again like honest men;
Or pack to their old playfellows: there, I take it,
They may, *cum privilegio*, wear away
The lag end of their lewdness, and be laughed at.
Sands. 'T is time to give 'em physic, their diseases
Are grown so catching.
Cham. What a loss our ladies
Will have of these trim vanities!
Lov. Ay, marry,
There will be woe indeed, lords: the sly whoresons
Have got a speeding trick to lay down ladies;
A French song and a fiddle has no fellow.
Sands. The devil fiddle 'em! I am glad they're going,
For, sure, there's no converting of 'em: now,
An honest country lord, as I am, beaten
A long time out of play, may bring his plain-song,
And have an hour of hearing; and, by 'r lady,
Held current music too.
Cham. Well said, Lord Sands:
Your colt's tooth is not cast yet.
Sands. No, my lord,
Nor shall not, while I have a stump.
Cham. Sir Thomas,
Whither were you a-going?
Lov. To the Cardinal's.
Your lordship is a guest too.
Cham. O, 't is true:
This night he makes a supper, and a great one,
To many lords and ladies; there will be
The beauty of this kingdom, I'll assure you.
Lov. That churchman bears a bounteous mind indeed.
A hand as fruitful as the land that feeds us;
His dews fall everywhere.
Cham. No doubt, he's noble;
He had a black mouth that said other of him.
Sands. He may, my lord—has wherewithal; in him
Sparing would show a worse sin than ill doctrine:

Men of his way should be most liberal;
They are set here for examples.
Cham. True, they are so;
But few now give so great ones. My barge stays;
Your lordship shall along.—Come, good Sir Thomas,
We shall be late else; which I would not be,
For I was spoke to, with Sir Henry Guildford,
This night to be comptrollers.
Sands. I am your lordship's.
[*Exeunt*

SCENE IV.—The Presence-chamber in York Place

Hautboys. A small table under a state for the CARDINAL, *a longer table for the guests. Then enter* ANNE BULLEN, *and divers other Ladies and Gentlemen, as guests, at one door; at another door, enter* SIR HENRY GUILDFORD

Guild. Ladies, a general welcome from his grace
Salutes ye all; this night he dedicates
To fair content, and you. None here, he hopes,
In all his noble bevy, has brought with her
One care abroad; he would have all as merry
As far 's good company, good wine, good welcome,
Can make good people.

Enter LORD CHAMBERLAIN, LORD SANDS, *and* SIR THOMAS LOVELL

O, my lord, you are tardy;
The very thought of this fair company
Clapped wings to me.
Cham. You are young, Sir Harry Guildford.
Sands. Sir Thomas Lovell, had the Cardinal
But half my lay-thoughts in him, some of these
Should find a running banquet ere they rested,
I think would better please 'em: by my life,
They are a sweet society of fair ones.
Lov. O, that your worship were but now confessor
To one or two of these.
Sands. I would I were;
They should find easy penance.
Lov. 'Faith, how easy?
Sands. As easy as a down-bed would afford it.
Cham. Sweet ladies, will it please you sit? Sir Harry,
Place you that side; I'll take the charge of this:
His grace is entering—Nay, you must not freeze;
Two women placed together makes cold weather:—
My Lord Sands, you are one will keep them waking;

Pray, sit between these ladies.
Sands. By my faith,
And thank your lordship.—By your leave, sweet ladies:
[*Seats himself between Anne Bullen and another lady*
If I chance to talk a little wild, forgive me;
I had it from my father.
Anne. Was he mad, sir?
Sands. O! very mad, exceeding mad, in love too;
But he would bite none: just as I do now,
He would kiss you twenty with a breath. [*Kisses her*
Cham. Well said, my lord.—
So, now you are fairly seated.—Gentlemen,
The penance lies on you, if these fair ladies
Pass away frowning.
Sands. For my little cure,
Let me alone.

Hautboys. Enter CARDINAL WOLSEY, *attended, and takes his state*

Wol. You are welcome, my fair guests: that noble lady
Or gentlemen that is not freely merry,
Is not my friend. This, to confirm my welcome;
And to you all, good health. [*Drinks*
Sands. Your grace is noble:—
Let me have such a bowl may hold my thanks,
And save me so much talking.
Wol. My Lord Sands,
I am beholding to you: cheer your neighbours.—
Ladies, you are not merry:—gentlemen,
Whose fault is this?
Sands. The red wine first must rise
In their fair cheeks, my lord; then, we shall have 'em
Talk us to silence.
Anne. You are a merry gamester,
My Lord Sands.
Sands. Yes, if I make my play.
Here's to your ladyship; and pledge it, madam,
For 't is to such a thing—
Anne You cannot show me.
Sands. I told your grace, they would talk anon.
[*Drum and trumpet. Chambers discharged*
Wol. What's that?
Cham. Look out there, some of ye.
Wol. What warlike voice,
And to what end is this?—Nay, ladies, fear not;
By all the laws of war you are privileged.

Enter a Servant

Cham. How now? what is 't?

Serv. A noble troop of strangers,
For so they seem; they've left their barge, and landed,
And hither make, as great ambassadors
From foreign princes.

Wol. Good Lord Chamberlain,
Go, give 'em welcome; you can speak the French tongue;
And, pray, receive 'em nobly, and conduct 'em
Into our presence, where this heaven of beauty
Shall shine at full upon them.—Some attend him.—

[*Exit Chamberlain. All rise, and tables removed*

You have now a broken banquet, but we'll mend it.
A good digestion to you all; once more,
I shower a welcome on ye:—Welcome all.

Hautboys. Enter the KING *and others, as Masquers, habited like shepherds, ushered by the* LORD CHAMBERLAIN. *They pass directly before the* CARDINAL, *and gracefully salute him*

A noble company: what are their pleasures?

Cham. Because they speak no English, thus they prayed
To tell your grace:—that, having heard by fame
Of this so noble and so fair assembly
This night to meet here, they could do no less,
Out of the great respect they bear to beauty,
But leave their flocks, and, under your fair conduct,
Crave leave to view these ladies, and entreat
An hour of revels with 'em.

Wol. Say, Lord Chamberlain,
They have done my poor house grace; for which I pay 'em
A thousand thanks, and pray 'em take their pleasures.

[*Ladies chosen. The King takes Anne Bullen*

K. Hen. The fairest hand I ever touched: O Beauty,
Till now I never knew thee! [*Music. Dance*

Wol. My lord!

Cham. Your grace?

Wol. Pray, tell them thus much from me:
There should be one amongst them by his person,
More worthy this place than myself; to whom,
If I but knew him, with my love and duty
I would surrender it.

Cham. I will, my lord.

[*Goes to the Masquers, and returns*

Wol. What say they?

Cham. Such a one, they all confess,
There is, indeed; which they would have your grace
Find out, and he will take it.

Wol. Let me see then,—
By all your good leaves, gentlemen; here I'll make
My royal choice.

K. Hen. [*Unmasking*] Ye have found him, Cardinal.
You hold a fair assembly; you do well, lord:
You are a churchman, or, I'll tell you, Cardinal,
I should judge now unhappily.
Wol. I am glad,
Your grace is grown so pleasant.
K. Hen. My Lord Chamberlain,
Pr'ythee, come hither. What fair lady's that?
Cham. An 't please your grace, Sir Thomas Bullen's daughter,
The Viscount Rochford; one of her highness' women.
K. Hen. By heaven, she is a dainty one.—Sweetheart,
I were unmannerly to take you out,
And not to kiss you.—A health, gentlemen!
Let it go round.
Wol. Sir Thomas Lovell, is the banquet ready
I' the privy chamber?
Lov. Yes, my lord.
Wol. Your grace,
I fear, with dancing is a little heated.
K. Hen. I fear, too much.
Wol. There's fresher air, my lord,
In the next chamber.
K. Hen. Lead in your ladies, every one.—Sweet partner,
I must not yet forsake you.—Let's be merry,
Good my Lord Cardinal: I have half a dozen healths
To drink to these fair ladies, and a measure
To lead 'em once again; and then let's dream
Who's best in favour.—Let the music knock it.
[*Exeunt, with trumpets*

ACT TWO

Scene I.—A Street

Enter two Gentlemen, meeting

First Gent. Whither away so fast?
Sec. Gent. O,—God save you.
E'en to the hall, to hear what shall become
Of the great Duke of Buckingham.
First Gent. I'll save you
That labour, sir. All's now done, but the ceremony
Of bringing back the prisoner.
Sec. Gent. Were you there?
First Gent. Yes, indeed, was I.
Sec. Gent. Pray, speak what has happened.
First Gent. You may guess quickly what.

Sec. Gent. Is he found guilty?
First Gent. Yes, truly is he, and condemned upon 't.
Sec. Gent. I am sorry for 't.
First Gent. So are a number more.
Sec. Gent. But, pray, how passed it?
First Gent. I'll tell you in a little. The great duke
Came to the bar; where to his accusations
He pleaded still not guilty, and alleged
Many sharp reasons to defeat the law.
The king's attorney, on the contrary,
Urged on the examinations, proofs, confessions
Of divers witnesses, which the duke desired
To have brought, *vivâ voce*, to his face:
At which appeared against him, his surveyor;
Sir Gilbert Peck his chancellor; and John Car,
Confessor to him; with that devil-monk,
Hopkins, that made this mischief.
Sec. Gent. That was he
That fed him with his prophecies?
First Gent. The same.
All these accused him strongly; which he fain
Would have flung from him, but, indeed, he could not:
And so his peers, upon this evidence,
Have found him guilty of high treason. Much
He spoke, and learnedly, for life; but all
Was either pitied in him or forgotten.
Sec. Gent. After all this, how did he bear himself?
First Gent. When he was brought again to the bar, to hear
His knell rung out, his judgment—he was stirred
With such an agony, he sweat extremely,
And something spoke in choler, ill, and hasty:
But he fell to himself again, and sweetly
In all the rest showed a most noble patience.
Sec. Gent. I do not think he fears death.
First Gent. Sure, he does not;
He never was so womanish: the cause
He may a little grieve at.
Sec. Gent. Certainly,
The Cardinal is the end of this.
First Gent. 'T is likely,
By all conjectures: first, Kildare's attainder,
Then Deputy of Ireland; who removed,
Earl Surrey was sent thither, and in haste too
Lest he should help his father.
Sec. Gent. That trick of state
Was a deep envious one.
First Gent. At his return
No doubt he will requite it. This is noted,
And generally—whoever the King favours,

The Cardinal instantly will find employment,
And far enough from court too.

Sec. Gent. All the commons
Hate him perniciously, and, o' my conscience,
Wish him ten fathom deep: this Duke as much
They love and dote on; call him bounteous Buckingham,
The mirror of all courtesy,—

First Gent. Stay there, sir,
And see the noble ruined man you speak of.

Enter BUCKINGHAM *from his arraignment; tip-staves before him; the axe with the edge towards him; halberds on each side; accompanied with* SIR THOMAS LOVELL, SIR NICHOLAS VAUX, SIR WILLIAM SANDS, *and common people, etc.*

Sec. Gent. Let's stand close, and behold him.

Buck. All good people,
You that thus far have come to pity me,
Hear what I say, and then go home and lose me.
I have this day received a traitor's judgment,
And by that name must die; yet, Heaven bear witness,
And if I have a conscience, let it sink me,
Even as the axe falls, if I be not faithful.
The law I bear no malice for my death;
'T has done upon the premises but justice:
But those that sought it I could wish more Christians:
Be what they will, I heartily forgive 'em:
Yet let them look they glory not in mischief,
Nor build their evils on the graves of great men;
For then my guiltless blood must cry against them.
For further life in this world I ne'er hope,
Nor will I sue, although the King have mercies
More than I dare make faults. You few that loved me,
And dare be bold to weep for Buckingham,
His noble friends and fellows,—whom to leave
Is only bitter to him, only, dying,—
Go with me, like good angels, to my end,
And, as the long divorce of steel falls on me,
Make of your prayers one sweet sacrifice,
And lift my soul to heaven.—Lead on, o' God's name.

Lov. I do beseech your grace for charity,
If ever any malice in your heart
Were hid against me, now to forgive me frankly.

Buck. Sir Thomas Lovell, I as free forgive you,
As I would be forgiven: I forgive all.
There cannot be those numberless offences
'Gainst me, that I cannot take peace with: no black envy
Shall make my grave. Commend me to his grace:
And, if he speak of Buckingham, pray, tell him,

You met him half in heaven. My vows and prayers
Yet are the King's; and, till my soul forsake,
Shall cry for blessings on him. May he live
Longer than I have time to tell his years!
Ever beloved, and loving, may his rule be!
And when old time shall lead him to his end,
Goodness and he fill up one monument!

Lov. To the water side I must conduct your grace;
Then, give my charge up to Sir Nicholas Vaux,
Who undertakes you to your end.

Vaux. Prepare there,
The Duke is coming; see the barge be ready,
And fit it with such furniture as suits
The greatness of his person.

Buck. Nay, Sir Nicholas,
Let it alone; my state now will but mock me.
When I came hither, I was Lord High Constable,
And Duke of Buckingham; now, poor Edward Bohun:
Yet I am richer than my base accusers,
That never knew what truth meant: I now seal it
And with that blood will make them one day groan for 't.
My noble father, Henry of Buckingham,
Who first raised head against usurping Richard
Flying for succour to his servant Banister,
Being distressed, was by that wretch betrayed,
And without trial fell: God's peace be with him!
Henry the Seventh succeeding, truly pitying
My father's loss, like a most royal prince,
Restored me to my honours, and, out of ruins,
Made my name once more noble. Now, his son,
Henry the Eighth, life, honour, name, and all
That made me happy, at one stroke has taken
For ever from the world. I had my trial,
And, must needs say, a noble one; which makes me
A little happier than my wretched father:
Yet thus far we are one in fortunes,—both
Fell by our servants, by those men we loved most:
A most unnatural and faithless service.
Heaven has an end in all: yet, you that hear me,
This from a dying man receive as certain:
Where you are liberal of your loves and counsels,
Be sure you be not loose; for those you make friends
And give your hearts to, when they once perceive
The least rub in your fortunes, fall away
Like water from ye, never found again
But where they mean to sink ye. All good people,
Pray for me! I must now forsake ye: the last hour
Of my long weary life is come upon me.
Farewell:
And when you would say something that is sad,

Speak how I fell.—I have done; and God forgive me!
[*Exeunt Duke and Train*

First Gent. O, this is full of pity.—Sir, it calls,
I fear, too many curses on their heads
That were the authors.

Sec. Gent. If the Duke be guiltless,
'T is full of woe: yet I can give you inkling
Of an ensuing evil, if it fall,
Greater than this.

First Gent. Good angels keep it from us!
What may it be?—You do not doubt my faith, sir?

Sec. Gent. This secret is so weighty, 't will require
A strong faith to conceal it.

First Gent. Let me have it:
I do not talk much.

Sec. Gent. I am confident;
You shall, sir: did you not of late days hear
A buzzing of a separation
Between the King and Katharine?

First Gent. Yes, but it held not;
For when the King once heard it, out of anger
He sent command to the Lord Mayor straight
To stop the rumour, and allay those tongues
That durst disperse it.

Sec. Gent. But that slander, sir,
Is found a truth now; for it grows again
Fresher than e'er it was; and held for certain,
The King will venture at it. Either the Cardinal,
Or some about him near, have, out of malice
To the good Queen, possessed him with a scruple
That will undo her: to confirm this too,
Cardinal Campeius is arrived and lately,
As all think, for this business.

First Gent. 'T is the Cardinal;
And merely to revenge him on the Emperor,
For not bestowing on him, at his asking,
The archbishoprick of Toledo, this is purposed.

Sec. Gent. I think you have hit the mark: but is 't not cruel,
That she should feel the smart of this? The Cardinal
Will have his will, and she must fall.

First Gent. 'T is woful.
We are too open here to argue this;
Let's think in private more. [*Exeunt*

Scene II.—An Ante-chamber in the Palace

Enter the Lord Chamberlain, *reading this letter*

Cham. 'My lord,—The horses your lordship sent for, with all the care I had, I saw well chosen, ridden, and furnished. They were young, and handsome, and of the best breed in the North. When they were ready to set out for London, a man of my Lord Cardinal's, by commission and main power, took 'em from me, with this reason,—his master would be served before a Subject, if not before the King; which stopped our mouths, sir.'
I fear, he will, indeed; well, let him have them:
He will have all, I think.

Enter the Dukes of Norfolk *and* Suffolk

Nor. Well met, my Lord Chamberlain.
Cham. Good day to both your graces.
Suf. How is the King employed?
Cham. I left him private,
Full of sad thoughts and troubles.
Nor. What's the cause?
Cham. It seems, the marriage with his brother's wife
Has crept too near his conscience.
Suf. No, his conscience
Has crept too near another lady.
Nor. 'T is so.
This is the Cardinal's doing, the King-Cardinal:
That blind priest, like the eldest son of Fortune,
Turns what he list. The King will know him one day.
Suf. 'Pray God, he do: he'll never know himself else.
Nor. How holily he works in all his business!
And with what zeal! for now he has cracked the league
Between us and the Emperor, the Queen's great-nephew,
He dives into the King's soul; and there scatters
Dangers, doubts, wringing of the conscience,
Fears, and despairs,—and all these for his marriage:
And out of all these to restore the King,
He counsels a divorce; a loss of her
That like a jewel has hung twenty years
About his neck, yet never lost her lustre;
Of her that loves him with that excellence
That angels love good men with; even of her
That, when the greatest stroke of fortune falls,
Will bless the King:—and is not this course pious?
Cham. Heaven keep me from such counsel! 'T is most true
These news are everywhere; every tongue speaks them,
And every true heart weeps for 't. All, that dare

Look into these affairs, see this main end,—
The French king's sister. Heaven will one day open
The King's eyes, that so long have slept upon
This bold bad man.

Suf. And free us from his slavery.

Nor. We had need pray,
And heartily, for our deliverance;
Or this imperious man will work us all
From princes into pages. All men's honours
Lie like one lump before him, to be fashioned
Into what pitch he please.

Suf. For me, my lords,
I love him not, nor fear him; there's my creed.
As I am made without him, so I'll stand,
If the King please: his curses and his blessings
Touch me alike, they're breath I not believe in.
I knew him, and I know him; so I leave him
To him that made him proud, the Pope.

Nor. Let's in;
And with some other business put the King
From these sad thoughts, that work too much upon him.—
My lord, you'll bear us company?

Cham. Excuse me;
The King hath sent me otherwise: besides,
You'll find a most unfit time to disturb him:
Health to your lordships.

Nor. Thanks, my good Lord Chamberlain.
[*Exit Lord Chamberlain*

NORFOLK *opens a folding door. The* KING *is discovered sitting, and reading pensively*

Suf. How sad he looks: sure, he is much afflicted.

K. Hen. Who is there? Ha!

Nor. 'Pray God, he be not angry.

K. Hen. Who's there, I say? How dare you thrust yourselves
Into my private meditations?
Who am I? Ha!

Nor. A gracious King, that pardons all offences
Malice ne'er meant: our breach of duty this way
Is business of estate; in which we come
To know your royal pleasure.

K. Hen. Ye are too bold.
Go to; I'll make ye know your times of business.
Is this an hour for temporal affairs? Ha!—

Enter WOLSEY *and* CAMPEIUS

Who's there!—My good lord Cardinal? O, my Wolsey.

The quiet of my wounded conscience;
Thou art a cure fit for a King.—[*To Campeius*] You're welcome,
Most learned Reverend Sir, into our kingdom;
Use us, and it:—[*To Wolsey*] My good lord, have great care
I be not found a talker.

Wol. Sir, you cannot.—
I would, your grace would give us but an hour
Of private conference.

K. Hen. [*To Norfolk and Suffolk*] We are busy. Go!

Nor. [*Aside to Suffolk*] This priest has no pride in him?

Suf. [*Aside to Norfolk*] Not to speak of.
I would not be so sick though for his place:
But this cannot continue.

Nor. [*Aside to Suffolk*] If it do,
I'll venture one have-at-him.

Suf. [*Aside to Norfolk*] I another.

[*Exeunt Norfolk and Suffolk*

Wol. Your grace has given a precedent of wisdom
Above all princes, in committing freely
Your scruple to the voice of Christendom.
Who can be angry now? what envy reach you?
The Spaniard, tied by blood and favour to her,
Must now confess, if they have any goodness,
The trial just and noble. All the clerks,
I mean the learned ones, in Christian kingdoms,
Have their free voices; Rome, the nurse of judgment,
Invited by your noble self, hath sent
One general tongue unto us, this good man,
This just and learned priest, Cardinal Campeius,
Whom once more I present unto your highness.

K. Hen. And once more in mine arms I bid him welcome,
And thank the holy conclave for their loves:
They have sent me such a man I would have wished for.

Cam. Your grace must needs deserve all strangers' loves,
You are so noble. To your highness' hand
I tender my commission, by whose virtue—
The court of Rome commanding—you, my Lord
Cardinal of York, are joined with me, their servant,
In the unpartial judging of this business.

K. Hen. Two equal men. The Queen shall be acquainted
Forthwith for what you come.—Where's Gardiner?—

Wol. I know, your majesty has always loved her
So dear in heart, not to deny her that
A woman of less place might ask by law,
Scholars allowed freely to argue for her.

K. Hen. Ay, and the best she shall have; and my favour

To him that does best: God forbid else.—Cardinal,
Pr'ythee, call Gardiner to me, my new secretary:
I find him a fit fellow. [*Exit Wolsey*

Re-enter WOLSEY *with* GARDINER

Wol. Give me your hand; much joy and favour to you:
You are the King's now.
Gard. But to be commanded
For ever by your grace, whose hand has raised me.
K. Hen. Come hither, Gardiner.
[*They converse apart*
Cam. My Lord of York, was not one Doctor Pace
In this man's place before him?
Wol. Yes, he was.
Cam. Was he not held a learned man?
Wol. Yes, surely.
Cam. Believe me, there's an ill opinion spread, then,
Even of yourself, Lord Cardinal.
Wol. How! of me?
Cam. They will not stick to say, you envied him,
And, fearing he would rise, he was so virtuous,
Kept him a foreign man still; which so grieved him,
That he ran mad, and died.
Wol. Heaven's peace be with him!
That's Christian care enough: for living murmurers
There's places of rebuke. He was a fool;
For he would needs be virtuous: that good fellow,
If I command him, follows my appointment:
I will have none so near else. Learn this, brother,
We live not to be griped by meaner persons.—
K. Hen. Deliver this with modesty to the Queen.
[*Exit Gardiner*
The most convenient place that I can think of—
For such receipt of learning, is Black-Friars:
There ye shall meet about this weighty business:—
My Wolsey, see it furnished:—O my lord,
Would it not grieve an able man, to leave
So sweet a bedfellow? But, conscience, conscience,—
O! 't is a tender place! and I must leave her. [*Exeunt*

SCENE III.—An Ante-chamber in the QUEEN's Apartments

Enter ANNE BULLEN *and an Old Lady*

Anne. Not for that neither: here 's the pang that pinches:
His highness having lived so long with her, and she
So good a lady, that no tongue could ever

Pronounce dishonour of her,—by my life,
She never knew harm-doing,—O, now, after
So many courses of the sun enthroned,
Still growing in majesty and pomp, the which
To leave 's a thousand-fold more bitter than
'T is sweet at first to acquire,—after this process,
To give her the avaunt! it is a pity
Would move a monster.

Old L. Hearts of most hard temper
Melt and lament for her.

Anne. O, God's will! much better.
She ne'er had known pomp: though 't be temporal,
Yet, if that quarrel, fortune, do divorce
It from the bearer, 't is a sufferance panging
As soul and body's severing.

Old L. Alas, poor lady!
She 's a stranger now again.

Anne. So much the more
Must pity drop upon her. Verily,
I swear, 't is better to be lowly born,
And range with humble livers in content,
Than to be perked up in a glistering grief,
And wear a golden sorrow.

Old L. Our content
Is our best having.

Anne. By my troth and maidenhead,
I would not be a Queen.

Old L. Beshrew me, I would,
And venture maidenhead for 't; and so would you,
For all this spice of your hypocrisy.
You, that have so fair parts of woman on you,
Have too a woman's heart; which ever yet
Affected eminence, wealth, sovereignty;
Which, to say sooth, are blessings, and which gifts—
Saving your mincing—the capacity
Of your soft cheveril conscience would receive,
If you might please to stretch it.

Anne. Nay, good troth,—

Old L. Yes, troth, and troth;—you would not be a Queen?

Anne. No, not for all the riches under heaven.

Old L. 'T is strange: a three-pence bowed would hire me,
Old as I am, to queen it. But, I pray you,
What think you of a Duchess? have you limbs
To bear that load of title?

Anne. No, in truth.

Old L. Then you are weakly made. Pluck off a little:
I would not be a young Count in your way,
For more than blushing comes to. If your back

Cannot vouchsafe this burden, 't is too weak
Ever to get a boy.
Anne. How you do talk!
I swear again, I would not be a Queen
For all the world.
Old L. In faith, for little England
You'd venture an emballing: I myself
Would for Carnarvonshire, although there 'longed
No more to the Crown but that. Lo, who comes here?

Enter the LORD CHAMBERLAIN

Cham. Good morrow, ladies; what were it worth to know
The secret of your conference?
Anne. My good lord,
Not your demand; it values not your asking:
Our mistress' sorrows we were pitying.
Cham. It was a gentle business, and becoming
The action of good women; there is hope
All will be well.
Anne. Now, I pray God, Amen!
Cham. You bear a gentle mind, and heavenly blessings
Follow such creatures. That you may, fair lady,
Perceive I speak sincerely, and high note's
Ta'en of your many virtues, the King's Majesty
Commends his good opinion of you to you, and
Does purpose honour to you no less flowing
Than Marchioness of Pembroke; to which title
A thousand pound a year, annual support,
Out of his grace he adds.
Anne. I do not know,
What kind of my obedience I should tender;
More than my all, is nothing; nor my prayers
Are not words duly hallowed; nor my wishes
More worth than empty vanities: yet prayers, and wishes
Are all I can return. 'Beseech your lordship
Vouchsafe to speak my thanks, and my obedience,
As from a blushing handmaid, to his highness,
Whose health and royalty I pray for.
Cham. Lady,
I shall not fail to approve the fair conceit
The King hath of you.—[*Aside*] I have perused her well:
Beauty and honour in her are so mingled,
That they have caught the King; and who knows yet
But from this lady may proceed a gem
To lighten all this isle?—[*To her*] I'll to the King,
And say, I spoke to you.
Anne. My honoured lord.
[*Exit Lord Chamberlain*

Old L. Why, this it is; see, see!
I have been begging sixteen years in court,
Am yet a courtier beggarly, nor could
Come pat betwixt too early and too late
For any suit of pounds; and you, O fate!
A very fresh-fish here, fie, fie, upon
This compelled fortune! have your mouth filled up,
Before you open it.
Anne. This is strange to me.
Old L. How tastes it? Is it bitter? Forty pence, no.
There was a lady once, 't is an old story,
That would not be a Queen, that would she not,
For all the mud in Egypt:—have you heard it?
Anne. Come, you are pleasant.
Old L. With your theme, I could
O'ermount the lark. The Marchioness of Pembroke!
A thousand pounds a year,—for pure respect!
No other obligation! By my life,
That promises more thousands: Honour's train
Is longer than his foreskirt. By this time,
I know, your back will bear a Duchess:—say,
Are you not stronger than you were?
Anne. Good lady,
Make yourself mirth with your particular fancy,
And leave me out on 't. 'Would I had no being,
If this salute my blood a jot: it faints me,
To think what follows.
The Queen is comfortless, and we forgetful
In our long absence. Pray, do not deliver
What here you've heard, to her.
Old L. What do you think me?
[*Exeunt*

Scene IV.—A Hall in Blackfriars

Trumpets, sennet, and cornets. Enter two Vergers, with short silver wands; next them, two Scribes, in the habit of doctors; after them, the Archbishop of Canterbury *alone; after him, the* Bishops of Lincoln, Ely, Rochester, *and* Saint Asaph: *next them, with some small distance, follows a Gentleman bearing the Purse, with the great Seal, and a cardinal's hat: then two Priests, bearing each a silver cross; then a Gentleman-Usher bareheaded, accompanied with a Sergeant-at-Arms, bearing a silver mace; then two Gentlemen bearing two great silver pillars: after them, side by side, the two* Cardinals. *Two Noblemen with the Sword and*

Mace. The KING *takes place under the Cloth of State; the two* CARDINALS *sit under him as Judges. The* QUEEN *takes place at some distance from the* KING. *The Bishops place themselves on each side the Court, in manner of a consistory; below them, the Scribes. The Lords sit next the Bishops. The rest of the Attendants stand in convenient order about the stage*

Wol. Whilst our Commission from Rome is read,
Let silence be commanded.
K. Hen. What's the need?
It hath already publicly been read,
And on all sides the authority allowed;
You may then spare that time.
Wol. Be't so.—Proceed.
Scribe. Say, Henry King of England, come into the Court.
Crier. Henry King of England, etc.
K. Hen. Here.
Scribe. Say, Katharine Queen of England, come into the Court.
Crier. Katharine Queen of England, etc.
[*The Queen makes no answer, rises out of her chair, goes about the court, comes to the King, and kneels at his feet; then speaks*
Q. Kath. Sir, I desire you do me right and justice,
And to bestow your pity on me; for
I am a most poor woman, and a stranger,
Born out of your dominions; having here
No judge indifferent, nor no more assurance
Of equal friendship and proceeding. Alas, sir,
In what have I offended you? what cause
Hath my behaviour given to your displeasure,
That thus you should proceed to put me off,
And take your good grace from me? Heaven witness,
I have been to you a true and humble wife,
At all times to your will conformable:
Ever in fear to kindle your dislike,
Yea, subject to your countenance, glad, or sorry,
As I saw it inclined. When was the hour
I ever contradicted your desire,
Or made it not mine too? Which of your friends
Have I not strove to love, although I knew
He were mine enemy? What friend of mine,
That had to him derived your anger, did I
Continue in my liking? nay, gave notice
He was from thence discharged. Sir, call to mind
That I have been your wife, in this obedience,
Upward of twenty years, and have been blest

With many children by you. If, in the course
And process of this time, you can report,
And prove it too, against mine honour aught,
My bond to wedlock, or my love and duty
Against your sacred person, in God's name
Turn me away; and let the foul'st contempt
Shut door upon me, and so give me up
To the sharpest kind of justice. Please you, sir.
The king, your father, was reputed for
A prince most prudent, of an excellent
And unmatched wit and judgment: Ferdinand,
My father, King of Spain, was reckoned one
The wisest prince that there had reigned by many
A year before: it is not to be questioned
That they had gathered a wise council to them
Of every realm, that did debate this business,
Who deemed our marriage lawful. Wherefore I humbly
Beseech you, sir, to spare me, till I may
Be by my friends in Spain advised, whose counsel
I will implore. If not, i' the name of God,
Your pleasure be fulfilled.

Wol. You have here, lady,—
And of your choice—these reverend fathers; men
Of singular integrity and learning,
Yea, the elect of the land, who are assembled
To plead your cause. It shall be therefore bootless,
That longer you desire the Court, as well
For your own quiet, as to rectify
What is unsettled in the King.

Cam. His grace
Hath spoken well, and justly: therefore, madam,
It's fit this Royal Session do proceed,
And that, without delay, their arguments
Be now produced and heard.

Q. Kath. Lord Cardinal,
To you I speak.

Wol. Your pleasure, madam?

Q. Kath. Sir,
I am about to weep; but, thinking that
We are a Queen, or long have dreamed so, certain
The daughter of a King, my drops of tears
I'll turn to sparks of fire.

Wol. Be patient yet.

Q. Kath. I will, when you are humble; nay, before,
Or God will punish me. I do believe,
Induced by potent circumstances, that
You are mine enemy; and make my challenge
You shall not be my judge. For it is you
Have blown this coal betwixt my lord and me,
Which God's dew quench.—Therefore, I say again,

I utterly abhor, yea, from my soul
Refuse, you for my judge, whom, yet once more,
I hold my most malicious foe, and think not
At all a friend to truth.

Wol. I do profess
You speak not like yourself; who ever yet
Have stood to charity, and displayed the effects
Of disposition gentle, and of wisdom
O'ertopping woman's power. Madam, you do me wrong:
I have no spleen against you; nor injustice
For you, or any: how far I have proceeded,
Or how far further shall, is warranted
By a Commission from the Consistory,
Yes, the whole Consistory of Rome. You charge me,
That I have blown this coal: I do deny it.
The King is present: if it be known to him,
That I gainsay my deed, how may he wound,
And worthily, my falsehood; yea, as much
As you have done my truth. If he know
That I am free of your report, he knows
I am not of your wrong. Therefore in him
It lies to cure me; and the cure is, to
Remove these thoughts from you: the which before
His highness shall speak in, I do beseech
You, gracious madam, to unthink your speaking,
And to say so no more.

Q. Kath. My lord, my lord,
I am a simple woman, much too weak
To oppose your cunning. You are meek, and humble-mouthed;
You sign your place and calling, in full seeming,
With meekness and humility; but your heart
Is crammed with arrogancy, spleen, and pride.
You have, by fortune and his highness' favours,
Gone slightly o'er low steps, and now are mounted
Where powers are your retainers; and your words,
Domestics to you, serve your will, as't please
Yourself pronounce their office. I must tell you,
You tender more your person's honour than
Your high profession spiritual: that again
I do refuse you for my judge, and here,
Before you all, appeal unto the Pope,
To bring my whole cause 'fore his Holiness,
And to be judged by him.

[*She curtsies to the King, and offers to depart*

Cam. The Queen is obstinate,
Stubborn to justice, apt to accuse it, and
Disdainful to be tried by it: 't is not well.
She's going away.

K. Hen. Call her again.

Crier. Katharine Queen of England, come into the Court.

Griffith. Madam, you are called back.

Q. Kath. What need you note it? pray you, keep your way:
When you are called, return.—Now the Lord help,
They vex me past my patience! Pray you, pass on:
I will not tarry; no, nor ever more
Upon this business my appearance make
In any of their Courts.

[*Exeunt Queen, Griffith, and her other Attendants*

K. Hen. Go thy ways, Kate:
That man i' the world who shall report he has
A better wife, let him in nought be trusted
For speaking false in that. Thou art, alone,
If thy rare qualities, sweet gentleness,
Thy meekness saint-like, wife-like government,
Obeying in commanding, and thy parts
Sovereign and pious else, could speak thee out,
The Queen of earthly Queens. She's noble born;
And like her true nobility she has
Carried herself towards me.

Wol. Most gracious sir,
In humblest manner I require your highness,
That it shall please you to declare, in hearing
Of all these ears, for where I am robbed and bound,
There must I be unloosed, although not there
At once and fully satisfied, whether ever I
Did broach this business to your highness, or
Laid any scruple in your way, which might
Induce you to the question on't? or ever
Have to you, but with thanks to God for such
A royal lady, spake one the least word, that might
Be to the prejudice of her present state,
Or touch of her good person?

K. Hen. My Lord Cardinal,
I do excuse you; yea, upon mine honour,
I free you from't. You are not to be taught
That you have many enemies, that know not
Why they are so, but, like to village curs,
Bark when their fellows do: by some of these
The Queen is put in anger. You are excused:
But will you be more justified? you ever
Have wished the sleeping of this business; never
Desired it to be stirred; but oft have hindered, oft,
The passages made toward it.—On my honour,
I speak, my good Lord Cardinal, to this point
And thus far clear him. Now, what moved me to't:
I will be bold with time, and your attention:—
Then, mark the inducement. Thus it came;—give heed to't.

My conscience first received a tenderness,
Scruple, and prick, on certain speeches uttered
By the Bishop of Bayonne, then French ambassador,
Who had been hither sent on the debating
A marriage 'twixt the Duke of Orleans and
Our daughter Mary. I' the progress of this business,
Ere a determinate resolution, he—
I mean, the bishop—did require a respite,
Wherein he might the King his Lord advertise
Whether our daughter were legitimate,
Respecting this our marriage with the dowager,
Sometimes our brother's wife. This respite shook
The bosom of my conscience, entered me,
Yea, with a splitting power, and made to tremble
The region of my breast; which forced such way,
That many mazed considerings did throng,
And pressed in with this caution. First, methought,
I stood not in the smile of Heaven, who had
Commanded nature, that my lady's womb,
If it conceived a male child by me, should
Do no more offices of life to't than
The grave does to the dead, for her male issue
Or died where they were made, or shortly after
This world had aired them. Hence I took a thought,
This was a judgment on me, that my kingdom,
Well worthy the best heir o' the world, should not
Be gladded in't by me. Then follows, that
I weighed the danger which my realms stood in
By this my issue's fail; and that gave to me
Many a groaning throe. Thus hulling in
The wild sea of my conscience, I did steer
Toward this remedy whereupon we are
Now present here together; that's to say,
I meant to rectify my conscience,—which
I then did feel full sick, and yet not well,—
By all the reverend fathers of the land,
And doctors learned. First, I began in private
With you, my Lord of Lincoln; you remember
How under my oppression I did reek,
When I first moved you.
Lin. Very well, my liege.
K. Hen. I have spoke long; be pleased yourself to say
How far you satisfied me.
Lin. So please your highness,
The question did at first so stagger me,—
Bearing a state of mighty moment in 't,
And consequence of dread,—that I committed
The daring'st counsel which I had, to doubt,
And did entreat your highness to this course,
Which you are running here.

K. Hen. I then moved you,
My Lord of Canterbury, and got your leave
To make this present summons.—Unsolicited
I left no reverend person in this Court;
But by particular consent proceeded,
Under your hands and seals: therefore, go on;
For no dislike i' the world against the person
Of the good Queen, but the sharp thorny points
Of my allegéd reasons drive this forward.
Prove but our marriage lawful, by my life
And kingly dignity, we are contented
To wear our mortal state to come with her,
Katharine our Queen, before the primest creature
That's paragoned o' the world.
Cam. So please your highness,
The Queen being absent, 't is a needful fitness
That we adjourn this Court till further day:
Meanwhile must be an earnest motion
Made to the Queen, to call back her appeal
She intends unto his Holiness.
K. Hen. [*Aside*] I may perceive,
These Cardinals trifle with me: I abhor
This dilatory sloth, and tricks of Rome.
My learned and well-beloved servant, Cranmer,
Pr'ythee, return: with thy approach, I know,
My comfort comes along.—Break up the Court:
I say, set on. [*Exeunt, in manner as they entered*

ACT THREE

Scene I.—London. The Palace at Bridewell. A Room in the Queen's Apartment

The Queen, *and her Women, at Work*

Q. Kath. Take thy lute, wench: my soul grows sad with troubles;
Sing, and disperse 'em, if thou canst. Leave working.

Song

Orpheus with his lute made trees,
And the mountain-tops that freeze,
Bow themselves, when he did sing:
To his music plants, and flowers
Ever sprung; as sun and showers
There had made a lasting spring.

Everything that heard him play,
Even the billows of the sea,
Hung their heads, and then lay by.
In sweet music is such art,
Killing care and grief of heart
Fall asleep, or, hearing, die.

Enter a Gentleman

Q. Kath. How now?
Gent. An't please your grace, the two great Cardinals
Wait in the presence.
Q. Kath. Would they speak with me?
Gent. They willed me say so, madam.
Q. Kath. Pray their graces
To come near. [*Exit Gentleman*] What can be their business
With me, a poor weak woman, fallen from favour?
I do not like their coming, now I think on't.
They should be good men; their affairs as righteous:
But all hoods make not monks.

Enter Wolsey *and* Campeius

Wol. Peace to your highness!
Q. Kath. Your graces find me here part of a housewife:
I would be all, against the worst may happen.
What are your pleasures with me, reverend lords?
Wol. May it please you, noble madam, to withdraw
Into your private chamber, we shall give you
The full cause of our coming.
Q. Kath. Speak it here.
There's nothing I have done yet, o' my conscience,
Deserves a corner: 'would all other women
Could speak this with as free a soul as I do!
My lords, I care not,—so much I am happy
Above a number,—if my actions
Were tried by every tongue, every eye saw them,
Envy and base opinion set against 'em,
I know my life so even. If your business
Seek me out, and that way I am wife in,
Out with it boldly: truth loves open dealing.
Wol. *Tanta est erga te mentis integritas, Regina Serenissima,—*
Q. Kath. O, good my lord, no Latin:
I am not such a truant since my coming,
As not to know the language I have lived in:
A strange tongue makes my cause more strange-suspicious;
Pray, speak in English. Here are some will thank you,
If you speak truth, for their poor mistress' sake:

Believe me, she has had much wrong. Lord Cardinal,
The willing'st sin I ever yet committed
May be absolved in English.
Wol. Noble lady,
I am sorry, my integrity should breed—
And service to his Majesty and you—
So deep suspicion where all faith was meant.
We come not by the way of accusation,
To taint that honour every good tongue blesses,
Nor to betray you any way to sorrow;
You have too much, good lady; but to know
How you stand minded in the weighty difference
Between the King and you, and to deliver
Like free and honest men, our just opinions,
And comforts to your cause.
Cam. Most honoured madam,
My Lord of York,—out of his noble nature,
Zeal and obedience he still bore your grace,
Forgetting, like a good man, your late censure
Both of his truth and him, which was too far,—
Offers, as I do, in a sign of peace,
His service and his counsel.
Q. Kath. [*Aside*] To betray me.—
My lords, I thank you both for your good wills,
Ye speak like honest men,—pray God, ye prove so!
But how to make ye suddenly an answer,
In such a point of weight, so near mine honour,—
More near my life, I fear,—with my weak wit,
And to such men of gravity and learning,
In truth, I know not. I was set at work
Among my maids; full little, God knows, looking
Either for such men, or such business.
For her sake that I have been, for I feel
The last fit of my greatness, good your graces,
Let me have time and counsel for my cause.
Alas, I am a woman, friendless, hopeless.
Wol. Madam, you wrong the King's love with these fears:
Your hopes and friends are infinite.
Q. Kath. In England
But little for my profit. Can you think, lords,
That any Englishman dare give me counsel?
Or be a known friend, 'gainst his highness' pleasure,—
Though he be grown so desperate to be honest,—
And live a subject? Nay, forsooth; my friends,
They that must weigh out my afflictions,
They that my trust must grow to, live not here:
They are, as all my other comforts, far hence,
In mine own country, lords.
Cam. I would, your grace

Would leave your griefs, and take my counsel.
Q. Kath. How, sir?
Cam. Put your main cause into the King's protection;
He's loving, and most gracious. 'T will be much
Both for your honour better, and your cause:
For if the trial of the law o'ertake ye,
You'll part away disgraced.
Wol. He tells you rightly.
Q. Kath. Ye tell me what ye wish for both,—my ruin.
Is this your Christian counsel? out upon ye!
Heaven is above all yet; there sits a Judge
That no King can corrupt.
Cam. Your rage mistakes us.
Q. Kath. The more shame for ye! holy men I thought ye,
Upon my soul, two reverend cardinal virtues;
But cardinal sins, and hollow hearts, I fear ye.
Mend them, for shame, my lords. Is this your comfort?
The cordial that ye bring a wretched lady?
A woman lost among ye, laughed at, scorned?
I will not wish ye half my miseries,
I have more charity; but say, I warned ye:
Take heed, for Heaven's sake, take heed, lest at once
The burden of my sorrows fall upon ye.
Wol. Madam, this is a mere distraction;
You turn the good we offer into envy.
Q. Kath. Ye turn me into nothing. Woe upon ye,
And all such false professors! Would you have me—
If you have any justice, any pity,
If ye be anything but churchmen's habits—
Put my sick cause into his hands that hates me?
Alas, he has banished me his bed already;
His love, too long ago: I am old, my lords,
And all the fellowship I hold now with him
Is only my obedience. What can happen
To me, above this wretchedness? all your studies
Make me a curse, like this.
Cam. Your fears are worse.
Q. Kath. Have I lived thus long—let me speak myself,
Since virtue finds no friends—a wife, a true one?
A woman—I dare say, without vain-glory—
Never yet branded with suspicion?
Have I with all my full affections
Still met the King? loved him next Heaven? obeyed him?
Been, out of fondness, superstitious to him?
Almost forgot my prayers, to content him?
And am I thus rewarded? 't is not well, lords.
Bring me a constant woman to her husband,
One that ne'er dreamed a joy beyond his pleasure,

And to that woman, when she has done most,
Yet will I add an honour,—a great patience.

Wol. Madam, you wander from the good we aim at.

Q. Kath. My lord, I dare not make myself so guilty,
To give up willingly that noble title
Your master wed me to: nothing but death
Shall e'er divorce my dignities.

Wol. 'Pray, hear me.

Q. Kath. 'Would I had never trod this English earth,
Or felt the flatteries that grow upon it!
Ye have angels' faces, but Heaven knows your hearts.
What will become of me now, wretched lady?
I am the most unhappy woman living.—
[*To her Women*] Alas! poor wenches, where are now your fortunes?
Shipwrecked upon a kingdom where no pity,
No friends, no hope, no kindred weep for me,
Almost no grave allowed me.—Like the lily,
That once was mistress of the field and flourished,
I'll hang my head, and perish.

Wol. If your grace
Could but be brought to know our ends are honest,
You'd feel more comfort. Why should we, good lady,
Upon what cause, wrong you? alas, our places,
The way of our profession is against it:
We are to cure such sorrows, not to sow them.
For goodness' sake, consider what you do;
How you may hurt yourself, ay, utterly
Grow from the King's acquaintance by this carriage.
The hearts of princes kiss obedience,
So much they love it; but to stubborn spirits
They swell and grow as terrible as storms.
I know you have a gentle, noble temper,
A soul as even as a calm: pray, think us
Those we profess, peace-makers, friends, and servants.

Cam. Madam, you'll find it so. You wrong your virtues
With these weak women's fears: a noble spirit,
As yours was put into you, ever casts
Such doubts, as false coin, from it. The King loves you;
Beware, you lose it not: for us, if you please
To trust us in your business, we are ready
To use our utmost studies in your service.

Q. Kath. Do what ye will, my lords: and, pray forgive me,
If I have used myself unmannerly.
You know, I am a woman, lacking wit
To make a seemly answer to such persons.
Pray, do my service to his Majesty:
He has my heart yet, and shall have my prayers,

While I shall have my life. Come, reverend fathers,
Bestow your counsels on me; she now begs,
That little thought, when she set footing here,
She should have bought her dignities so dear. [*Exeunt*

Scene II.—Ante-chamber to the King's Apartment

Enter the Duke of Norfolk, *the* Duke of Suffolk, *the* Earl of Surrey, *and the* Lord Chamberlain

Nor. If you will now unite in your complaints,
And force them with a constancy, the Cardinal
Cannot stand under them: if you omit
The offer of this time, I cannot promise
But that you shall sustain more new disgraces,
With these you bear already.
Sur. I am joyful
To meet the least occasion that may give me
Remembrance of my father-in-law, the Duke,
To be revenged on him.
Suf. Which of the peers
Have uncontemned gone by him, or at least
Strangely neglected? when did he regard
The stamp of nobleness in any person,
Out of himself?
Cham. My lords, you speak your pleasures.
What he deserves of you and me, I know;
What we can do to him,—though now the time
Gives way to us,—I much fear. If you cannot
Bar his access to the King, never attempt
Anything on him, for he hath a witchcraft
Over the King in's tongue.
Nor. O, fear him not;
His spell in that is out: the King hath found
Matter against him that for ever mars
The honey of his language. No, he's settled,
Not to come off, in his displeasure.
Sur. Sir,
I should be glad to hear such news as this
Once every hour.
Nor. Believe it, this is true.
In the divorce, his contrary proceedings
Are all unfolded; wherein he appears
As I would wish mine enemy.
Sur. How came
His practices to light?
Suf. Most strangely.
Sur. O, how? how?
Suf. The Cardinal's letter to the Pope miscarried,

And came to the eye o' the King; wherein was read,
How that the Cardinal did entreat His Holiness
To stay the judgment o' the divorce; for if
It did take place, 'I do,' quoth he, 'perceive,
My King is tangled in affection to
A creature of the Queen's, Lady Anne Bullen.'

Sur. Has the King this?

Suf. Believe it.

Sur. Will this work?

Cham. The King in this perceives him, how he coasts,
And hedges his own way. But in this point
All his tricks founder, and he brings his physic
After his patient's death: the King already
Hath married the fair lady.

Sur. 'Would he had!

Suf. May you be happy in your wish, my lord;
For, I profess, you have 't.

Sur. Now all my joy
Trace the conjunction!

Suf. My Amen to 't!

Nor. All men's.

Suf. There's order given for her coronation:
Marry, this is yet but young, and may be left
To some ears unrecounted.—But, my lords,
She is a gallant creature, and complete
In mind and feature: I persuade me, from her
Will fall some blessing to this land, which shall
In it be memorized.

Sur. But, will the King
Digest this letter of the Cardinal's?
The Lord forbid!

Nor. Marry, Amen!

Suf. No, no:
There be moe wasps that buzz about his nose,
Will make this sting the sooner. Cardinal Campeius
Is stolen away to Rome; hath ta'en no leave;
Has left the cause o' the King unhandled, and
Is posted, as the agent of our Cardinal,
To second all his plot. I do assure you,
The King cried, 'Ha!' at this.

Cham. Now, God incense him,
And let him cry, 'Ha!' louder!

Nor. But, my lord,
When returns Cranmer?

Suf. He is returned, in his opinions, which
Have satisfied the King for his divorce,
Together with all famous colleges
Almost in Christendom. Shortly, I believe,
His second marriage shall be published, and
Her coronation. Katherine no more

Shall be called Queen, but Princess Dowager,
And widow to Prince Arthur.
Nor. This same Cranmer's
A worthy fellow, and hath ta'en much pain
In the King's business.
Suf. He has; and we shall see him
For it an Archbishop.
Nor. So I hear.
Suf. 'T is so.
The Cardinal—

Enter WOLSEY *and* CROMWELL

Nor. Observe, observe; he's moody.
Wol. The packet, Cromwell,
Gave't you the King?
Crom. To his own hand, in's bedchamber.
Wol. Looked he o' th' inside of the papers?
Crom. Presently
He did unseal them, and the first he viewed,
He did it with a serious mind; a heed
Was in his countenance. You he bade
Attend him here this morning.
Wol. Is he ready
To come abroad?
Crom. I think, by this he is.
Wol. Leave me awhile.— [*Exit Cromwell*
It shall be to the Duchess of Alençon,
The French King's sister; he shall marry her.—
Anne Bullen? No; I'll no Anne Bullens for him:
There's more in't than fair visage.—Bullen!
No, we'll no Bullens.—Speedily I wish
To hear from Rome.—The Marchioness of Pembroke!—
Nor. He's discontented.
Suf. May be, he hears the King
Does whet his anger to him.
Sur. Sharp enough,
Lord, for thy justice!—
Wol. The late Queen's gentlewoman, a knight's daughter,
To be her mistress' mistress! the queen's queen!—
This candle burns not clear: 't is I must snuff it;
Then, out it goes.—What though I know her virtuous,
And well deserving? yet I know her for
A spleeny Lutheran; and not wholesome to
Our cause, that she should lie i' the bosom of
Our hard-ruled King. Again, there is sprung up
An heretic, an arch one, Cranmer; one
Hath crawled into the favour of the King,
And is his oracle.

Nor. He's vexed at something.
Suf. I would, 't were something that would fret the string,
The master-cord on 's heart!

Enter the KING, *reading a schedule; and* LOVELL

Suf. The King, the King!
K. Hen. What piles of wealth hath he accumulated
To his own portion! and what expense by the hour
Seems to flow from him! How, i' the name of thrift,
Does he rake this together?—Now, my lords,
Saw you the Cardinal?
Nor. My lord, we have
Stood here observing him. Some strange commotion
Is in his brain: he bites his lip, and starts;
Stops on a sudden, looks upon the ground,
Then lays his finger on his temple; straight,
Springs out into fast gait; then stops again,
Strikes his breast hard; and anon, he casts
His eye against the moon: in most strange postures
We have seen him set himself.
K. Hen. It may well be:
There is a mutiny in 's mind. This morning
Papers of state he sent me to peruse,
As I required; and wot you what I found
There, on my conscience, put unwittingly?
Forsooth an inventory, thus importing,—
The several parcels of his plate, his treasure,
Rich stuffs, and ornaments of household, which
I find at such proud rate, that it outspeaks
Possession of a subject.
Nor. It's Heaven's will:
Some spirit put this paper in the packet,
To bless your eye withal.
K. Hen. If we did think
His contemplation were above the earth,
And fixed on spiritual object, he should still
Dwell in his musings: but, I am afraid,
His thinkings are below the moon, not worth
His serious considering.
[*He takes his seat, and whispers Lovell, who goes to Wolsey*
Wol. Heaven forgive me!—
Ever God bless your highness!
K. Hen. Good my lord,
You are full of heavenly stuff, and bear the inventory
Of your best graces in your mind; the which
You were now running o'er: you have scarce time
To steal from spiritual leisure a brief span
To keep your earthly audit. Sure, in that

I deem you an ill husband, and am glad
To have you therein my companion.
Wol. Sir,
For holy offices I have a time; a time
To think upon the part of business, which
I bear i' the state; and nature does require
Her times of preservation, which, perforce,
I, her frail son, amongst my brethren mortal,
Must give my tendance to.
K. Hen. You have said well.
Wol. And ever may your highness yoke together,
As I will lend you cause, my doing well
With my well-saying!
K. Hen. 'T is well said again;
And 't is a kind of good deed, to say well:
And yet words are no deeds. My father loved you;
He said he did, and with his deed did crown
His word upon you. Since I had my office,
I have kept you next my heart; have not alone
Employed you where high profits might come home,
But pared my present havings, to bestow
My bounties upon you.
Wol. [*Aside*] What should this mean?
Sur. [*Aside, to the others*] The Lord increase this business!
K. Hen. Have I not made you
The prime man of the State? I pray you, tell me,
If what I now pronounce you have found true:
And, if you may confess it, say withal,
If you are bound to us, or no. What say you?
Wol. My sovereign, I confess, your royal graces,
Showered on me daily, have been more than could
My studied purposes requite; which went
Beyond all man's endeavours: my endeavours
Have ever come too short of my desires,
Yet filed with my abilities. Mine own ends
Have been mine so, that evermore they pointed
To the good of your most sacred person and
The profit of the state. For your great graces
Heaped upon me, poor undeserver, I
Can nothing render but allegiant thanks,
My prayers to Heaven for you, my loyalty,
Which ever has, and ever shall be growing,
Till death, that winter, kill it.
K. Hen. Fairly answered;
A loyal and obedient subject is
Therein illustrated. The honour of it
Does pay the act of it, as, i' the contrary,
The foulness is the punishment. I presume,
That, as my hand has opened bounty to you,

My heart dropped love, my power rained honour, more
On you than any; so your hand, and heart,
Your brain, and every function of your power,
Should, notwithstanding that your bond of duty,
As 't were in love's particular, be more
To me, your friend, than any.
Wol. I do profess,
That for your highness' good I ever laboured
More than mine own: that am, have, and will be—
Though all the world should crack their duty to you,
And throw it from their soul; though perils did
Abound, as thick as thought could make 'em, and
Appear in forms more horrid,—yet my duty,
As doth a rock against the chiding flood,
Should the approach of this wild river break,
And stand unshaken yours.
K. Hen. 'T is nobly spoken.
Take notice, lords, he has a loyal breast,
For you have seen him open't.—Read o'er this:
[*Giving him papers*
And, after, this: and then to breakfast with
What appetite you have.
[*Exit King, frowning upon the Cardinal. The nobles throng after him, smiling, and whispering*
Wol. What should this mean?
What sudden anger's this? how have I reaped it?
He parted frowning from me, as if ruin
Leaped from his eyes: so looks the chaféd lion
Upon the daring huntsmen that has galled him;
Then makes him nothing. I must read this paper;
I fear, the story of his anger.—'T is so:
This paper has undone me!—'T is the account
Of all that world of wealth I have drawn together
For mine own ends; indeed, to gain the Popedom,
And fee my friends in Rome. O negligence,
Fit for a fool to fall by! What cross devil
Made me put this main secret in the packet
I sent the King!—Is there no way to cure this?
No new device to beat this from his brains?
I know 't will stir him strongly;—yet I know
A way, if it take right, in spite of fortune
Will bring me off again.—What's this?—To the Pope!
The letter, as I live, with all the business
I writ to his Holiness.—Nay then, farewell!
I have touched the highest point of all my greatness;
And, from that full meridian of my glory,
I haste now to my setting: I shall fall
Like a bright exhalation in the evening,
And no man see me more.

Re-enter the DUKES OF NORFOLK *and* SUFFOLK, *the* EARL OF SURREY, *and the* LORD CHAMBERLAIN

Nor. Hear the King's pleasure, Cardinal; who commands you
To render up the Great Seal presently
Into our hands, and to confine yourself
To Asher House, my Lord of Winchester's,
Till you hear further from his highness.
Wol. Stay:
Where's your commission, lords? words cannot carry
Authority so weighty.
Suf. Who dare cross 'em,
Bearing the King's will from his mouth expressly?
Wol. Till I find more than will or words to do it,—
I mean your malice,—know, officious lords,
I dare, and must deny it. Now I feel
Of what coarse metal ye are moulded,—envy.
How eagerly ye follow my disgraces,
As if it fed ye! and how sleek and wanton
Ye appear in everything may bring my ruin!
Follow your envious courses, men of malice;
You've Christian warrant for them, and, no doubt,
In time will find their fit rewards. That Seal,
You ask with such a violence, the King—
Mine, and your master—with his own hand gave me;
Bade me enjoy it, with the place and honours,
During my life; and, to confirm his goodness,
Tied it by letters-patents:—now, who'll take it?
Sur. The King that gave it.
Wol. It must be himself, then.
Sur. Thou'rt a proud traitor, priest.
Wol. Proud lord, thou liest:
Within these forty hours, Surrey durst better
Have burnt that tongue than said so.
Sur. Thy ambition,
Thou scarlet Sin, robbed this bewailing land
Of noble Buckingham, my father-in-law:
The heads of all thy brother Cardinals—
With thee, and all thy best parts bound together—
Weighed not a hair of his. Plague of your policy!
You sent me Deputy for Ireland,
Far from his succour, from the King, from all
That might have mercy on the fault thou gav'st him,
Whilst your great goodness, out of holy pity,
Absolved him with an axe.
Wol. This, and all else
This talking lord can lay upon my credit,
I answer, is most false. The Duke by law
Found his deserts. How innocent I was

From my private malice in his end,
His noble jury and foul cause can witness.
If I loved many words, lords, I should tell you,
You have as little honesty as honour,
That in the way of loyalty and truth
Toward the King, my ever royal master,
Dare mate a sounder man than Surrey can be,
And all that love his follies.

Sur. By my soul,
Your long coat, priest, protects you; thou shouldst feel
My sword i' the life-blood of thee else.—My lords,
Can ye endure to hear this arrogance?
And from this fellow? If we live thus tamely,
To be thus jaded by a piece of scarlet,
Farewell nobility; let his grace go forward,
And dare us with his cap like larks.

Wol. All goodness
Is poison to thy stomach.

Sur. Yes, that goodness
Of gleaning all the land's wealth into one,
Into your own hands, Cardinal, by extortion;
The goodness of your intercepted packets,
You writ to the Pope, against the King; your goodness,
Since you provoke me, shall be most notorious.—
My Lord of Norfolk,—as you are truly noble,
As you respect the common good, the state
Of our despised nobility, our issues—
Who, if he live, will scarce be gentlemen—
Produce the grand sum of his sins, the articles
Collected from his life:—I'll startle you
Worse than the sacring bell, when the brown wench
Lay kissing in your arms, Lord Cardinal.

Wol. How much, methinks, I could despise this man,
But that I am bound in charity against it.

Nor. Those articles, my lord, are in the King's hand;
But, thus much, they are foul ones.

Wol. So much fairer
And spotless shall mine innocence arise,
When the King knows my truth.

Sur. This cannot save you:
I thank my memory, I yet remember
Some of these articles; and out they shall.
Now, if you can, blush, and cry guilty, Cardinal,
You'll show a little honesty.

Wol. Speak on, sir;
I dare your worst objections: if I blush,
It is to see a nobleman want manners.

Sur. I had rather want those, than my head.—Have at you.
First, that without the King's assent or knowledge

You wrought to be a Legate; by which power
You maimed the jurisdiction of all Bishops.
Nor. Then, that in all you writ to Rome, or else
To foreign princes, *Ego et Rex meus*
Was still inscribed; in which you brought the King
To be your servant.
Suf. Then, that without the knowledge
Either of King or Council, when you went
Ambassador to the Emperor, you made bold
To carry into Flanders the Great Seal.
Sur. Item, you sent a large commission
To Gregory de Cassado, to conclude,
Without the King's will or the State's allowance,
A league between his highness and Ferrara.
Suf. That, out of mere ambition, you have caused
Your holy hat to be stamped on the King's coin.
Sur. Then, that you have sent innumerable substance,—
By what means got, I leave to your own conscience,—
To furnish Rome, and to prepare the ways
You have for dignities; to the mere undoing
Of all the kingdom. Many more there are;
Which, since they are of you, and odious,
I will not taint my mouth with.
Cham. O my lord,
Press not a falling man too far; 't is virtue:
His faults lie open to the laws; let them,
Not you, correct him. My heart weeps to see him
So little of his great self.
Sur. I forgive him.
Suf. Lord Cardinal, the King's further pleasure is,—
Because all those things you have done of late
By your power legatine within this kingdom,
Fall into the compass of a *Præmunire*,—
That therefore such a writ be sued against you;
To forfeit all your goods, lands, tenements,
Chattels, and whatsoever, and to be
Out of the King's protection.—This is my charge.
Nor. And so we'll leave you to your meditations,
How to live better. For your stubborn answer,
About the giving back the Great Seal to us,
The King shall know it, and, no doubt, shall thank you.
So, fare you well, my little good Lord Cardinal.
[*Exeunt all but Wolsey*
Wol. So, farewell to the little good you bear me.
Farewell! a long farewell, to all my greatness!
This is the state of man: to-day he puts forth
The tender leaves of hope, to-morrow blossoms,
And bears his blushing honours thick upon him:
The third day comes a frost, a killing frost,
And, when he thinks, good easy man, full surely

His greatness is a-ripening,—nips his root,
And then he falls, as I do. I have ventured,
Like little wanton boys that swim on bladders,
This many summers in a sea of glory,
But far beyond my depth: my high-blown pride
At length broke under me, and now has left me
Weary, and old with service, to the mercy
Of a rude stream, that must for ever hide me.
Vain pomp and glory of this world, I hate ye:
I feel my heart new opened. O, how wretched
Is that poor man that hangs on princes' favours!
There is, betwixt that smile we would aspire to,
That sweet aspect of princes, and their ruin,
More pangs and fears than wars or women have;
And when he falls, he falls like Lucifer,
Never to hope again.—

Enter CROMWELL, *and stands amazed*

Why, how now, Cromwell?
Crom. I have no power to speak, sir.
Wol. What! amazed
At my misfortunes? can thy spirit wonder
A great man should decline? Nay, an you weep,
I am fallen indeed.
Crom. How does your grace?
Wol. Why, well.
Never so truly happy, my good Cromwell.
I know myself now; and I feel within me
A peace above all earthly dignities,
A still and quiet conscience. The King has cured me,
I humbly thank his grace; and from these shoulders,
These ruined pillars, out of pity, taken
A load would sink a navy,—too much honour.
O, 't is a burden, Cromwell, 't is a burden,
Too heavy for a man that hopes for heaven.
Crom. I am glad your grace has made that right use of it.
Wol. I hope I have: I am able now, methinks,
Out of a fortitude of soul I feel,
To endure more miseries, and greater far,
Than my weak-hearted enemies dare offer.
What news abroad?
Crom. The heaviest, and the worst,
Is your displeasure with the King.
Wol. God bless him!
Crom. The next is, that Sir Thomas More is chosen
Lord Chancellor in your place.
Wol. That's somewhat sudden;
But he's a learned man. May he continue

Long in his highness' favour, and do justice
For truth's sake, and his conscience; that his bones,
When he has run his course and sleeps in blessings,
May have a tomb of orphans' tears wept on 'em!—
What more?

Crom. That Cranmer is returned with welcome,
Installed Lord Archbishop of Canterbury.

Wol. That's news indeed.

Crom. Last, that the Lady Anne,
Whom the King hath in secrecy long married,
This day was viewed in open, as his Queen,
Going to chapel; and the voice is now
Only about her coronation.

Wol. There was the weight that pulled me down, O Cromwell,
The King has gone beyond me: all my glories
In that one woman I have lost for ever.
No sun shall ever usher forth mine honours,
Or gild again the noble troops that waited
Upon my smiles. Go, get thee from me, Cromwell;
I am a poor fall'n man, unworthy now
To be thy lord and master. Seek the King;
That sun, I pray, may never set! I have told him
What and how true thou art: he will advance thee.
Some little memory of me will stir him—
I know his noble nature—not to let
Thy hopeful service perish too. Good Cromwell,
Neglect him not; make use now, and provide
For thine own future safety.

Crom. O my lord,
Must I then leave you? must I needs forego
So good, so noble, and so true a master?
Bear witness all that have not hearts of iron,
With what a sorrow Cromwell leaves his lord.
The King shall have my service; but my prayers,
For ever and for ever, shall be yours.

Wol. Cromwell, I did not think to shed a tear
In all my miseries; but thou hast forced me,
Out of thy honest truth, to play the woman.
Let's dry our eyes; and thus far hear me, Cromwell:
And—when I am forgotten, as I shall be,
And sleep in dull cold marble, where no mention
Of me more must be heard of—say, I taught thee,
Say, Wolsey,—that once trod the ways of glory
And sounded all the depths and shoals of honour,—
Found thee a way, out of his wreck, to rise in;
A sure and safe one, though thy master missed it.
Mark but my fall, and that that ruined me.
Cromwell, I charge thee, fling away ambition:
By that sin fell the angels; how can man, then,

The image of his Maker, hope to win by 't?
Love thyself last: cherish those hearts that hate thee.
Corruption wins not more than honesty.
Still in thy right hand carry gentle peace,
To silence envious tongues. Be just, and fear not.
Let all the ends thou aim'st at be thy country's,
Thy God's, and truth's: then if thou fall'st, O Cromwell,
Thou fall'st a blessed martyr. Serve the King;
And—pr'ythee lead me in:
There take an inventory of all I have,
To the last penny; 't is the King's: my robe,
And my integrity to Heaven, is all
I dare now call my own. O Cromwell, Cromwell!
Had I but served my God with half the zeal
I served my King, He would not in mine age
Have left me naked to mine enemies.

Crom. Good sir, have patience.

Wol. So I have. Farewell
The hopes of Court! my hopes in Heaven do dwell.

[*Exeunt*

ACT FOUR

Scene I.—A Street in Westminster

Enter two Gentlemen, meeting

First Gent. You're well met once again.

Sec. Gent. So are you.

First Gent. You come to take your stand here, and behold
The Lady Anne pass from her coronation?

Sec. Gent. 'T is all my business. At our last encounter,
The Duke of Buckingham came from his trial.

First Gent. 'T is very true; but that time offered sorrow;
This, general joy.

Sec. Gent. 'T is well: the citizens,
I am sure, have shown at full their royal minds—
As, let 'em have their rights, they are ever forward—
In celebration of this day with shows,
Pageants, and sights of honour.

First Gent. Never greater;
Nor, I'll assure you, better taken, sir.

Sec. Gent. May I be bold to ask what that contains.
That paper in your hand?

First Gent. Yes; 't is the list
Of those that claim their offices this day,
By custom of the coronation.

The Duke of Suffolk is the first, and claims
To be High-Steward; next, the Duke of Norfolk,
He to be Earl Marshal. You may read the rest.
Sec. Gent. I thank you, sir: had I not known those
customs,
I should have been beholding to your paper.
But, I beseech you, what's become of Katherine,
The Princess Dowager? how goes her business?
First Gent. That I can tell you too. The Archbishop
Of Canterbury, accompanied with other
Learned and reverend fathers of his order,
Held a late court at Dunstable, six miles off
From Ampthill, where the Princess lay; to which
She was often cited by them, but appeared not:
And, to be short, for not-appearance, and
The King's late scruple, by the main assent
Of all these learned men she was divorced,
And the late marriage made of none effect:
Since which she was removed to Kimbolton,
Where she remains now, sick.
Sec. Gent. Alas, good lady!—[*Trumpets*
The trumpets sound: stand close, the Queen is coming.
[*Hautboys*

THE ORDER OF THE CORONATION

A lively flourish of trumpets

1. *Two Judges*
2. LORD CHANCELLOR, *with purse and Mace before him*
3. *Choristers, singing* [*Music*
4. MAYOR OF LONDON, *bearing the Mace. Then, Garter in his coat of arms, and on his head a gilt copper crown*
5. MARQUESS DORSET, *bearing a sceptre of gold; on his head a demi-coronal of gold. With him the* EARL OF SURREY, *bearing the Rod of Silver with the Dove, crowned with an earl's coronet. Collars of SS.*
6. DUKE OF SUFFOLK, *in his robe of estate, his coronet on his head, bearing a long white wand, as High-Steward. With him, the* DUKE OF NORFOLK, *with the rod of marshalship, a coronet on his head. Collars of SS.*
7. *A canopy borne by four of the Cinque-ports; under it, the* QUEEN *in her robe, in her hair, richly adorned with pearl, crowned. On each side of her, the* BISHOPS OF LONDON *and* WINCHESTER

8. *The old* Duchess of Norfolk, *in a coronal of gold, wrought with flowers, bearing the* Queen's *train*

9. *Certain Ladies or Countesses, with plain circlets of gold without flowers*

Sec. Gent. A royal train, believe me.—These I know;—
Who's that, that bears the Sceptre?
First Gent. Marquess Dorset:
And that the Earl of Surrey, with the Rod.
Sec. Gent. A bold brave gentleman. That should be
The Duke of Suffolk.
First Gent. 'T is the same: High-Steward.
Sec. Gent. And that my Lord of Norfolk?
First Gent. Yes.
Sec. Gent. [*Looking on the Queen*] Heaven bless thee!
Thou hast the sweetest face I ever looked on.—
Sir, as I have a soul, she is an angel;
Our King has all the Indies in his arms,
And more, and richer, when he strains that lady:
I cannot blame his conscience.
First. Gent. They, that bear
The cloth of honour over her, are four barons
Of the Cinque-ports.
Sec. Gent. Those men are happy; and so are all are near her.
I take it, that she carries up the train
Is that old noble lady, Duchess of Norfolk.
First Gent. It is; and all the rest are countesses.
Sec. Gent. Their coronets say so. These are stars indeed:
And sometimes falling ones.
First Gent. No more of that.
[*Exit Procession, with a great flourish of trumpets*

Enter a third Gentleman

God save you, sir! Where have you been broiling?
Third Gent. Among the crowd i' the Abbey; where a finger
Could not be wedged in more: I am stifled
With the mere rankness of their joy.
Sec. Gent. You saw the ceremony?
Third Gent. That I did.
First Gent. How was it?
Third Gent. Well worth the seeing.
Sec. Gent. Good sir, speak it to us.
Third Gent. As well as I am able. The rich stream
Of lords, and ladies, having brought the Queen
To a prepared place in the choir, fell off
A distance from her; while her grace sat down

To rest awhile, some half an hour or so,
In a rich chair of state, opposing freely
The beauty of her person to the people.
Believe me, sir, she is the goodliest woman
That ever lay by man: which when the people
Had the full view of, such a noise arose
As the shrouds make at sea in a stiff tempest,
As loud, and to as many tunes: hats, cloaks,
Doublets, I think, flew up; and had their faces
Been loose, this day they had been lost. Such joy
I never saw before. Great-bellied women,
That had not half a week to go, like rams
In the old time of war, would shake the press,
And make 'em reel before 'em. No man living
Could say, 'This is my wife,' there; all were woven
So strangely in one piece.

Sec. Gent. But what followed?

Third Gent. At length her grace rose, and with modest paces
Came to the altar; where she kneeled and saint-like
Cast her fair eyes to heaven, and prayed devoutly.
Then rose again, and bowed her to the people:
When by the Archbishop of Canterbury
She had all the royal makings of a Queen;
As holy oil, Edward Confessor's crown,
The rod, and bird of peace, and all such emblems
Laid nobly on her: which performed, the choir,
With all the choicest music of the kingdom,
Together sung *Te Deum*. So she parted,
And with the same full state paced back again
To York Place, where the feast is held.

First Gent. Sir,
You must no more call it York Place, that's past;
For, since the Cardinal fell, that title's lost:
'T is now the King's, and called White Hall.

Third Gent. I know it;
But 't is so lately altered, that the old name
Is fresh about me.

Sec. Gent. What two reverend Bishops
Were those that went on each side of the Queen?

Third Gent. Stokesly and Gardiner; the one, of Winchester,
Newly preferred from the King's Secretary;
The other, London.

Sec. Gent. He of Winchester
Is held no great good lover of the Archbishop's,
The virtuous Cranmer.

Third Gent. All the land knows that:
However, yet there's no great breach; when it comes,
Cranmer will find a friend will not shrink from him.

Sec. Gent. Who may that be, I pray you?
Third Gent. Thomas Cromwell;
A man in much esteem with the King, and truly
A worthy friend.—The King
Has made him master of the jewel-house,
And one, already, of the Privy-Council.
Sec. Gent. He will deserve more.
Third Gent. Yes, without all doubt.
Come, gentlemen, ye shall go my way, which
Is to the Court, there ye shall be my guests:
Something I can command. As I walk thither,
I'll tell ye more.
Both. You may command us, sir. [*Exeunt*

Scene II.—Kimbolton

Enter Katherine, *Dowager, sick; led between* Griffith *and* Patience

Grif. How does your grace?
Kath. O Griffith, sick to death:
My legs, like loaden branches, bow to the earth,
Willing to leave their burden: reach a chair:—
So,—now, methinks, I feel a little ease.
Didst thou not tell me, Griffith, as thou ledd'st me,
That the great child of honour, Cardinal Wolsey,
Was dead?
Grif. Yes, madam; but, I think, your grace,
Out of the pain you suffered, gave no ear to 't.
Kath. Pr'ythee, good Griffith, tell me how he died:
If well, he stepped before me, happily,
For my example.
Grif. Well, the voice goes, madam:
For after the stout Earl Northumberland
Arrested him at York, and brought him forward,
As a man sorely tainted, to his answer,
He fell sick suddenly, and grew so ill
He could not sit his mule.
Kath. Alas, poor man!
Grif. At last, with easy roads, he came to Leicester;
Lodged in the Abbey, where the reverend Abbot,
With all his convent, honourably received him:
To whom he gave these words,—'O father Abbot,
An old man, broken with the storms of state,
Is come to lay his weary bones among ye;
Give him a little earth for charity!'
So went to bed, where eagerly his sickness
Pursued him still; and three nights after this,—
About the hour of eight, which he himself

Foretold should be his last,—full of repentance,
Continual meditations, tears, and sorrows,
He gave his honours to the world again,
His blessed part to Heaven, and slept in peace.
Kath. So may he rest: his faults lie gently on him!
Yet thus far, Griffith, give me leave to speak him,
And yet with charity.—He was a man
Of an unbounded stomach, ever ranking
Himself with princes; one that by suggestion
Tied all the kingdom: simony was fair-play;
His own opinion was his law: i' the presence
He would say untruths, and be ever double,
Both in his words and meaning. He was never,
But where he meant to ruin, pitiful:
His promises were, as he then was, mighty;
But his performance, as he is now, nothing.
Of his own body he was ill, and gave
The clergy ill example.
Grif. Noble madam,
Men's evil manners live in brass; their virtues
We write in water. May it please your highness
To hear me speak his good now?
Kath. Yes, good Griffith;
I were malicious else.
Grif. This Cardinal,
Though from an humble stock, undoubtedly
Was fashioned to much honour from his cradle.
He was a scholar, and a ripe and good one;
Exceeding wise, fair-spoken, and persuading;
Loftly and sour to them that loved him not;
But, to those men that sought him, sweet as summer:
And though he were unsatisfied in getting,—
Which was a sin,—yet in bestowing, madam,
He was most princely. Ever witness for him
Those twins of learning, that he raised in you,
Ipswich, and Oxford! one of which fell with him,
Unwilling to outlive the good that did it;
The other, though unfinished, yet so famous,
So excellent in art, and still so rising,
That Christendom shall ever speak his virtue.
His overthrow heaped happiness upon him;
For then, and not till then, he felt himself,
And found the blessedness of being little:
And, to add greater honours to his age
Than man could give him, he died fearing God.
Kath. After my death I wish no other herald,
No other speaker of my living actions,
To keep mine honour from corruption,
But such an honest chronicler as Griffith.
Whom I most hated living, thou hast made me,

With thy religious truth and modesty.
Now in his ashes honour. Peace be with him!—
Patience, be near me still; and set me lower:
I have not long to trouble thee.—Good Griffith,
Cause the musicians play me that sad note
I named my knell, whilst I sit meditating
On that celestial harmony I go to. [*Sad and solemn Music*

Grif. She is asleep. Good wench, let's sit down quiet,
For fear we wake her:—softly, gentle Patience.

The Vision. Enter, solemnly tripping one after another, six personages, clad in white robes, wearing on their heads garlands of bays, and golden visards on their faces; branches of bays, or palm, in their hands. They first congee unto her, then dance; and, at certain changes, the first two hold a spare garland over her head; at which the other four make reverent curtsies: then, the two that held the garland deliver the same to the other next two, who observe the same order in their changes, and holding the garland over her head. Which done, they deliver the same garland to the last two, who likewise observe the same order: at which (as it were by inspiration) she makes in her sleep signs of rejoicing, and holdeth up her hands to heaven. And so in their dancing they vanish, carrying the garland with them. The music continues

Kath. Spirits of peace, where are ye? are ye all gone,
And leave me here in wretchedness behind ye?

Grif. Madam, we are here.

Kath. It is not you I call for:
Saw ye none enter, since I slept?

Grif. None, madam.

Kath. No? Saw you not, even now, a blessed troop
Invite me to a banquet; whose bright faces
Cast thousand beams upon me, like the sun?
They promised me eternal happiness,
And brought me garlands, Griffith, which I feel
I am not worthy yet to wear: I shall,
Assuredly.

Grif. I am most joyful, madam, such good dreams
Possess your fancy.

Kath. Bid the music leave,
They are harsh and heavy to me. [*Music ceases*

Pat. Do you note.
How much her grace is altered on the sudden?
How long her face is drawn? how pale she looks,
And of an earthy colour? Mark her eyes!

Grif. She is going, wench. Pray, pray.
Pat. Heaven comfort her!

Enter a Messenger

Mess. An't like your grace,—
Kath. You are a saucy fellow:
Deserve we no more reverence?
Grif. You are to blame,
Knowing she will not lose her wonted greatness,
To use so rude behaviour: go to, kneel.
Mess. I humbly do entreat your highness' pardon;
My haste made me unmannerly. There is staying
A gentleman, sent from the King to see you.
Kath. Admit him entrance, Griffith: but this fellow
Let me ne'er see again. [*Exeunt Griffith and Messenger*

Re-enter GRIFFITH, *with* CAPUCIUS

If my sight fail not,
You should be lord ambassador from the Emperor,
My royal nephew, and your name Capucius.
Cap. Madam, the same, your servant.
Kath. O my lord,
The times, and titles, now are altered strangely
With me, since first you knew me. But, I pray you,
What is your pleasure with me?
Cap. Noble lady,
First, mine own service to your grace; the next,
The King's request that I would visit you;
Who grieves much for your weakness, and by me
Sends you his princely commendations,
And heartily entreats you take good comfort.
Kath. O my good lord, that comfort comes too late;
'T is like a pardon after execution.
That gentle physic, given in time, had cured me;
But now I am past all comforts here, but prayers.
How does his highness?
Cap. Madam, in good health.
Kath. So may he ever do; and ever flourish,
When I shall dwell with worms, and my poor name
Banished the kingdom!—Patience, is that letter,
I caused you write, yet sent away?
Pat. No, madam.
[*Giving it to Katharine*
Kath. Sir, I most humbly pray you to deliver
This to my Lord the King.
Cap. Most willing, madam.
Kath. In which I have commended to his goodness
The model of our chaste loves, his young daughter,—
The dews of heaven fall thick in blessings on her!

Beseeching him to give her virtuous breeding,—
She is young, and of noble modest nature;
I hope she will deserve well,—and a little
To love her for her mother's sake, that loved him,
Heaven knows how dearly. My next poor petition
Is, that his noble grace would have some pity
Upon my wretched women, that so long
Have followed both my fortunes faithfully:
Of which there is not one, I dare avow—
And now I should not lie—but will deserve,
For virtue and true beauty of the soul,
For honesty and decent carriage,
A right good husband, let him be a noble;
And, sure, those men are happy that shall have them.
The last is, for my men; they are the poorest,
But poverty could never draw them from me;—
That they may have their wages duly paid them,
And something over to remember me by:
If Heaven had pleased to have given me longer life,
And able means, we had not parted thus.
These are the whole contents:—and, good my lord,
By that you love the dearest in this world,
As you wish Christian peace to souls departed,
Stand these poor people's friend, and urge the King
To do me this last right.

Cap. By Heaven, I will,
Or let me lose the fashion of a man!

Kath. I thank you, honest lord. Remember me
In all humility unto his highness:
Say to him, his long trouble now is passing
Out of this world; tell him, in death I blessed him,
For so I will.—Mine eyes grow dim.—Farewell,
My lord.—Griffith, farewell.—Nay, Patience,
You must not leave me yet: I must to bed;
Call in more women.—When I am dead, good wench,
Let me be used with honour: strew me over
With maiden flowers, that all the world may know
I was a chaste wife to my grave: embalm me,
Then lay me forth: although unqueened, yet like
A Queen, and a daughter to a King, inter me.
I can no more.— [*Exeunt, leading Katharine*

ACT FIVE

Scene I.—London. A Gallery in the Palace

Enter Gardiner, *Bishop of Winchester, a Page with a torch before him, met by* Sir Thomas Lovell

Gar. It's one o'clock, boy, is 't not?
Boy. It hath struck.
Gar. These should be hours for necessities,
Not for delights; times to repair our nature
With comforting repose, and not for us
To waste these times.—Good hour of night, Sir Thomas:
Whither so late?
Lov. Came you from the King, my lord?
Gar. I did, Sir Thomas; and left him at primero
With the Duke of Suffolk.
Lov. I must to him too,
Before he go to bed. I'll take my leave.
Gar. Not yet, Sir Thomas Lovell. What's the matter?
It seems you are in haste: an if there be
No great offence belongs to 't, give your friend
Some touch of your late business. Affairs that walk—
As they say spirits do—at midnight, have
In them a wilder nature than the business
That seeks despatch by day.
Lov. My lord, I love you,
And durst commend a secret to your ear
Much weightier than this work. The Queen's in labour,
They say, in great extremity; and feared,
She'll with the labour end.
Gar. The fruit she goes with
I pray for heartily that it may find
Good time, and live: but for the stock, Sir Thomas,
I wish it grubbed up now.
Lov. Methinks, I could
Cry the Amen; and yet my conscience says
She's a good creature, and, sweet lady, does
Deserve our better wishes.
Gar. But, sir, sir,—
Hear me, Sir Thomas: you are a gentleman
Of mine own way; I know you wise, religious;
And, let me tell you, it will ne'er be well,
'T will not, Sir Thomas Lovell, take 't of me,
Till Cranmer, Cromwell, her two hands, and she,
Sleep in their graves.
Lov. Now, sir, you speak of two
The most remarked i' the kingdom. As for Cromwell,
Beside that of the jewel-house, he's made Master

O' the Rolls, and the King's Secretary; further, sir,
Stands in the gap and trade of more preferments,
With which the time will load him. The Archbishop
Is the King's hand and tongue; and who dare speak
One syllable against him?
Gar. Yes, yes, Sir Thomas,
There are that dare; and I myself have ventured
To speak my mind of him: and, indeed, this day,—
Sir, I may tell it you, I think,—I have
Incensed the lords o' the council, that he is—
For so I know he is, they know he is—
A most arch heretic, a pestilence
That does infect the land: with which they moved
Have broken with the King; who hath so far
Given ear to our complaint, of his great grace
And princely care, foreseeing those fell mischiefs
Our reasons laid before him; hath commanded,
To-morrow morning to the council-board
He be convented. He's a rank weed, Sir Thomas,
And we must root him out. From your affairs
I hinder you too long: good night, Sir Thomas.
Lov. Many good nights, my lord. I rest your servant.
[*Exeunt Gardiner and Page*

Enter the KING *and the* DUKE OF SUFFOLK

K. Hen. Charles, I will play no more to-night:
My mind 's not on 't; you are too hard for me.
Suf. Sir, I did never win of you before.
K. Hen. But little, Charles;
Nor shall not when my fancy 's on my play.
Now, Lovell, from the Queen what is the news?
Lov. I could not personally deliver to her
What you commanded me, but by her woman
I sent your message; who returned her thanks
In the great'st humbleness, and desired your highness
Most heartily to pray for her.
K. Hen. What say'st thou? Ha!
To pray for her? What! is she crying out?
Lov. So said her woman; and that her sufferance made
Almost each pang a death.
K. Hen. Alas, good lady!
Suf. God safely quit her of her burden, and
With gentle travail, to the gladding of
Your highness with an heir!
K. Hen. 'T is midnight, Charles:
Pr'ythee, to bed; and in thy prayers remember
The estate of my poor Queen. Leave me alone;
For I must think of that, which company
Would not be friendly to.

Suf. I wish your highness
A quiet night, and my good mistress will
Remember in my prayers.
K. Hen. Charles, good night.—
[*Exit Suffolk*

Enter Sir Anthony Denny

Well, sirs, what follows?
Den. Sir, I have brought my lord the Archbishop,
As you commanded me.
K. Hen. Ha! Canterbury?
Den. Ay, my good lord.
K. Hen. 'T is true: where is he, Denny?
Den. He attends your highness' pleasure.
K. Hen. Bring him to us. [*Exit Denny*
Lov. [*Aside*] This is about that which the Bishop spake:
I am happily come hither.

Re-enter Denny *with* Cranmer

K. Hen. Avoid the gallery.
[*Lovell seems to stay*
Ha!—I have said.—Be gone.
What!— [*Exeunt Lovell and Denny*
Cran. I am fearful:—wherefore frowns he thus?
'T is his aspéct of terror: all's not well.
K. Hen. How now, my lord? You do desire to know
Wherefore I sent for you.
Cran. It is my duty
To attend your highness' pleasure.
K. Hen. 'Pray you, arise,
My good and gracious Lord of Canterbury.
Come, you and I must walk a turn together;
I have news to tell you. Come, come, give me your hand.
Ah, my lord, I grieve at what I speak,
And am right sorry to repeat what follows.
I have, and most unwillingly, of late
Heard many grievous, I do say, my lord,
Grievous complaints of you; which, being considered,
Have moved us and our Council, that you shall
This morning come before us; where, I know,
You cannot with such freedom purge yourself,
But that, till further trial in those charges
Which will require your answer, you must take
Your patience to you, and be well contented
To make your house our Tower: you a brother of us,
It fits we thus proceed, or else no witness
Would come against you.

Cran. I humbly thank your highness,
And am right glad to catch this good occasion
Most thoroughly to be winnowed, where my chaff
And corn shall fly asunder; for, I know,
There's none stands under more calumnious tongues,
Than I myself, poor man.
K. Hen. Stand up, good Canterbury:
Thy truth and thy integrity is rooted
In us, thy friend. Give me thy hand, stand up:
Pr'ythee, let's walk. Now, by my halidom,
What manner of man are you? My lord, I looked
You would have given me your petition, that
I should have ta'en some pains to bring together
Yourself and your accusers; and to have heard you,
Without indurance, further.
Cran. Most dread liege,
The good I stand on is my truth and honesty:
If they shall fail, I with mine enemies
Will triumph o'er my person, which I weigh not,
Being of those virtues vacant. I fear nothing
What can be said against me.
K. Hen. Know you not
How your state stands i' the world, with the whole world?
Your enemies
Are many, and not small; their practices
Must bear the same proportion: and not ever
The justice and the truth o' the question carries
The due o' the verdict with it. At what ease
Might corrupt minds procure knaves as corrupt
To swear against you? such things have been done.
You are potently opposed, and with a malice
Of as great size. Ween you of better luck,
I mean in perjured witness, than your Master,
Whose minister you are, whiles here He lived
Upon this naughty earth? Go to, go to:
You take a precipice for no leap of danger,
And woo your own destruction.
Cran. God, and your Majesty,
Protect mine innocence, or I fall into
The trap is laid for me!
K. Hen. Be of good cheer;
They shall no more prevail than we give way to.
Keep comfort to you; and this morning, see
You do appear before them. If they shall chance,
In charging you with matters, to commit you,
The best persuasions to the contrary
Fail not to use, and with what vehemency
The occasion shall instruct you: if entreaties
Will render you no remedy, this ring
Deliver them, and your appeal to us

There make before them.—Look, the good man weeps:
He's honest, on mine honour. God's blest mother!
I swear, he is true-hearted; and a soul
None better in my kingdom.—Get you gone,
And do as I have bid you. [*Exit Cranmer*
—He has strangled
His language in his tears.

Enter an Old Lady

Gent. [*Within*] Come back: what mean you?
Old L. I'll not come back; the tidings that I bring
Will make my boldness manners.—Now, good angels
Fly o'er thy royal head, and shade thy person
Under their blessed wings!
K. Hen. Now, by thy looks
I guess thy message. Is the queen delivered?
Say, ay; and of a boy.
Old L. Ay, ay, my liege;
And of a lovely boy: the God of heaven
Both now and ever bless her!—'t is a girl,—
Promises boys hereafter. Sir, your Queen
Desires your visitation, and to be
Acquainted with this stranger: 't is as like you
As cherry is to cherry.
K. Hen. Lovell!

Re-enter LOVELL

Lov. Sir.
K. Hen. Give her an hundred marks. I'll to the Queen. [*Exit*
Old L. An hundred marks! By this light, I'll ha' more.
An ordinary groom is for such payment.
I will have more, or scold it out of him.
Said I for this, the girl was like to him?
I will have more, or else unsay't; and now,
While it is hot, I'll put it to the issue. [*Exeunt*

SCENE II.—Lobby before the Council-chamber

Enter CRANMER: *Servants, Door-keeper, etc., attending*

Cran. I hope, I am not too late; and yet the gentleman
That was sent to me from the Council prayed me
To make great haste. All fast? what means this? Ho!
Who waits there?—Sure, you know me?
D. Keep. Yes, my lord;
But yet I cannot help you.

Cran. Why?
D. Keep. Your grace must wait till you be called for.

Enter DOCTOR BUTTS

Cran. So.
Butts. This is a piece of malice. I am glad
I came this way so happily: the King
Shall understand it presently. [*Exit*
Cran. [*Aside*] 'T is Butts,
The King's physician. As he passed along,
How earnestly he cast his eyes upon me.
'Pray Heaven, he sound not my disgrace! For certain,
This is of purpose laid by some that hate me,—
God turn their hearts! I never sought their malice,—
To quench mine honour: they would shame to make me
Wait else at door, a fellow-counsellor,
Among boys, grooms, and lackeys. But their pleasures
Must be fulfilled, and I attend with patience.

Enter the KING *and* BUTTS, *at a window above*

Butts. I'll show your grace the strangest sight—
K. Hen. What's that, Butts?
Butts. I think your highness saw this many a day.
K. Hen. Body o' me, where is it?
Butts. There, my lord:
The high promotion of his grace of Canterbury;
Who holds his state at door, 'mongst pursuivants,
Pages, and footboys.
K. Hen. Ha! 'T is he, indeed.
Is this the honour they do one another?
'T is well, there's one above them yet. I had thought,
They had parted so much honesty among them—
At least good manners—as not thus to suffer
A man of his place, and so near our favour,
To dance attendance on their lordships' pleasures,
And at the door too, like a post with packets.
By holy Mary, Butts, there's knavery:
Let 'em alone, and draw the curtain close;
We shall hear more anon. [*Exeunt*

SCENE III.—The Council-chamber

Enter the LORD CHANCELLOR, *the* DUKE OF SUFFOLK, DUKE OF NORFOLK, EARL OF SURREY, LORD CHAMBERLAIN, GARDINER, *and* CROMWELL. *The* CHANCELLOR *places himself at the upper end of the table on the left hand; a seat being left void above him, as for the* ARCHBISHOP OF

CANTERBURY. *The rest seat themselves in order on each side,* CROMWELL *at the lower end, as secretary*

Chan. Speak to the business, master secretary:
Why are we met in council?
Crom. Please your honours,
The chief cause concerns his grace of Canterbury.
Gar. Has he had knowledge of it?
Crom. Yes.
Nor. Who waits there?
D. Keep. Without, my noble lords?
Gar. Yes.
D. Keep. My lord Archbishop;
And has done half an hour, to know your pleasures.
Chan. Let him come in.
D. Keep. Your grace may enter now.
[*Cranmer approaches the council-table*
Chan. My good lord Archbishop, I am very sorry
To sit here at this present, and behold
That chair stand empty: but we all are men,
In our own natures frail, and capable
Of our flesh, few are angels: out of which frailty
And want of wisdom, you, that best should teach us,
Have misdemeaned yourself, and not a little,
Toward the King first, then his laws, in filling
The whole realm, by your teaching, and your chaplains,—
For so we are informed,—with new opinions,
Divers and dangerous; which are heresies,
And, not reformed, may prove pernicious.
Gar. Which reformation must be sudden too,
My noble lords; for those that tame wild horses
Pace them not in their hands to make them gentle,
But stop their mouths with stubborn bits, and spur them
Till they obey the manage. If we suffer,
Out of our easiness and childish pity
To one man's honour, this contagious sickness,
Farewell all physic: and what follows then?
Commotions, uproars, with a general taint
Of the whole state; as, of late days, our neighbours,
The upper Germany, can dearly witness,
Yet freshly pitied in our memories.
Cran. My good lords, hitherto, in all the progress
Both of my life and office, I have laboured,
And with no little study, that my teaching,
And the strong course of my authority
Might go one way, and safely; and the end
Was ever to do well: nor is there living—
I speak it with a single heart, my lords—
A man, that more detests, more stirs against,
Both in his private conscience and his place,

Defacers of the public peace, than I do.
'Pray Heaven, the King may never find a heart
With less allegiance in it! Men that make
Envy and crooked malice nourishment
Dare bite the best. I do beseech your lordships
That, in this case of justice, my accusers,
Be what they will, may stand forth face to face,
And freely urge against me.

Suf. Nay, my lord,
That cannot be: you are a counsellor,
And, by that virtue, no man dare accuse you.

Gar. My lord, because we have business of more moment,
We will be short with you. 'T is his highness' pleasure,
And our consent, for better trial of you,
From hence you be committed to the Tower;
Where, being but a private man again,
You shall know many dare accuse you boldly,
More than, I fear, you are provided for.

Cran. Ah, my good Lord of Winchester, I thank you;
You are always my good friend: if your will pass,
I shall both find your lordship judge and juror,
You are so merciful. I see your end:
'T is my undoing. Love and meekness, lord,
Become a churchman better than ambition;
Win straying souls with modesty again,
Cast none away. That I shall clear myself,
Lay all the weight ye can upon my patience,
I make as little doubt, as you do conscience
In doing daily wrongs. I could say more,
But reverence to your calling makes me modest.

Gar. My lord, my lord, you are a sectary;
That's the plain truth: your painted gloss discovers,
To men that understood you, words and weakness.

Crom. My Lord of Winchester, you are a little,
By your good favour, too sharp: men so noble,
However faulty, yet should find respect
For what they have been: 't is a cruelty
To load a falling man.

Gar. Good master Secretary,
I cry your honour mercy: you may, worst
Of all this table, say so.

Crom. Why, my lord?

Gar. Do not I know you for a favourer
Of this new sect? ye are not sound.

Crom. Not sound?

Gar. Not sound, I say.

Crom. 'Would you were half so honest
Men's prayers then would seek you, not their fears.

Gar. I shall remember this bold language.

Crom. Do.

Remember your bold life too.
Chan. This is too much;
Forbear, for shame, my lords.
Gar. I have done.
Crom. And I.
Chan. Then thus for you, my lord:—it stands agreed,
I take it, by all voices, that forthwith
You be conveyed to the Tower a prisoner,
There to remain till the King's further pleasure
Be known unto us. Are you all agreed, lords?
All. We are.
Cran. Is there no other way of mercy,
But I must needs to the Tower, my lords?
Gar. What other
Would you expect? You are strangely troublesome.
Let some o' the guard be ready there.

Enter Guard

Cran. For me?
Must I go like a traitor thither?
Gar. Receive him,
And see him safe i' the Tower.
Cran. Stay, good my lords;
I have a little yet to say.—Look there, my lords:
By virtue of that ring I take my cause
Out of the gripes of cruel men, and gave it
To a most noble judge, the King my master.
Chan. This is the King's ring.
Sur. 'T is no counterfeit.
Suf. 'T is the right ring, by Heaven! I told ye all,
When we first put this dangerous stone a-rolling,
'T would fall upon ourselves.
Nor. Do you think, my lords,
The King will suffer but the little finger
Of this man to be vexed?
Chan. 'T is now too certain:
How much more is his life in value with him!
'Would I were fairly out on 't!
Crom. My mind gave me,
In seeking tales and informations
Against this man, whose honesty the devil
And his disciples only envy at,
Ye blew the fire that burns ye. Now, have at ye!

Enter the KING, *frowning on them; he takes his seat*

Gar. Dread sovereign, how much are we bound to Heaven
In daily thanks, that gave us such a prince;
Not only good and wise, but most religious:

One that, in all obedience, makes the church
The chief aim of his honour; and, to strengthen
That holy duty, out of dear respect,
His royal self in judgment comes to hear
The cause betwixt her and this great offender.

K. Hen. You were ever good at sudden commendations,
Bishop of Winchester. But know, I come not
To hear such flatteries now, and in my presence;
They are too thin and bare to hide offences.
To me you cannot reach. You play the spaniel,
And think with wagging of your tongue to win me;
But, whatsoe'er thou tak'st me for, I'm sure,
Thou hast a cruel nature, and a bloody.—
[*To Cranmer*] Good man, sit down. Now let me see the proudest,
He that dares most, but wag his finger at thee:
By all that's holy, he had better starve
Than but once think this place becomes thee not.

Sur. May it please your grace,—

K. Hen. No, sir, it does not please me.
I had thought, I had had men of some understanding
And wisdom of my Council; but I find none.
Was it discretion, lords, to let this man,
This good man,—few of you deserve that title,—
This honest man, wait like a lousy footboy
At chamber-door? and one as great as you are?
Why, what a shame was this! Did my commission
Bid ye so far forget yourselves? I gave ye
Power, as he was a Councillor to try him,
Not as a groom. There's some of ye, I see,
More out of malice than integrity,
Would try him to the utmost, had ye mean;
Which ye shall never have while I live.

Chan. Thus far,
My most dread sovereign, may it like your grace
To let my tongue excuse all. What was purposed
Concerning his imprisonment, was rather—
If there be faith in men—meant for his trial
And fair purgation to the world, than malice,
I'm sure, in me.

K. Hen. Well, well, my lords, respect him;
Take him, and use him well; he's worthy of it.
I will say thus much for him,—if a prince
May be beholding to a subject, I
Am, for his love and service, so to him.
Make me no more ado, but all embrace him:
Be friends, for shame, my lords!—My Lord of Canterbury,
I have a suit which you must not deny me;
That is, a fair young maid that yet wants baptism,
You must be god-father, and answer for her.

Cran. The greatest monarch now alive may glory
In such an honour: how may I deserve it,
That am a poor and humble subject to you?
K. Hen. Come, come, my lord, you'd spare your spoons. You shall have
Two noble partners with you; the old Duchess of Norfolk
And Lady Marquess Dorset: will these please you?
Once more, my Lord of Winchester, I charge you,
Embrace, and love this man.
Gar. With a true heart,
And brother-love, I do it.
Cran. And let Heaven
Witness, how dear I hold this confirmation.
K. Hen. Good man, those joyful tears show thy true heart.
The common voice, I see, is verified
Of thee, which says thus, 'Do my Lord of Canterbury
A shrewd turn, and he is your friend for ever.'—
Come, lords, we trifle time away; I long
To have this young one made a Christian.
As I have made ye one, lords, one remain:
So I grow stronger, you more honour gain. [*Exeunt*

SCENE IV.—The Palace Yard

Noise and tumult within. Enter Porter and his Man

Port. You'll leave your noise anon, ye rascals. Do you take the Court for Paris-garden? Ye rude slaves, leave your gaping.

[*Within*] Good master Porter, I belong to the larder.

Port. Belong to the gallows, and be hanged, you rogue! —Is this a place to roar in?—Fetch me a dozen crab-tree staves, and strong ones: these are but switches to them.— I'll scratch your heads: you must be seeing christenings? Do you look for ale and cakes here, you rude rascals?

Man. Pray, sir, be patient: 't is as much impossible,
Unless we sweep them from the door with cannons,
To scatter 'em, as 't is to make 'em sleep
On May-day morning; which will never be.
We may as well push against Paul's as stir them.
Port. How got they in, and be hanged?
Man. Alas, I know not; how gets the tide in?
As much as one sound cudgel of four foot—
You see the poor remainder—could distribute,
I made no spare, sir.
Port. You did nothing, sir.
Man. I am not Samson, nor Sir Guy, nor Colbrand,
To mow them down before me; but if I spared any

That had a head to hit, either young or old,
He or she, cuckold or cuckold-maker,
Let me ne'er hope to see a chine again;
And that I would not for a cow, God save her.

[*Within*] Do you hear, master porter?

Port. I shall be with you presently, good master puppy.—Keep the door close, sirrah.

Man. What would you have me do?

Port. What should you do, but knock 'em down by the dozens? Is this Moorfields to muster in? or have we some strange Indian with the great tool come to Court, the women so besiege us? Bless me, what a fry of fornication is at door! On my Christian conscience, this one christening will beget a thousand; here will be father, god-father, and all together.

Man. The spoons will be the bigger, sir. There is a fellow somewhat near the door, he should be a brazier by his face, for o' my conscience, twenty of the dog-days now reign in 's nose: all that stand about him are under the line, they need no other penance. That fire-drake did I hit three times on the head, and three times was his nose discharged against me: he stands there, like a mortar-piece, to blow us. There was a haberdasher's wife of small wit near him, that railed upon me till her pink'd porringer fell off her head, for kindling such a combustion in the state. I missed the meteor once, and hit that woman, who cried out: Clubs! when I might see from far some forty truncheoners draw to her succour, which were the hope o' the Strand, where she was quartered. They fell on; I made good my place; at length they came to the broom-staff to me: I defied em still; when suddenly a file of boys behind 'em, loose shot, delivered such a shower of pebbles, that I was fain to draw mine honour in, and let 'em win the work: the devil was amongst 'em, I think, surely.

Port. These are the youths that thunder at a playhouse, and fight for bitten apples; that no audience, but the Tribulation of Tower Hill, or the Limbs of Limehouse, their dear brothers, are able to endure. I have some of 'em in *Limbo Patrum*, and there they are like to dance these three days, besides the running banquet of two beadles that is to come.

Enter the LORD CHAMBERLAIN

Cham. Mercy o' me, what a multitude are here!
They grow still, too; from all parts they are coming,
As if we kept a fair here! Where are these porters,
These lazy knaves?—Ye have made a fine hand, fellows
There is a trim rabble let in. Are all these

Your faithful friends o' the suburbs? We shall have
Great store of room, no doubt, left for the ladies,
When they pass back from the christening.

Port. An 't please your honour,
We are but men; and what so many may do,
Not being torn in pieces, we have done:
An army cannot rule 'em.

Cham. As I live,
If the King blame me for 't, I'll lay ye all
By the heels, and suddenly; and on your heads
Clap round fines for neglect. Ye are lazy knaves;
And here ye lie, baiting of bombards, when
Ye should do service. Hark! the trumpets sound;
They're come already from the christening.
Go, break among the press, and find a way out
To let the troop pass fairly, or I'll find
A Marshalsea shall hold you play these two months.

Port. Make way there for the princess.

Man. You great fellow,
Stand close up, or I'll make your head ache.

Port. You i' the camlet, get up o' the rail
I'll pick you o'er the pales else. [*Exeunt*

SCENE V.—The Palace

Enter trumpets, sounding; then two Aldermen, LORD MAYOR, GARTER, CRANMER, DUKE OF NORFOLK, *with his marshal's staff,* DUKE OF SUFFOLK, *two Noblemen bearing great standing-bowls for the christening-gifts; then, four Noblemen bearing a canopy, under which the* DUCHESS OF NORFOLK, *god-mother, bearing the child richly habited in a mantle, etc., train borne by a Lady; then follows the* MARCHIONESS OF DORSET, *the other god-mother, and Ladies. The troop pass once about the stage, and* GARTER *speaks*

Gart. Heaven, from thy endless goodness, send prosperous life, long, and ever happy, to the high and mighty Princess of England, Elizabeth

Flourish. Enter KING *and Train*

Cran. [*Kneeling*] And to your royal grace and the good Queen,
My noble partners, and myself, thus pray:
All comfort, joy, in this most gracious lady,
Heaven ever laid up to make parents happy,
May hourly fall upon ye!

K. Hen. Thank you, good Lord Archbishop;
What is her name?
Cran. Elizabeth.
K. Hen. Stand up, lord.—
[*The King kisses the child*
With this kiss take my blessing: God protect thee!
Into whose hand I give thy life.
Cran. Amen.
K. Hen. My noble gossips, ye have been too prodigal.
I thank ye heartily: so shall this lady,
When she has so much English.
Cran. Let me speak, sir,
For Heaven now bids me; and the words I utter
Let none think flattery, for they'll find 'em truth.
This royal infant,—Heaven still move about her!—
Though in her cradle, yet now promises
Upon this land a thousand thousand blessings,
Which time shall bring to ripeness. She shall be—
But few now living can behold that goodness—
A pattern to all princes living with her,
And all that shall succeed: Saba was never
More covetous of wisdom and fair virtue,
Than this pure soul shall be: all princely graces
That mould up such a mighty piece as this is,
With all the virtues that attend the good,
Shall still be doubled on her: Truth shall nurse her;
Holy and heavenly thoughts still counsel her:
She shall be loved, and feared: her own shall bless her;
Her foes shake like a field of beaten corn,
And hang their heads with sorrow: good grows with her:
In her days every man shall eat in safety,
Under his own vine, what he plants; and sing
The merry songs of peace to all his neighbours.
God shall be truly known; and those about her
From her shall read the perfect ways of honour,
And by those claim their greatness, not by blood.
Nor shall this peace sleep with her: but as when
The bird of wonder dies, the maiden phœnix,
Her ashes new create another heir
As great in admiration as herself:
So shall she leave her blessedness to one,
When Heaven shall call her from this cloud of darkness,
Who, from the sacred ashes of her honour,
Shall star-like rise, as great in fame as she was,
And so stand fixed. Peace, plenty, love, truth, terror,
That were the servants to this chosen infant,
Shall then be his, and like a vine grow to him:
Wherever the bright sun of Heaven shall shine,
His honour and the greatness of his name
Shall be, and make new nations: he shall flourish,

And, like a mountain cedar, reach his branches
To all the plains about him. Our children's children
Shall see this, and bless Heaven.

K. Hen Thou speakest wonders.

Cran. She shall be, to the happiness of England,
An aged princess; many days shall see her,
And yet no day without a deed to crown it.
'Would I had known no more! but she must die—
She must, the saints must have her;—yet a virgin,
A most unspotted lily shall she pass
To the ground, and all the world shall mourn her.

K. Hen. O lord Archbishop,
Thou has made me now a man: never, before
This happy child, did I get anything.
This oracle of comfort has so pleased me,
That, when I am in heaven, I shall desire
To see what this child does, and praise my Maker.
I thank ye all. To you, my good Lord Mayor,
And your good brethren, I am much beholding:
I have received much honour by your presence,
And ye shall find me thankful.—Lead the way, lords:
Ye must all see the Queen, and she must thank ye,
She will be sick else. This day, no man think
'Has business at his house, for all shall stay:
This little one shall make it holiday. [*Exeunt*

EPILOGUE

'T is ten to one, this play can never please
All that are here. Some come to take their ease,
And sleep an act or two; but those, we fear,
We have frighted with our trumpets; so, 't is clear,
They'll say, 't is naught: others, to hear the city
Abused extremely, and to cry,—'That's witty!'
Which we have not done neither; that, I fear,
All the expected good we're like to hear
For this play, at this time, is only in
The merciful construction of good women;
For such a one we showed 'em. If they smile,
And say, 't will do, I know, within a while
All the best men are ours; for 't is ill hap,
If they hold, when their ladies bid 'em clap.

THE LIFE AND DEATH
OF
KING JOHN

DRAMATIS PERSONÆ

KING JOHN
PRINCE HENRY, *his son*
ARTHUR, *Duke of Bretagne*
WILLIAM MARESHALL, *Earl of Pembroke*
GEFFREY FITZ-PETER, *Earl of Essex*
WILLIAM LONGSWORD, *Earl of Salisbury*
ROBERT BIGOT, *Earl of Norfolk*
HUBERT DE BURGH, *Chamberlain to the King*
ROBERT FAULCONBRIDGE
PHILIP FAULCONBRIDGE
JAMES GURNEY, *servant to Lady Faulconbridge*
PETER *of Pomfret*

PHILIP, *King of France*
LEWIS, *the Dauphin*
ARCHDUKE OF AUSTRIA
CARDINAL PANDULPH, *the Pope's Legate*
MELUN, *a French Lord*
CHATILLON, *ambassador from France*

QUEEN ELINOR, *widow of King Henry II.*
CONSTANCE, *mother to Arthur*
BLANCH, *daughter to Alphonso, King of Castile*
LADY FAULCONBRIDGE

Lords, Ladies, Citizens of Angiers, Sheriff, Heralds, Officers, Soldiers, Messengers, and Attendants

SCENE—*Sometimes in England, and sometimes in France*

THE LIFE AND DEATH OF

KING JOHN

ACT ONE

Scene I.—Northampton. A Room of State in the Palace

Enter King John, Queen Elinor, Pembroke, Essex, Salisbury, *and others, with* Chatillon

K. John. Now, say, Chatillon, what would France with us?
Chat. Thus, after greeting, speaks the King of France,
In my behaviour, to the majesty,
The borrowed majesty, of England here.
Eli. A strange beginning:—'borrowed majesty'!
K. John. Silence, good mother; hear the embassy.
Chat. Philip of France, in right and true behalf
Of thy deceaséd brother Geffrey's son,
Arthur Plantagenet, lays most lawful claim
To this fair island, and the territories;
To Ireland, Poictiers, Anjou, Touraine, Maine;
Desiring thee to lay aside the sword
Which sways usurpingly these several titles,
And put the same into young Arthur's hand,
Thy nephew and right royal sovereign.
K. John. What follows if we disallow of this?
Chat. The proud control of fierce and bloody war,
To enforce these rights so forcibly withheld.
K. John. Here have we war for war and blood for blood,
Controlment for controlment: so answer France.
Chat. Then take my king's defiance from my mouth,
The farthest limit of my embassy.
K. John. Bear mine to him, and so depart in peace.
Be thou as lightning in the eyes of France;
For ere thou canst report I will be there,
The thunder of my cannon shall be heard.
So, hence: Be thou the trumpet of our wrath,
And sullen presage of your own decay.—

An honourable conduct let him have;
Pembroke, look to 't. Farewell, Chatillon.
[*Exeunt Chatillon and Pembroke*

Eli. What now, my son? Have I not ever said
How that ambitious Constance would not cease
Till she had kindled France, and all the world,
Upon the right and party of her son?
This might have been prevented, and made whole
With very easy arguments of love,
Which now the manage of two kingdoms must
With fearful bloody issue arbitrate.

K. John. Our strong possession and our right for us.

Eli. Your strong possession much more than your right,
Or else it must go wrong with you and me:
So much my conscience whispers in your ear,
Which none but Heaven and you and I shall hear.

Enter the Sheriff of Northamptonshire, who whispers ESSEX

Essex. My liege, here is the strangest controversy,
Come from the country to be judged by you,
That e'er I heard: shall I produce the men?

K. John. Let them approach.— [*Exit Sheriff*
Our abbeys, and our priories shall pay
This expedition's charge.—

Re-enter Sheriff, with ROBERT FAULCONBRIDGE, *and* PHILIP *his bastard brother*

What men are you?

Bast. Your faithful subject I, a gentleman
Born in Northamptonshire, and eldest son,
As I suppose, to Robert Faulconbridge,
A soldier, by the honour-giving hand
Of Cœur-de-Lion knighted in the field.

K. John. What art thou?

Rob. The son and heir to that same Faulconbridge.

K. John. Is that the elder, and art thou the heir?
You came not of one mother then, it seems.

Bast. Most certain of one mother, mighty king;
That is well known: and, as I think, one father:
But, for the certain knowledge of that truth
I put you o'er to Heaven, and to my mother:
Of that I doubt, as all men's children may.

Eli. Out on thee, rude man, thou dost shame thy mother,
And wound her honour with this diffidence.

Bast. I, madam! no, I have no reason for it:
That is my brother's plea and none of mine;
The which if he can prove, 'a pops me out

At least from fair five hundred pound a year.
Heaven guard my mother's honour, and my land!

K. John. A good blunt fellow.—Why, being younger born,
Doth he lay claim to thine inheritance?

Bast. I know now why, except to get the land:
But, once, he slandered me with bastardy.
But whe'r I be as true begot, or no,
That still I lay upon my mother's head;
But, that I am as well begot, my liege,—
Fair fall the bones that took the pains for me!—
Compare our faces, and be judge yourself.
If old Sir Robert did beget us both,
And were our father, and this son like him;—
O old Sir Robert, father, on my knee
I give Heaven thanks I was not like to thee!

K. John. Why, what a madcap hath Heaven lent us here!

Eli. He hath a trick of Cœur-de-Lion's face;
The accent of his tongue affecteth him.
Do you not read some tokens of my son
In the large composition of this man?

K. John. Mine eye hath well examinéd his parts,
And finds them perfect Richard.—Sirrah, speak:
What doth move you to claim your brother's land?

Bast. Because he hath a half-face like my father,
With that half-face would he have all my land,
A half-face groat five hundred pound a year!

Rob. My gracious liege, when that my father lived,
Your brother did employ my father much,—

Bast. Well, sir; by this you cannot get my land:
Your tale must be, how he employed my mother.

Rob. And once despatched him in an embassy
To Germany, there, with the emperor,
To treat of high affairs touching that time.
The advantage of his absence took the king,
And in the mean time sojourned at my father's;
Where how he did prevail I shame to speak,
But truth is truth: large lengths of seas and shores
Between my father and my mother lay,
As I have heard my father speak himself,
When this same lusty gentleman was got.
Upon his death-bed he by will bequeathed
His lands to me; and took it on his death
That this, my mother's son, was none of his;
An if he were, he came into the world
Full fourteen weeks before the course of time.
Then, good my liege, let me have what is mine,
My father's land, as was my father's will.

K. John. Sirrah, your brother is legitimate;

Your father's wife did after wedlock bear him;
And if she did play false the fault was hers,
Which fault lies on the hazards of all husbands
That marry wives. Tell me, how if my brother,
Who, as you say, took pains to get this son,
Had of your father claimed this son for his?
In sooth, good friend, your father might have kept
This calf, bred from his cow, from all the world;
In sooth, he might: then, if he were my brother's,
My brother might not claim him, nor your father,
Being none of his, refuse him. This concludes:
My mother's son did get your father's heir;
Your father's heir must have your father's land.

Rob. Shall then my father's will be of no force
To dispossess that child which is not his?

Bast. Of no more force to dispossess me, sir,
Than was his will to get me, as I think.

Eli. Whether hadst thou rather be a Faulconbridge,
And, like thy brother, to enjoy thy land,
Or the reputed son of Cœur-de-Lion,
Lord of thy presence, and no land beside?

Bast. Madam, an if my brother had my shape
And I had his, Sir Robert his, like him;
And if my legs were two such riding-rods,
My arms such eel-skins stuffed, my face so thin
That in mine ear I durst not stick a rose
Lest men should say, 'Look, where three-farthings goes,'
And, to his shape, were heir to all this land,
Would I might never stir from off this place
I'd give it every foot to have this face:
I would not be Sir Nob in any case.

Eli. I like thee well. Wilt thou forsake thy fortune,
Bequeath thy land to him, and follow me?
I am a soldier, and now bound to France.

Bast. Brother, take you my land, I'll take my chance.
Your face hath got five hundred pounds a year,
Yet sell your face for fivepence, and 't is dear.—
Madam, I'll follow you unto the death.

Eli. Nay, I would have you go before me thither.

Bast. Our country manners give our betters way.

K. John. What is thy name?

Bast. Philip, my liege; so is my name begun;
Philip, good old Sir Robert's wife's eldest son.

K. John. From henceforth bear his name whose form thou bearest:
Kneel thou down, Philip, but arise more great;
Arise Sir Richard, and Plantagenet.

Bast. Brother by the mother's side, give me your hand:
My father gave me honour, yours gave land.—
Now blessèd be the hour, by night or day,

When I was got Sir Robert was away!
Eli. The very spirit of Plantagenet!
I am thy grandam, Richard: call me so.
Bast. Madam, by chance, but not by truth; what though?
Something about, a little from the right,
In at the window, or else o'er the hatch:
Who dares not stir by day, must walk by night,
And have is have, however men do catch.
Near or far off, well won is still well shot,
And I am I, howe'er I was begot.
K. John. Go, Faulconbridge: now hast thou thy desire;
A landless knight makes thee a landed squire.—
Come, madam, and come, Richard: we must speed
For France, for France, for it is more than need.
Bast. Brother, adieu: good fortune come to thee,
For thou was got i' the way of honesty.—
[*Exeunt all but the Bastard*
A foot of honour better than I was,
But many a many foot of land the worse.
Well, now can I make any Joan a lady.
'Good den, Sir Richard.'—'God-a-mercy, fellow'—
And if his name be George, I'll call him Peter;
For new-made honour doth forget men's names:
'T is too respective, and too sociable,
For your conversion. Now, your traveller,
He and his toothpick, at my worship's mess;
And when my knightly stomach is sufficed,
Why then I suck my teeth, and catechise
My pickéd man of countries:—'My dear sir,'
Thus, leaning on mine elbow, I begin,
'I shall beseech you'—that is Question now;
And then comes Answer like an absey-book:
'O sir,' says Answer, 'at your best command;
At your employment; at your service, sir:'
'No, sir,' says Question, 'I, sweet sir, at yours:'
And so, ere Answer knows what Question would,
Saving in dialogue of compliment
And talking of the Alps and Apennines,
The Pyrenean, and the river Po,
It draws toward supper in conclusion so.
But this is worshipful society,
And fits the mounting spirit, like myself;
For he is but a bastard to the time
That doth not smack of observation;—
And so am I, whether I smack, or no;—
And not alone in habit and device,
Exterior form, outward accoutrement,
But from the inward motion to deliver
Sweet, sweet, sweet poison for the age's tooth:

Which, though I will not practise to deceive,
Yet, to avoid deceit, I mean to learn;
For it shall strew the footsteps of my rising.—
But who comes in such haste, in riding-robes?
What woman-post is this? hath she no husband
That will take pains to blow a horn before her?

Enter LADY FAULCONBRIDGE *and* JAMES GURNEY

O me! it is my mother.—How now, good lady?
What brings you here to court so hastily?
Lady F. Where is that slave, thy brother? where is he,
That holds in chase mine honour up and down?
Bast. My brother Robert? old Sir Robert's son?
Colbrand the giant, that same mighty man?
Is it Sir Robert's son, that you seek so?
Lady F. Sir Robert's son! Ay, thou unreverent boy,
Sir Robert's son; why scorn'st thou at Sir Robert?
He is Sir Robert's son, and so art thou.
Bast. James Gurney, wilt thou give us leave awhile?
Gur. Good leave, good Philip.
Bast. Philip? sparrow! James,
There's toys abroad: anon I'll tell thee more.—
[*Exit Gurney*
Madam, I was not old Sir Robert's son:
Sir Robert might have eat his part in me
Upon Good Friday, and ne'er broke his fast.
Sir Robert could do well: marry, to confess,
Could he get me? Sir Robert could not do it:
We know his handiwork.—Therefore, good mother,
To whom am I beholding for these limbs?
Sir Robert never holp to make this leg.
Lady F. Hast thou conspiréd with thy brother too,
That for thine own gain shouldst defend mine honour?
What means this scorn, thou most untoward knave?
Bast. Knight, knight, good mother,—Basilisco-like.
What! I am dubbed; I have it on my shoulder.
But, mother, I am not Sir Robert's son;
I have disclaimed Sir Robert, and my land;
Legitimation, name, and all is gone.
Then, good my mother, let me know my father:
Some proper man, I hope; who was it, mother?
Lady F. Hast thou denied thyself a Faulconbridge?
Bast. As faithfully as I deny the devil.
Lady. King Richard Cœur-de-Lion was thy father.
By long and vehement suit I was seduced
To make room for him in my husband's bed.—
Heaven lay not my transgression to my charge!—
Thou art the issue of my dear offence
Which was so strongly urged, past my defence.

Bast. Now, by this light, were I to get again,
Madam, I would not wish a better father.
Some sins do bear their privilege on earth,
And so doth yours; your fault was not your folly:
Needs must you lay your heart at his dispose
Subjected tribute to commanding love,
Against whose fury and unmatchéd force
The aweless lion could not wage the fight,
Nor keep his princely heart from Richard's hand.
He that perforce robs lions of their hearts,
May easily win a woman's. Ay, my mother,
With all my heart I thank thee for my father!
Who lives and dares but say thou didst not well
When I was got, I'll send his soul to hell.
Come, lady, I will show thee to my kin;
And they shall say, when Richard me begot,
If thou hadst said him nay, it had been sin:
Who says it was, he lies: I say, 't was not. [*Exeunt*

ACT TWO

SCENE I.—France. Before the Walls of Angiers

Enter, on one side, the ARCHDUKE OF AUSTRIA, *and Forces; on the other,* PHILIP, *King of France, and Forces;* LEWIS, *the Dauphin,* CONSTANCE, ARTHUR, *and Attendants*

Lew. Before Angiers well met, brave Austria.—
Arthur, that great forerunner of thy blood,
Richard, that robbed the lion of his heart,
And fought the holy wars in Palestine,
By this brave duke came early to his grave:
And, for amends to his posterity,
At our importance hither is he come,
To spread his colours, boy, in thy behalf,
And to rebuke the usurpation
Of thy unnatural uncle, English John.
Embrace him, love him, give him welcome hither.
Arth. God shall forgive you Cœur-de-Lion's death,
The rather, that you give his offspring life,
Shadowing their right under your wings of war.
I give you welcome with a powerless hand,
But with a heart full of unstainéd love:
Welcome before the gates of Angiers, duke.
Lew. A noble boy! Who would not do thee right?
Aust. Upon thy cheek lay I this zealous kiss,
As seal to this indenture of my love,

That to my home I will no more return
Till Angiers and the right thou hast in France,
Together with that pale, that white-faced shore,
Whose foot spurns back the ocean's roaring tides
And coops from other lands her islanders,
Even till that England, hedged in with the main,
That water-wallèd bulwark, still secure
And confident from foreign purposes,
Even till that utmost corner of the west
Salute thee for her king: till then, fair boy,
Will I not think of home, but follow arms.
Const. O, take his mother's thanks, a widow's thanks,
Till your strong hand shall help to give him strength,
To make a more requital to your love.
Aust. The peace of Heaven is theirs that lift their swords
In such a just and charitable war.
K. Phi. Well then, to work. Our cannon shall be bent
Against the brows of this resisting town.
Call for our chiefest men of discipline,
To cull the plots of best advantages.
We'll lay before this town our royal bones,
Wade to the market-place in Frenchmen's blood,
But we will make it subject to this boy.
Const. Stay for an answer to your embassy,
Lest unadvised you stain your swords with blood.
My Lord Chatillon may from England bring
That right in peace which here we urge in war;
And then we shall repent each drop of blood
That hot rash haste so indirectly shed.

Enter CHATILLON

K. Phi. A wonder, lady!—lo, upon thy wish,
Our messenger, Chatillon, is arrived,—
What England says, say briefly, gentle lord,
We coldly pause for thee: Chatillon, speak.
Chat. Then turn your forces from this paltry siege,
And stir them up against a mightier task.
England, impatient of your just demands,
Hath put himself in arms. The adverse winds,
Whose leisure I have stayed, have given him time
To land his legions all as soon as I:
His marches are expedient to this town,
His forces strong, his soldiers confident.
With him along is come the mother-queen,
An Até, stirring him to blood and strife;
With her her niece, the Lady Blanch of Spain;
With them a bastard of the king's deceased:
And all the unsettled humours of the land,
Rash, inconsiderate, fiery voluntaries,

With ladies' faces and fierce dragons' spleens,
Have sold their fortunes at their native homes,
Bearing their birthrights proudly on their backs,
To make a hazard of new fortunes here.
In brief, a braver choice of dauntless spirits
Than now the English bottoms have waft o'er,
Did never float upon the swelling tide
To do offence and scath in Christendom.
[*Drums heard within*
The interruption of their churlish drums
Cuts off more circumstance: they are at hand
To parley, or to fight: therefore, prepare.
K. Phi. How much unlooked for is this expedition!
Aust. By how much unexpected, by so much
We must awake endeavour for defence,
For courage mounteth with occasion:
Let them be welcome then, we are prepared.

Enter KING JOHN, ELINOR, BLANCH, *the* BASTARD, PEMBROKE, *and Forces*

K. John. Peace be to France, if France in peace permit
Our just and lineal entrance to our own;
If not, bleed France, and peace ascend to heaven,
Whiles we, God's wrathful agent, do correct
Their proud contempt that beat his peace to heaven.
K. Phi. Peace be to England, if that war return
From France to England, there to live in peace.
England we love; and, for that England's sake,
With burden of our armour here we sweat:
This toil of ours should be a work of thine;
But thou from loving England art so far
That thou has under-wrought his lawful king,
Cut off the sequence of posterity,
Outfacéd infant state, and done a rape
Upon the maiden virtue of the crown.
Look here upon thy brother Geffrey's face:
These eyes, these brows, were moulded out of his;
This little abstract doth contain that large
Which died in Geffrey, and the hand of time
Shall draw this brief into as huge a volume.
That Geffrey was thy elder brother born,
And this his son; England was Geffrey's right,
And this Geffrey's. In the name of God,
How comes it then, that thou art called a king,
When living blood doth in these temples beat
Which owe the crown that thou o'ermasterest?
K. John. From whom hast thou this great commission, France,
To draw my answer from thy articles?

K. Phi. From that supernal Judge, that stirs good thoughts
In any breast of strong authority
To look into the blots and stains of right.
That Judge hath made me guardian to this boy:
Under whose warrant I impeach thy wrong,
And by whose help I mean to chastise it.
K. John. Alack, thou dost usurp authority.
K. Phi. Excuse: it is to beat usurping down.
Eli. Who is it, thou dost call usurper, France?
Const. Let me make answer:—thy usurping son.
Eli. Out, insolent! thy bastard shall be king
That thou may'st be a queen and check the world!
Const. My bed was ever to thy son as true
As thine was to thy husband, and this boy
Liker in feature to his father Geffrey,
Than thou and John, in manners being as like
As rain to water, or devil to his dam.
My boy a bastard! By my soul, I think,
His father never was so true begot:
It cannot be, an if thou wert his mother.
Eli. There's a good mother, boy, that blots thy father.
Const. There's a good grandam, boy, that would blot thee.
Aust. Peace!
Bast. Hear the crier.
Aust. What the devil art thou?
Bast. One that will play the devil, sir, with you
An 'a may catch your hide and you alone.
You are the hare of whom the proverb goes,
Whose valour plucks dead lions by the beard.
I'll smoke your skin-coat, an I catch you right.
Sirrah, look to 't; i' faith, I will, i' faith.
Blanch. O, well did he become that lion's robe,
That did disrobe the lion of that robe.
Bast. It lies as slightly on the back of him
As great Alcides' shows upon an ass.—
But, ass, I'll take that burden from your back,
Or lay on that shall make your shoulders crack.
Aust. What cracker is this same that deafs our ears
With this abundance of superfluous breath?
K. Phi. Lewis, determine what we shall do, straight.
Lew. Women and fools, break off your conference.—
King John, this is the very sum of all:
England, and Ireland, Anjou, Touraine, Maine,
In right of Arthur do I claim of thee.
Wilt thou resign them, and lay down thy arms?
K. John. My life as soon: I do defy thee, France.—
Arthur of Bretagne, yield thee to my hand,
And, out of my dear love, I'll give thee more

Than e'er the coward hand of France can win.
Submit thee, boy.
Eli. Come to thy grandam, child.
Const. Do, child, go to it grandam, child;
Give grandam kingdom, and it grandam will
Give it a plum, a cherry, and a fig:
There's a good grandam.
Arth. Good my mother, peace!
I would that I were low laid in my grave:
I am not worth this coil that's made for me.
Eli. His mother shames him so, poor boy, he weeps.
Const. Now shame upon you, whe'r she does or no!
His grandam's wrongs, and not his mother's shames,
Draw those Heaven-moving pearls from his poor eyes,
Which Heaven shall take in nature of a fee:
Ay, with these crystal beads Heaven shall be bribed
To do him justice, and revenge on you.
Eli. Thou monstrous slanderer of Heaven and earth!
Const. Thou monstrous injurer of Heaven and earth!
Call not me slanderer: thou, and thine, usurp
The dominations, royalties, and rights
Of this oppressed boy. This is thy eld'st son's son,
Infortunate in nothing but in thee:
Thy sins are visited in this poor child;
The canon of the law is laid on him,
Being but the second generation
Removéd from thy sin-conceiving womb.
K. John. Bedlam, have done!
Const. I have but this to say,—
That he's not only plaguéd for her sin,
But God hath made her sin and her the plague
On this removéd issue; plagued for her,
And with her plague, her sin; his injury
Her injury, the beadle to her sin,
All punished in the person of this child,
And all for her. A plague upon her!
Eli. Thou unadviséd scold, I can produce
A will, that bars the title of thy son.
Const. Ay, who doubts that? a will: a wicked will;
A woman's will; a cankered grandam's will!
K. Phi. Peace, lady; pause, or be more temperate.
It ill beseems this presence, to cry, Ay me,
To these ill tunéd repetitions.—
Some trumpet summon hither to the walls
These men of Angiers: let us hear them speak
Whose title they admit, Arthur's or John's.

Trumpets sound. Enter Citizens upon the walls

Cit. Who is it that hath warned us to the walls?

K. Phi. 'T is France, for England.
K. John. England, for itself.
You men of Angiers, and my loving subjects.—
K. Phi. You loving men of Angiers, Arthur's subjects,
Our trumpet called you to this gentle parle.—
K. John. For our advantage; therefore hear us first.—
These flags of France that are advancéd here
Before the eye and prospect of your town,
Have hither marched to your endamagement:
The cannons have their bowels full of wrath,
And ready mounted are they to spit forth
Their iron indignation 'gainst your walls:
All preparation for a bloody siege
And merciless proceeding by these French,
Confront your city's eyes, your winking gates;
And, but for our approach, those sleeping stones
That as a waist do girdle you about,
By the compulsion of their ordinance
By this time from their fixéd beds of lime
Had been dishabited, and wide havoc made
For bloody power to rush upon your peace.
But, on the sight of us, your lawful king,
Who painfully with much expedient march
Have brought a countercheck before your gates,
To save unscratched your city's threatened cheeks,
Behold, the French amazed vouchsafe a parle;
And now, instead of bullets wrapped in fire,
To make a shaking fever in your walls,
They shoot but calm words, folded up in smoke,
To make a faithless error in your ears:
Which trust accordingly, kind citizens,
And let us in, your king, whose laboured spirits,
Forwearied in this action of swift speed,
Crave harbourage within your city walls.
K. Phi. When I have said, make answer to us both.
Lo, in this right hand, whose protection
Is most divinely vowed upon the right
Of him it holds, stands young Plantagenet,
Son to the elder brother of this man,
And king o'er him and all that he enjoys.
For this down-trodden equity, we tread
In warlike march these greens before your town,
Being no further enemy to you
Than the constraint of hospitable zeal
In the relief of this oppressed child
Religiously provokes. Be pleaséd then
To pay that duty which you truly owe
To him that owes it, namely, this young prince;
And then our arms, like to a muzzled bear,
Save in aspéct, have all offence sealed up:

Our cannons' malice vainly shall be spent
Against the invulnerable clouds of heaven;
And with a blessèd and unvexed retire,
With unhacked swords, and helmets all unbruised,
We will bear home that lusty blood again
Which here we came to spout against your town,
And leave your children, wives, and you, in peace.
But if you fondly pass our proffered offer,
'T is not the roundure of your old-faced walls
Can hide you from our messengers of war,
Though all these English, and their discipline,
Were harboured in their rude circumference.
Then, tell us, shall your city call us lord,
In that behalf which we have challenged it,
Or shall we give the signal to our rage,
And stalk in blood to our possession?

Cit. In brief, we are the King of England's subjects:
For him, and in his right we hold this town.

K. John. Acknowledge then the king, and let me in.

Cit. That can we not; but he that proves the king,
To him will we prove loyal: till that time
Have we rammed up our gates against the world.

K. John. Doth not the crown of England prove the king?
And if not that, I bring you witnesses,
Twice fifteen thousand hearts of England's breed,—

Bast. Bastards, and else.

K. John. To verify our title with their lives.

K. Phi. As many, and as well-born bloods as those,—

Bast. Some bastards too.

K. Phi. Stand in his face to contradict his claim.

Cit. Till you compound whose right is worthiest,
We for the worthiest hold the right from both.

K. John. Then God forgive the sin of all those souls
That to their everlasting residence,
Before the dew of evening fall, shall fleet
In dreadful trial of our kingdom's king!

K. Phi. Amen, Amen.—Mount, chevaliers! to arms!

Bast. Saint George, that swinged the dragon, and e'er since
Sits on his horseback at mine hostess' door,
Teach us some fence!—[*To Austria*] Sirrah, were I at home,
At your den, sirrah, with your lioness,
I would set an oxhead to your lion's hide,
And make a monster of you.

Aust. Peace, no more.

Bast. O, tremble, for you hear the lion roar.

K. John. Up higher to the plain; where we 'll set forth
In best appointment all our regiments.

Bast. Speed then, to take advantage of the field.
K. Phi. It shall be so;—[*to Lewis*] and at the other hill
Command the rest to stand.—God, and our right! [*Exeunt*

Scene II.—The Same

Alarums and Excursions; then a Retreat. Enter a French Herald with trumpets, to the gates

F. Her. You men of Angiers, open wide your gates,
And let young Arthur, Duke Bretagne, in,
Who by the hand of France this day hath made
Much work for tears in many an English mother
Whose sons lie scattered on the bleeding ground;
Many a widow's husband grovelling lies,
Coldly embracing the discoloured earth;
And victory, with little loss, doth play
Upon the dancing banners of the French,
Who are at hand, triumphantly displayed,
To enter conquerors and to proclaim
Arthur of Bretagne England's king and yours.

Enter an English Herald, with trumpets

E. Her. Rejoice, you men of Angiers, ring your bells:
King John, your king and England's, doth approach,
Commander of this hot malicious day.
Their armours that marched hence so silver bright
Hither return all gilt with Frenchmen's blood.
There stuck no plume in any English crest
That is removéd by a staff of France;
Our colours do return in those same hands
That did display them when we first marched forth;
And, like a jolly troop of huntsmen come
Our lusty English, all with purpled hands,
Dyed in the dying slaughter of their foes.
Open your gates, and give the victors way.
Cit. Heralds, from off our towers we might behold,
From first to last, the onset and retire
Of both your armies; whose equality
By our best eyes cannot be censuréd:
Blood hath bought blood and blows have answered blows;
Strength matched with strength and power confronted power:
Both are alike; and both alike we like:
One must prove greatest. While they weigh so even,
We hold our town for neither; yet for both.

Enter, at one side, KING JOHN, *with his Power,* ELINOR, BLANCH, *and the* BASTARD; *at the other,* KING PHILIP, LEWIS, AUSTRIA, *and Forces*

K. John. France, hast thou yet more blood to cast away?
Say, shall the current of our right roam on,
Whose passage, vexed with thy impediment,
Shall leave his native channel and o'erswell
With course disturbed even thy confining shores,
Unless thou let his silver water keep
A peaceful progress to the ocean.
K. Phi. England, thou hast not saved one drop of blood
In this hot trial more than we of France;
Rather, lost more: and by this hand I swear,
That sways the earth this climate overlooks,
Before we will lay down our just-borne arms,
We'll put thee down 'gainst whom these arms we bear,
Or add a royal number to the dead;
Gracing the scroll that tells of this war's loss
With slaughter coupled to the name of kings.
Bast. Ha! majesty, how high thy glory towers,
When the rich blood of kings is set on fire!
O, now doth Death line his dead chaps with steel;
The swords of soldiers are his teeth, his fangs;
And now he feasts, mousing the flesh of men,
In undetermined differences of kings.—
Why stand these royal fronts amazéd thus?
Cry, havoc, kings, back to the stainéd field,
You equal-potents, fiery-kindled spirits!
Then let confusion of one part confirm
The other's peace; till then, blows, blood, and death!
K. John. Whose party do the townsmen yet admit?
K. Phi. Speak citizens, for England; who's your king?
Cit. The King of England, when we know the king.
K. Phi. Know him in us, that here hold up his right.
K. John. In us, that are our own great deputy,
And bear possession of our person here,
Lord of our presence, Angiers, and of you.
Cit. A greater power than we denies all this;
And till it be undoubted, we do lock
Our former scruple in our strong-barred gates,
Kings of our fear; until our fears, resolved,
Be by some certain king purged and deposed.
Bast. By Heaven, these scroyles of Angiers flout you, kings,
And stand securely on their battlements,
As in a theatre, whence they gape and point
At your industrious scenes and acts of death.

Your royal presences be ruled by me;
Do like the mutinies of Jerusalem,
Be friends awhile, and both conjointly bend
Your sharpest deeds of malice on this town.
By east and west let France and England mount
Their battering cannon chargéd to the mouths,
Till their soul-fearing clamours have brawled down
The flinty ribs of this contemptuous city:
I'd play incessantly upon these jades,
Even till unfencéd desolation
Leave them as naked as the vulgar air.
That done, dissever your united strengths,
And part your mingled colours once again;
Turn face to face, and bloody point to point;
Then, in a moment, Fortune shall cull forth
Out of one side her happy minion
To whom in favour she shall give the day,
And kiss him with a glorious victory.
How like you this wild counsel, mighty states?
Smacks it not something of the policy?

K. John. Now, by the sky that hangs above our heads,
I like it well.—France, shall we knit our powers,
And lay this Angiers even with the ground,
Then, after, fight who shall be king of it?

Bast. And if thou hast the mettle of a king,
Being wronged as we are by this peevish town,
Turn thou the mouth of thy artillery,
As we will ours, against these saucy walls;
And when that we have dashed them to the ground,
Why, then defy each other, and, pell-mell,
Make work upon ourselves, for heaven, or hell.

K. Phi. Let it be so.—Say, where will you assault?

K. John. We from the west will send destruction
Into this city's bosom.

Aust. I from the north.

K. Phi. Our thunder from the south
Shall rain their drift of bullets on this town.

Bast. [*Aside*] O prudent discipline! From north to south,
Austria and France shoot in each other's mouth:
I'll stir them to it.—Come, away, away!

Cit. Hear us, great kings: vouchsafe awhile to stay,
And I shall show you peace, and fair-faced league;
Win you this city without stroke or wound;
Rescue those breathing lives to die in beds,
That here come sacrifices for the field.
Persévere not, but hear me, mighty kings.

K. John. Speak on, with favour: we are bent to hear.

Cit. That daughter there of Spain, the Lady Blanch,
Is niece to England. Look upon the years

Of Lewis the Dauphin, and that lovely maid.
If lusty love should go in quest of beauty,
Where should he find it fairer than in Blanch?
If zealous love should go in search of virtue,
Where should he find it purer than in Blanch?
If love ambitious sought a match of birth,
Whose veins bound richer blood than Lady Blanch?
Such as she is, in beauty, virtue, birth,
Is the young Dauphin every way complete:
If not complete of, say, he is not she;
And she again wants nothing, to name want,
If want it be not that she is not he:
He is the half part of a blessèd man,
Left to be finishèd by such as she;—
And she a fair divided excellence,
Whose fulness of perfection lies in him.
O, two such silver currents, when they join,
Do glorify the banks that bound them in;
And two such shores to two such streams made one,
Two such controlling bounds, shall you be, kings,
To these two princes, if you marry them.
This union shall do more than battery can
To our fast closèd gates; for, at this match,
With swifter spleen than powder can enforce,
The mouth of passage shall we fling wide ope,
And give you entrance; but, without this match,
The sea enragèd is not half so deaf,
Lions more confident, mountains and rocks
More free from motion, no, not Death himself
In mortal fury half so peremptory,
As we to keep this city.
Bast. Here's a stay,
That shakes the rotten carcase of old Death
Out of his rags! Here's a large mouth, indeed,
That spits forth death, and mountains, rocks, and seas,
Talks as familiarly of roaring lions
As maids of thirteen do of puppy-dogs.
What cannoneer begot this lusty blood?
He speaks plain cannon, fire, and smoke, and bounce;
He gives the bastinado with his tongue;
Our ears are cudgelled: not a word of his,
But buffets better than a fist of France.
'Zounds! I was never so bethumped with words,
Since I first called my brother's father, dad.
Eli. Son, list to this conjunction, make this match.
Give with our niece a dowry large enough;
For by this knot thou shalt so surely tie
Thy now unsured assurance to the crown,
That yon green boy shall have no sun to ripe
The bloom that promiseth a mighty fruit.

I see a yielding in the looks of France;
Mark, how they whisper: urge them while their souls
Are capable of this ambition,
Lest zeal, now melted, by the windy breath
Of soft petitions, pity, and remorse,
Cool and congeal again to what it was.
Cit. Why answer not the double majesties
This friendly treaty of our threatened town?
K. Phi. Speak England first, that hath been forward first
To speak unto this city: what say you?
K. John. If that the Dauphin there, thy princely son,
Can in this book of beauty read, I love,
Her dowry shall weigh equal with a queen:
For Anjou, and fair Touraine, Maine, Poictiers,
And all that we upon this side the sea—
Except this city now by us besieged—
Find liable to our crown and dignity,
Shall gild her bridal bed, and make her rich
In titles, honours, and promotions,
As she in beauty, education, blood,
Holds hands with any princess of the world.
K. Phi. What say'st thou, boy? look in the lady's face.
Lew. I do, my lord; and in her eye I find
A wonder, or a wondrous miracle,
The shadow of myself formed in her eye,
Which, being but the shadow of your son,
Becomes a sun, and makes your son a shadow.
I do protest, I never loved myself,
Till now infixéd I beheld myself,
Drawn in the flattering table of her eye.
[*Whispers with Blanch*
Bast. 'Drawn in the flattering table of her eye,'
Hanged in the frowning wrinkle of her brow,
And quartered in her heart, he doth espy
Himself love's traitor: this is pity now,
That hanged, and drawn, and quartered, there should be,
In such a love, so vile a lout as he.
Blanch. My uncle's will in this respect is mine.
If he sees aught in you that makes him like
That anything he sees which moves his liking,
I can with ease translate it to my will;—
Or, if you will, to speak more properly,
I will enforce it easily to my love.
Further I will not flatter you, my lord,
That all I see in you is worthy love,
Than this,—that nothing do I see in you,
Though churlish thoughts themselves should be your judge,
That I can find should merit any hate.
K. John. What say these young ones? What say you,
my niece?

Blanch. That she is bound in honour still to do
What you in wisdom still vouchsafe to say.
K. John. Speak then, Prince Dauphin: can you love this lady?
Lew. Nay, ask me if I can refrain from love;
For I do love her most unfeignedly.
K. John. Then do I give Volquessen, Touraine, Maine,
Poictiers, and Anjou, these five provinces,
With her to thee; and this addition more,
Full thirty thousand marks of English coin.—
Philip of France, if thou be pleased withal,
Command thy son and daughter to join hands.
K. Phi. It likes us well.—Young princes, close your hands.
Aust. And your lips too; for I am well assured
That I did so when I was first affied.
K. Phi. Now, citizens of Angiers, ope your gates,
Let in that amity which you have made;
For at Saint Mary's Chapel presently
The rites of marriage shall be solemnized.—
Is not the Lady Constance in this troop?
I know, she is not; for this match, made up,
Her presence would have interrupted much.
Where is she, and her son? tell me, who knows.
Lew. She is sad and passionate at your highness' tent.
K. Phi. And, by my faith, this league, that we have made,
Will give her sadness very little cure.—
Brother of England, how may we content
This widow lady? In her right we came,
Which we, God knows, have turned another way,
To our own vantage.
K. John. We will heal up all;
For we'll create young Arthur Duke of Bretagne,
And Earl of Richmond, and this rich fair town
We make him lord of.—Call the Lady Constance:
Some speedy messenger bid her repair
To our solemnity.—I trust, we shall,
If not fill up the measure of her will,
Yet in some measure satisfy her so,
That we shall stop her exclamation.
Go we, as well as haste will suffer us,
To this unlooked-for unpreparéd pomp.
[*Exeunt all but the Bastard. The citizens retire from the walls*
Bast. Mad world! mad kings! mad composition!
John, to stop Arthur's title in the whole,
Hath willingly departed with a part:
And France, whose armour conscience buckled on,
Whom zeal and charity brought to the field

As God's own soldier, rounded in the ear
With that same purpose-changer, that sly devil,
That broker that still breaks the pate of faith,
That daily break-vow, he that wins of all,
Of kings, of beggars, old men, young men, maids,—
Who having no external thing to lose
But the word maid, cheats the poor maid of that;—
That smooth-faced gentleman, tickling Commodity,
Commodity, the bias of the world;
The world, who of itself is peiséd well,
Made to run even, upon even ground,
Till this advantage, this vile-drawing bias,
This sway of motion, this Commodity,
Makes it take head from all indifferency,
From all direction, purpose, course, intent;
And this same bias, this Commodity,
This bawd, this broker, this all-changing word,
Clapped on the outward eye of fickle France,
Hath drawn him from his own determined aid,
From a resolved and honourable war,
To a more base and vile-concluded peace.—
And why rail I on this Commodity?
But for because he hath not wooed me yet.
Not that I have the power to clutch my hand,
When his fair angels would salute my palm;
But for my hand, as unattempted yet,
Like a poor beggar, raileth on the rich.
Well, whiles I am a beggar, I will rail,
And say, there is no sin but to be rich;
And being rich, my virtue then shall be,
To say, there is no vice but beggary.
Since kings break faith upon commodity,
Gain, be my lord, for I will worship thee! [*Exit*

ACT THREE

Scene I.—The Same. The French King's Tent

Enter Constance, Arthur, *and* Salisbury

Const. Gone to be married! gone to swear a peace!
False blood to false blood joined! gone to be friends!
Shall Lewis have Blanch, and Blanch those provinces?
It is not so; thou hast misspoke, misheard:
Be well advised, tell o'er thy tale again:
It cannot be; thou dost but say 't is so.
I trust I may not trust thee, for thy word
Is but the vain breath of a common man:
Believe me I do not believe thee, man:

I have a king's oath to the contrary.
Thou shalt be punished for thus frighting me;
For I am sick, and capable of fears;
Oppressed with wrongs, and therefore full of fears;
A widow, husbandless, subject to fears;
A woman, naturally born to fears;
And though thou now confess thou didst but jest,
With my vexed spirits I cannot take a truce,
But they will quake and tremble all this day.
What dost thou mean by shaking of thy head?
Why dost thou look so sadly on my son?
What means that hand upon that breast of thine?
Why holds thine eye that lamentable rheum,
Like a proud river peering o'er his bounds?
Be these sad signs confirmers of thy words?
Then speak again; not all thy former tale,
But this one word, whether thy tale be true.

Sal. As true as I believe you think them false
That give you cause to prove my saying true.

Const. O, if thou teach me to believe this sorrow,
Teach thou this sorrow how to make me die;
And let belief and life encounter so
As doth the fury of two desperate men,
Which in the very meeting fall, and die.—
Lewis marry Blanch! O boy, then where art thou?
France friend with England, what becomes of me?—
Fellow, be gone; I cannot brook thy sight:
This news hath made thee a most ugly man.

Sal. What other harm have I, good lady, done,
But spoke the harm that is by others done?

Const. Which harm within itself so heinous is,
As it makes harmful all that speak of it.

Arth. I do beseech you, madam, be content.

Const. If thou, that bidd'st me be content, were grim,
Ugly, and slanderous to thy mother's womb,
Full of unpleasing blots and sightless stains,
Lame, foolish, crooked, swart, prodigious,
Patched with foul moles, and eye-offending marks,
I would not care, I then would be content;
For then I should not love thee; no, nor thou
Become thy great birth, nor deserve a crown.
But thou art fair; and at thy birth, dear boy,
Nature and Fortune joined to make thee great:
Of Nature's gifts thou may'st with lilies boast
And with the half-blown rose. But Fortune, O,
She is corrupted, changed, and won from thee:
She adulterates hourly with thine uncle John;
And with her golden hand hath plucked on France
To tread down fair respect of sovereignty,
And made his majesty the bawd to theirs

France is a bawd to Fortune, and King John;
That strumpet Fortune, that usurping John!—
Tell me, thou fellow, is not France forsworn?
Envenom him with words, or get thee gone,
And leave those woes alone, which I alone
Am bound to underbear.

Sal. Pardon me, madam,
I may not go without you to the kings.

Const. Thou may'st, thou shalt: I will not go with thee.
I will instruct my sorrows to be proud,
For grief is proud, and makes his owner stoop.
To me and to the state of my great grief
Let kings assemble; for my grief's so great
That no supporter but the huge firm earth
Can hold it up: here I and sorrows sit,
Here is my throne, bid kings come bow to it.
[*Seats herself on the ground*

Enter King John, King Philip, Lewis, Blanch, Elinor, *the* Bastard, Austria, *and Attendants*

K. Phi. 'T is true, fair daughter, and this blessed day
Ever in France shall be kept festival:
To solemnise this day, the glorious sun
Stays in his course, and plays the alchymist,
Turning, with splendour of his precious eye,
The meagre cloddy earth to glittering gold.
The yearly course that brings this day about
Shall never see it but a holy day.

Const. [*Rising*] A wicked day, and not a holy day!
What hath this day deserved? what hath it done,
That it in golden letters should be set,
Among the high tides, in the calendar?
Nay, rather, turn this day out of the week,
This day of shame, oppression, perjury:
Or if it must stand still, let wives with child
Pray that their burdens may not fall this day,
Lest that their hopes prodigiously be crossed.
But on this day, let seamen fear no wrack;
No bargains break, that are not this day made;
This day all things begun come to ill end,
Yea, faith itself to hollow falsehood change!

K. Phi. By Heaven. lady, you shall have no cause
To curse the fair proceedings of this day.
Have I not pawned to you my majesty?

Const. You have beguiled me with a counterfeit
Resembling majesty, which, being touched and tried,
Proves valueless. You are forsworn, forsworn:
You came in arms to spill mine enemies' blood,
But now in arms you strengthen it with yours:

The grappling vigour and rough frown of war
Is cold in amity and painted peace,
And our oppression hath made up this league.—
Arm, arm, you heavens, against these perjured kings!
A widow cries: be husband to me, heavens!
Let not the hours of this ungodly day
Wear out the day in peace; but, ere sunset,
Set armèd discord 'twixt these perjured kings!
Hear me, O, hear me!

Aust. Lady Constance, peace!

Const. War! war! no peace! Peace is to me a war,
O Limoges! O Austria! thou dost shame
That bloody spoil: thou slave, thou wretch, thou coward;
Thou little-valiant, great in villainy!
Thou ever strong upon the stronger side!
Thou Fortune's champion, that dost never fight
But when her humorous ladyship is by
To teach thee safety! Thou art perjured too,
And sooth'st up greatness. What a fool art thou,
A ramping fool, to brag, and stamp, and swear
Upon my party! Thou cold-blooded slave,
Hast thou not spoke like thunder on my side;
Been sworn my soldier: bidding me depend
Upon thy stars, thy fortune, and thy strength?
And dost thou now fall over to my foes?
Thou wear a lion's hide! doff it for shame,
And hang a calf's-skin on those recreant limbs.

Aust. O, that a man should speak those words to me!

Bast. And hang a calf's-skin on those recreant limbs.

Aust. Thou dar'st not say so, villain, for thy life.

Bast. And hang a calf's-skin on those recreant limbs.

K. John. We like not this; thou dost forget thyself.

Enter PANDULPH

K. Phi. Here comes the holy Legate of the Pope.

Pand. Hail, you anointed deputies of Heaven!—
To thee, King John, my holy errand is.
I, Pandulph, of fair Milan Cardinal,
And from Pope Innocent the Legate here,
Do in his name religiously demand
Why thou against the Church, our holy mother,
So wilfully dost spurn; and force perforce,
Keep Stephen Langton, chosen archbishop
Of Canterbury, from that holy see:
This, in our foresaid holy Father's name,
Pope Innocent, I do demand of thee.

K. John. What earthly name to interrogatories
Can task the free breath of a sacred King?
Thou canst not, Cardinal, devise a name

So slight, unworthy, and ridiculous,
To charge me to an answer, as the Pope.
Tell him this tale; and from the mouth of England
Add thus much more,—that no Italian priest
Shall tithe or toil in our dominions;
But as we, under Heaven, are supreme head,
So, under Him that Great Supremacy,
Where we do reign we will alone uphold,
Without the assistance of a mortal hand.
So tell the Pope, all reverence set apart
To him and his usurped authority.
K. Phi. Brother of England, you blaspheme in this.
K. John. Though you and all the kings of Christendom
Are led so grossly by this meddling priest,
Dreading the curse that money may buy out,
And, by the merit of vile gold, dross, dust,
Purchase corrupted pardon of a man;
Who, in that sale, sells pardon from himself;
Though you and all the rest, so grossly led,
This juggling witchcraft with revenue cherish:
Yet I alone, alone do me oppose
Against the Pope, and count his friends my foes.
Pand. Then by the lawful power that I have,
Thou shalt stand cursed, and excommunicate:
And blessèd shall he be that doth revolt
From his allegiance to an heretic;
And meritorious shall that hand be called,
Canonisèd, and worshipped as a saint,
That takes away by any secret course
Thy hateful life.
Const. O, lawful let it be
That I have room with Rome to curse awhile.
Good Father Cardinal, cry thou Amen
To my keen curses; for, without my wrong,
There is no tongue hath power to curse him right.
Pand. There's law and warrant, lady, for my curse.
Const. And for mine too: when law can do no right,
Let it be lawful that law bar no wrong.
Law cannot give my child his kingdom here,
For he that holds his kingdom holds the law:
Therefore, since law itself is perfect wrong,
How can the law forbid my tongue to curse?
Pand. Philip of France, on peril of a curse,
Let go the hand of that arch-heretic,
And raise the power of France upon his head
Unless he do submit himself to Rome.
Eli. Look'st thou pale, France? do not let go thy hand.
Const. Look to that, Devil! lest that France repent,
And, by disjoining hands, hell lose a soul.
Aust. King Philip, listen to the Cardinal.

Bast. And hang a calf's-skin on his recreant limbs.
Aust. Well, ruffian, I must pocket up these wrongs,
Because—
Bast. Your breeches best may carry them.
K. John. Philip, what say'st thou to the Cardinal?
Const. What should he say, but as the Cardinal?
Lew. Bethink you, father,—for the difference
Is purchase of a heavy curse from Rome,
Or the light loss of England for a friend:
Forego the easier.
Blanch. That's the curse of Rome.
Const. O Lewis, stand fast! the devil tempts thee here,
In likeness of a new-uptrimmèd bride.
Blanch. The Lady Constance speaks not from her faith,
But from her need.
Const. O, if thou grant my need,
Which only lives but by the death of faith,
That need must needs infer this principle,
That faith would live again by death of need:
O, then, tread down my need, and faith mounts up;
Keep my need up, and faith is trodden down.
K. John. The king is moved, and answers not to this.
Const. O, be removed from him, and answer well.
Aust. Do so, King Philip, hang no more in doubt.
Bast. Hang nothing but a calf's-skin, most sweet lout.
K. Phi. I am perplexed, and know not what to say.
Pand. What canst thou say, but will perplex thee more
If thou stand excommunicate and cursed?
K. Phi. Good reverend Father, make my person yours,
And tell me how you would bestow yourself.
This royal hand and mine are newly knit,
And the conjunction of our inward souls
Married in league, coupled and linked together
With all religious strength of sacred vows;
The latest breath that gave the sound of words
Was deep-sworn faith, peace, amity, true love
Between our kingdoms and our royal selves;
And even before this truce, but new before,—
No longer than we well could wash our hands
To clap this royal bargain up of peace,—
Heaven knows they were besmeared and over-stained
With slaughter's pencil, where revenge did paint
The fearful difference of incensèd kings:
And shall these hands, so lately purged of blood,
So newly joined in love, so strong in both,
Unyoke this seizure and this kind regret;
Play fast and loose with faith, so jest with Heaven;
Make such unconstant children of ourselves
As now again to snatch our palm from palm,
Unswear faith sworn, and on the marriage-bed

Of smiling peace to march a bloody host,
And make a riot on the gentle brow
Of true sincerity? O, holy sir,
My reverend Father, let it not be so!
Out of your grace, devise, ordain, impose
Some gentle order, and then we shall be blessed
To do your pleasure, and continue friends.
Pand. All form is formless, order orderless,
Save what is opposite to England's love.
Therefore, to arms! be champion of our Church,
Or let the Church, our Mother, breathe her curse,
A Mother's curse, on her revolting son.
France, thou may'st hold a serpent by the tongue,
A chaféd lion by the mortal paw,
A fasting tiger safer by the tooth,
Than keep in peace that hand which thou dost hold.
K. Phi. I may disjoin my hand, but not my faith.
Pand. So mak'st thou faith an enemy to faith;
And, like a civil war, sett'st oath to oath,
Thy tongue against thy tongue. O, let thy vow
First made to Heaven first be to Heaven performed;
That is, to be the champion of our Church.
What since thou swor'st, is sworn against thyself,
And may not be performéd by thyself:
For that which thou hast sworn to do amiss,
Is not amiss when it is truly done:
And being not done, where doing tends to ill,
The truth is then most done not doing it.
The better act, of purposes mistook,
Is to mistake again; though indirect,
Yet indirection thereby grows direct,
And falsehood falsehood cures, as fire cools fire
Within the scorchéd veins of one new-burned.
It is religion that doth make vows kept,
But thou hast sworn against religion:
By what thou swear'st against the thing thou swear'st,—
And mak'st an oath the surety for thy truth
Against an oath to truth—thou art unsure;
To swear swears only not to be forsworn,
Else, what a mockery should it be to swear!
But thou dost swear only to be forsworn,
And most forsworn, to keep what thou dost swear.
Therefore, thy later vow, against thy first,
Is in thyself rebellion to thyself;
And better conquest never canst thou make
Than arm thy constant and thy nobler parts
Against these giddy loose suggestions:
Upon which better part our prayers come in,
If thou vouchsafe them; but, if not, then know,
The peril of our curses light on thee

So heavy, as thou shalt not shake them off,
But in despair die under their black weight.

Aust. Rebellion, flat rebellion!

Bast. Will 't not be?
Will not a calf's-skin stop that mouth of thine?

Lew. Father, to arms!

Blanch. Upon thy wedding-day?
Against the blood that thou hast marriéd?
What! shall our feast be kept with slaughtered men?
Shall braying trumpets and loud churlish drums,
Clamours of hell, be measures to our pomp?
O husband, hear me!—ah, alack, how new
Is husband in my mouth!—even for that name,
Which till this time my tongue did ne'er pronounce,
Upon my knee I beg, go not to arms
Against mine uncle.

Const. O, upon my knee,
Made hard with kneeling, I do pray to thee,
Thou virtuous Dauphin, alter not the doom
Forethought by Heaven!

Blanch. Now shall I see thy love. What motive may
Be stronger with thee than the name of wife?

Const. That which upholdeth him that thee upholds,
His honour. O, thine honour, Lewis, thine honour.

Lew. I muse your majesty doth seem so cold,
When such profound respects do pull you on.

Pand. I will denounce a curse upon his head.

K. Phi. Thou shalt not need.—England, I will fall from thee.

Const. O fair return of banished majesty!

Eli. O foul revolt of French inconstancy!

K. John. France, thou shalt rue this hour, within this hour.

Bast. Old Time the clock-setter, that bald sexton Time,
Is it as he will? well then, France shall rue.

Blanch. The sun's o'ercast with blood: fair day, adieu!
Which is the side that I must go withal?
I am with both; each army hath a hand,
And in their rage, I having hold of both,
They whirl asunder, and dismember me.
Husband, I cannot pray that thou may'st win:
Uncle, I needs must pray that thou may'st lose;
Father, I may not wish the fortune thine;
Grandam, I will not wish thy wishes thrive:
Whoever wins, on that side shall I lose;
Assuréd loss, before the match be played.

Lew. Lady, with me, with me thy fortune lies.

Blanch. There where my fortune lives, there my life dies.

K. John. Cousin, go draw our puissance together.—
[*Exit Bastard*
France, I am burned up with inflaming wrath;
A rage whose heat hath this condition
That nothing can allay, nothing but blood,
The blood, and dearest-valued blood, of France.
K. Phi. Thy rage shall burn thee up, and thou shalt turn
To ashes, ere our blood shall quench that fire.
Look to thyself, thou art in jeopardy.
K. John. No more than he that threats. To arms let's hie! [*Exeunt*

SCENE II.—The Same. Plains near Angiers

Alarums; Excursions. Enter the BASTARD, *with* AUSTRIA'S *head*

Bast. Now, by my life, this day grows wondrous hot;
Some airy devil hovers in the sky
And pours down mischief. Austria's head lie there,
While Philip breathes.

Enter KING JOHN, ARTHUR, *and* HUBERT

K. John. Hubert, keep this boy.—Philip, make up:
My mother is assailèd in our tent,
And ta'en, I fear.
Bast. My lord, I rescued her;
Her highness is in safety, fear you not.
But on, my liege; for very little pains
Will bring this labour to an happy end. [*Exeunt*

SCENE III.—The Same

Alarums; Excursions; Retreat. Enter KING JOHN, ELINOR, ARTHUR, *the* BASTARD, HUBERT *and Lords*

K. John. [*To Elinor*] So shall it be; your grace shall stay behind,
So strongly guarded.—[*To Arthur*] Cousin, look not sad;
Thy grandam loves thee, and thy uncle will
As dear be to thee as thy father was.
Arth. O, this will make my mother die with grief.
K. John. [*To the Bastard*] Cousin, away for England: haste before;
And, ere our coming, see thou shake the bags
Of hoarding abbots; imprisoned angels
Set at liberty: the fat ribs of peace

Must by the hungry now be fed upon:
Use our commission in his utmost force.

Bast. Bell, book, and candle shall not drive me back,
When gold and silver becks me to come on.
I leave your highness.—Grandam, I will pray
(If ever I remember to be holy)
For your fair safety: so I kiss your hand.

Eli. Farewell, gentle cousin.

K. John. Coz, farewell. [*Exit Bastard*

Eli. Come hither, little kinsman; hark, a word.
[*She takes Arthur aside*

K. John. Come hither, Hubert.—O my gentle Hubert,
We owe thee much: within this wall of flesh
There is a soul counts thee her creditor,
And with advantage means to pay thy love:
And, my good friend, thy voluntary oath
Lives in this bosom, dearly cherishéd.—
Give me thy hand.—I had a thing to say,—
But I will fit it with some better time.
By Heaven, Hubert, I am almost ashamed
To say what good respect I have of thee.

Hub. I am much bounden to your majesty.

K. John. Good friend, thou hast no cause to say so yet;
But thou shalt have: and creep time ne'er so slow,
Yet it shall come for me to do thee good.—
I had a thing to say,—but let it go:
The sun is in the heaven, and the proud day,
Attended with the pleasures of the world,
Is all too wanton and too full of gawds
To give me audience:—if the midnight bell
Did, with his iron tongue and brazen mouth,
Sound on into the drowsy ear of night;
If this same were a churchyard where we stand,
And thou possesséd with a thousand wrongs;—
Or if that surly spirit, melancholy,
Had baked thy blood, and made it heavy thick,—
Which, else, runs tickling up and down the veins
Making that idiot, laughter, keep men's eyes.
And strain their cheeks to idle merriment,
A passion hateful to my purposes;—
Or if that thou couldst see me without eyes,
Hear me without thine ears, and make reply
Without a tongue, using conceit alone,
Without eyes, ears, and harmful sound of words,—
Then, in despite of brooded-watchful day,
I would into thy bosom pour my thoughts.—
But ah, I will not:—yet I love thee well;
And, by my troth, I think, thou lov'st me well.

Hub. So well, that what you bid me undertake,
Though that my death were adjunct to my act,

By Heaven, I would do it.
K. John. Do not I know, thou wouldst?
Good Hubert, Hubert,—Hubert, throw thine eye
On yon young boy.—I'll tell thee what, my friend,—
He is a very serpent in my way,
And wheresoe'er this foot of mine doth tread,
He lies before me. Dost thou understand me?
Thou art his keeper.
Hub. And I'll keep him so,
That he shall not offend your majesty.
K. John. Death.
Hub. My lord?
K. John. A grave.
Hub. He shall not live.
K. John. Enough.
I could be merry now. Hubert, I love thee;
Well, I'll not say what I intend for thee:
Remember.—Madam, fare you well:
I'll send those powers o'er to your majesty.
Eli. My blessing go with thee!
K. John. For England, cousin: go.
Hubert shall be your man, attend on you
With all true duty.—On toward Calais, ho! [*Exeunt*

SCENE IV.—The Same. The FRENCH KING'S Tent

Enter KING PHILIP, LEWIS, PANDULPH, *and Attendants*

K. Phi. So by a roaring tempest on the flood
A whole armado of connected sail
Is scattered and disjoined from fellowship.
Pand. Courage and comfort: all shall yet go well.
K. Phi. What can go well, when we have run so ill?
Are we not beaten? Is not Angiers lost?
Arthur ta'en prisoner? divers dear friends slain?
And bloody England into England gone,
O'erbearing interruption, spite of France?
Lew. What he hath won, that hath he fortified:
So hot a speed with such advice disposed,
Such temperate order in so fierce a cause,
Doth want example. Who hath read, or heard,
Of any kindred action like to this?
K. Phi. Well could I bear that England had this praise,
So we could find some pattern of our shame.

Enter CONSTANCE

Look, who comes here? a grave unto a soul;
Holding the eternal spirit, against her will,

In the vile prison of afflicted breath.—
I pr'ythee, lady, go away with me.

Const. Lo now, now see the issue of your peace!

K. Phi. Patience, good lady: comfort, gentle Constance!

Const. No, I defy all counsel, all redress,
But that which ends all counsel, true redress,
Death, death,—O amiable lovely death!
Thou odoriferous stench, sound rottenness,
Arise forth from the couch of lasting night,
Thou hate and terror to prosperity,
And I will kiss thy detestable bones,
And put my eye-balls in thy vaulty brows,
And ring these fingers with thy household worms,
And stop this gap of breath with fulsome dust,
And be a carrion monster like thyself!
Come, grin on me; and I will think thou smil'st,
And buss thee as thy wife! Misery's love,
O, come to me!

K. Phi. O fair affliction, peace!

Const. No, no, I will not, having breath to cry.
O that my tongue were in the thunder's mouth,
Then with a passion would I shake the world
And rouse from sleep that fell anatomy,
Which cannot hear a lady's feeble voice,
Which scorns a modern invocation.

Pand. Lady, you utter madness, and not sorrow.

Const. Thou art unholy to belie me so.
I am not mad: this hair I tear is mine;
My name is Constance; I was Geffrey's wife:
Young Arthur is my son, and he is lost!
I am not mad:—I would to Heaven I were,
For then 't is like I should forget myself;
O, if I could, what grief should I forget!
Preach some philosophy to make me mad,
And thou shalt be canónized, Cardinal;
For, being not mad, but sensible of grief,
My reasonable part produces reason
How I may be delivered of these woes,
And teaches me to kill or hang myself.
If I were mad, I should forget my son,
Or madly think a babe of clouts were he.
I am not mad: too well, too well I feel
The different plague of each calamity.

K. Phi. Bind up those tresses. O, what love I note
In the fair multitude of those her hairs!
Where but by chance a silver drop hath fallen,
Even to that drop ten thousand wiry friends
Do glue themselves in sociable grief,
Like true, inseparable, faithful loves,

Sticking together in calamity.
Const. To England, if you will.
K. Phi. Bind up your hairs.
Const. Yes, that I will; and wherefore will I do it?
I tore them from their bonds, and cried aloud,
'O, that these hands could so redeem my son,
As they have given these hairs their liberty!'
But now I envy at their liberty,
But will again commit them to their bonds,
Because my poor child is a prisoner.—
And, Father Cardinal, I have heard you say
That we shall see and know our friends in heaven.
If that be true, I shall see my boy again;
For, since the birth of Cain, the first male child,
To him that did but yesterday suspire,
There was not such a gracious creature born.
But now will canker sorrow eat my bud,
And chase the native beauty from his cheek,
And he will look as hollow as a ghost,
As dim and meagre as an ague's fit,
And so he 'll die; and, rising so again,
When I shall meet him in the court of heaven,
I shall not know him: therefore, never, never
Must I behold my pretty Arthur more.
Pand. You hold too heinous a respect of grief.
Const. He talks to me that never had a son.
K. Phi. You are as fond of grief as of your child.
Const. Grief fills the room up of my absent child,
Lies in his bed, walks up and down with me;
Puts on his pretty looks, repeats his words,
Remembers me of all his gracious parts,
Stuffs out his vacant garments with his form:
Then have I reason to be fond of grief.
Fare you well: had you such a loss as I,
I could give better comfort than you do.—
I will not keep this form upon my head
When there is such disorder in my wit.
O Lord! my boy, my Arthur, my fair son!
My life, my joy, my food, my all the world!
My widow-comfort, and my sorrow's cure! [*Exit*
K. Phi. I fear some outrage, and I'll follow her. [*Exit*
Lew. There's nothing in this world can make me joy.
Life is as tedious as a twice-told tale
Vexing the dull ear of a drowsy man;
And bitter shame hath spoiled the sweet world's taste,
That it yields nought but shame and bitterness.
Pand. Before the curing of a strong disease,
Even in the instant of repair and health,
The fit is strongest: evils that take leave,
On their departure most of all show evil.

What have you lost by losing of this day?
Lew. All days of glory, joy, and happiness.
Pand. If you had won it, certainly, you had.
No, no: when Fortune means to men most good,
She looks upon them with a threatening eye.
'T is strange to think how much King John hath lost
In this which he accounts so clearly won.
Are not you grieved that Arthur is his prisoner?
Lew. As heartily, as he is glad he hath him.
Pand. Your mind is all as youthful as your blood.
Now hear me speak with a prophetic spirit;
For even the breath of what I mean to speak
Shall blow each dust, each straw, each little rub,
Out of the path which shall directly lead
Thy foot to England's throne; and therefore mark.
John hath seized Arthur: and it cannot be,
That whiles warm life plays in that infant's veins
The misplaced John should entertain an hour,
One minute, nay, one quiet breath of rest.
A sceptre, snatched with an unruly hand,
Must be as boisterously maintained as gained;
And he that stands upon a slippery place
Makes nice of no vile hold to stay him up:
That John may stand, then, Arthur needs must fall;
So be it, for it cannot be but so.
Lew. But what shall I gain by young Arthur's fall?
Pand. You, in the right of Lady Blanch your wife,
May then make all the claim that Arthur did.
Lew. And lose it, life and all, as Arthur did.
Pand. How green you are, and fresh in this old world!
John lays you plots: the times conspire with you;
For he that steeps his safety in true blood
Shall find but bloody safety and untrue.
This act so evilly borne, shall cool the hearts
Of all his people and freeze up their zeal,
That none so small advantage shall step forth
To check his reign, but they will cherish it:
No natural exhalation in the sky,
No scope of Nature, no distempered day,
No common wind, no customéd event,
But they will pluck away his natural cause,
And call them meteors, prodigies, and signs,
Abortives, presages, and tongues of heaven.
Plainly denouncing vengeance upon John.
Lew. May be, he will not touch young Arthur's life,
But hold himself safe in his prisonment.
Pand. O, sir, when he shall hear of your approach,
If that young Arthur be not gone already,
Even at that news he dies; and then the hearts
Of all his people shall revolt from him,

And kiss the lips of unacquainted change,
And pick strong matter of revolt and wrath
Out of the bloody fingers' ends of John.
Methinks I see this hurly all on foot:
And, O, what better matter breeds for you
Than I have named?—The bastard Faulconbridge
Is now in England ransacking the Church,
Offending charity: if but a dozen French
Were there in arms, they would be as a call
To train ten thousand English to their side,
Or as a little snow tumbled about
Anon becomes a mountain. O noble Dauphin,
Go with me to the king. 'T is wonderful
What may be wrought out of their discontent,
Now that their souls are topful of offence.
For England, go; I will whet on the king.
Lew. Strong reasons make strong actions. Let us go:
If you say, ay, the king will not say, no. [*Exeunt*

ACT FOUR

Scene I.—Northampton. A Room in the Castle

Enter Hubert *and two Attendants*

Hub. Heat me these irons hot; and look thou stand
Within the arras: when I strike my foot
Upon the bosom of the ground, rush forth,
And bind the boy which you shall find with me
Fast to the chair: be heedful. Hence, and watch.
First Atten. I hope, your warrant will bear out the deed.
Hub. Uncleanly scruples: fear not you: look to 't.—
[*Exeunt Attendants*
Young lad, come forth; I have to say with you.

Enter Arthur

Arth. Good morrow, Hubert.
Hub. Good morrow, little prince.
Arth. As little prince—having so great a title
To be more prince—as may be.—You are sad.
Hub. Indeed, I have been merrier.
Arth. Mercy on me,
Methinks no body should be sad but I:
Yet I remember, when I was in France,
Young gentlemen would be as sad as night,
Only for wantonness. By my christendom,
So I were out of prison, and kept sheep,

I should be as merry as the day is long;
And so I would be here, but that I doubt
My uncle practises more harm to me:
He is afraid of me, and I of him.
Is it my fault that I was Geffrey's son?
No, indeed, is 't not; and I would to Heaven
I were your son, so you would love me, Hubert.

Hub. [*Aside*] If I talk to him, with his innocent prate
He will awake my mercy, which lies dead:
There I will be sudden, and despatch.

Arth. Are you sick, Hubert? you look pale to-day.
In sooth, I would you were a little sick,
That I might sit all night and watch with you:
I warrant, I love you more than you do me.

Hub. [*Aside*] His words do take possession of my bosom.—
Read here, young Arthur. [*Showing a paper*
[*Aside*] How now, foolish rheum,
Turning dispiteous torture out of door
I must be brief, lest resolution drop
Out at mine eyes in tender womanish tears.—
Can you not read it? is it not fair writ?

Arth. Too fairly, Hubert, for so foul effect.
Must you with hot irons burn out both mine eyes?

Hub. Young boy, I must.

Arth. And will you?

Hub. And I will.

Arth. Have you the heart? When your head did but ache,
I knit my handkerchief about your brows,—
The best I had, a princess wrought it me,—
And I did never ask it you again;
And with my hand at midnight held your head,
And, like the watchful minutes to the hour,
Still and anon cheered up the heavy time,
Saying, 'What lack you?' and, 'Where lies your grief?'
Or, 'What good love may I perform for you?'
Many a poor man's son would have lain still
And ne'er have spoke a loving word to you,
But you at your sick-service had a prince.
Nay, you may think my love was crafty love,
And call it cunning: do, an if you will.
If Heaven be pleased that you will use me ill,
Why, then you must.—Will you put out mine eyes?
These eyes that never did, nor never shall,
So much as frown on you?

Hub. I have sworn to do it,
And with hot irons must I burn them out.

Arth. Ah! none but in this iron age would do it.
The iron of itself, though heat red-hot,

Approaching near these eyes would drink my tears,
And quench his fiery indignation
Even in the matter of mine innocence;
Nay, after that, consume away in rust
But for containing fire to harm mine eye.
Are you more stubborn-hard than hammered iron?
And if an angel should have come to me
And told me, Hubert should put out mine eyes,
I would not have believed him; no tongue but Hubert's.
Hub. Come forth. [*Stamps*

Re-enter Attendants, with cords, irons, etc.

Do as I bid you do.
Arth. O, save me, Hubert, save me! my eyes are out,
Even with the fierce looks of these bloody men.
Hub. Give me the iron, I say, and bind him here.
Arth. Alas! what need you be so boisterous-rough?
I will not struggle; I will stand stone-still.
For Heaven's sake, Hubert, let me not be bound.
Nay, hear me, Hubert: drive these men away,
And I will sit as quiet as a lamb;
I will not stir, nor wince, nor speak a word,
Nor look upon the iron angerly.
Thrust but these men away, and I'll forgive you,
Whatever torment you do put me to.
Hub. Go, stand within: let me alone with him.
First Atten. I am best pleased to be from such a deed.
[*Exeunt Attendants*
Arth. Alas, I then have chid away my friend:
He hath a stern look, but a gentle heart.—
Let him come back, that his compassion may
Give life to yours.
Hub. Come, boy, prepare yourself.
Arth. Is there no remedy?
Hub. None but to lose your eyes.
Arth. O Heaven,—that there were but a mote in yours,
A grain, a dust, a gnat, a wandering hair,
Any annoyance in that precious sense!
Then, feeling what small things are boisterous there,
Your vile intent must needs seem horrible.
Hub. Is this your promise? go to, hold your tongue.
Arth. Hubert, the utterance of a brace of tongues
Must needs want pleading for a pair of eyes:
Let me not hold my tongue; let me not, Hubert:
Or, Hubert, if you will, cut out my tongue,
So I may keep mine eyes. O, spare mine eyes;
Though to no use, but still to look on you.
Lo, by my troth, the instrument is cold,
And would not harm me.

Hub. I can heat it, boy.
Arth. No, in good sooth; the fire is dead with grief,
Being create for comfort, to be used
In undeserved extremes: see else yourself;
There is no malice in this burning coal;
The breath of heaven hath blown his spirit out,
And strewed repentant ashes on his head.
Hub. But with my breath I can revive it, boy.
Arth. An if you do, you will but make it blush
And glow with shame of your proceedings, Hubert:
Nay, it, perchance, will sparkle in your eyes;
And like a dog that is compelled to fight,
Snatch at his master that doth tarre him on.
All things that you should use to do me wrong,
Deny their office: only you do lack
That mercy which fierce fire and iron extends,
Creatures of note for mercy-lacking uses.
Hub. Well, see to live, I will not touch thine eyes
For all the treasure that thine uncle owes:
Yet am I sworn, and I did purpose, boy,
With this same very iron to burn them out.
Arth. O, now you look like Hubert: all this while
You were disguised.
Hub. Peace! no more. Adieu.
Your uncle must not know but you are dead:
I'll fill these doggéd spies with false reports.
And, pretty child, sleep doubtless, and secure
That Hubert, for the wealth of all the world,
Will not offend thee.
Arth. O Heaven!—I thank you, Hubert.
Hub. Silence! no more. Go closely in with me;
Much danger do I undergo for thee. [*Exeunt*

SCENE II.—The Same. A Room of State in the Palace

Enter KING JOHN, *crowned;* PEMBROKE, SALISBURY, *and other Lords. The* KING *takes his State*

K. John. Here once again we sit, once again crowned,
And looked upon, I hope, with cheerful eyes.
Pem. This 'once again,' but that your highness pleased,
Was once superfluous: you were crowned before,
And that high royalty was ne'er plucked off,
The faiths of men ne'er stainéd with revolt;
Fresh expectation troubled not the land
With any longed-for change, or better state.
Sal. Therefore, to be possessed with double pomp,
To guard a title that was rich before,
To gild refinéd gold, to paint the lily,

To throw a perfume on the violet,
To smooth the ice, or add another hue
Unto the rainbow, or with taper-light
To seek the beauteous eye of heaven to garnish,
Is wasteful and ridiculous excess.
Pem. But that your royal pleasure must be done,
This act is as an ancient tale new-told,
And in the last repeating troublesome,
Being urgéd at a time unseasonable.
Sal. In this, the antique and well-noted face
Of plain old form is much disfiguréd;
And, like a shifted wind unto a sail,
It makes the course of thoughts to fetch about,
Startles and frights consideration,
Makes sound opinion sick, and truth suspected,
For putting on so new a fashioned robe.
Pem. When workmen strive to do better than well,
They do confound their skill in covetousness;
And, oftentimes, excusing of a fault
Doth make the fault the worse by the excuse:
As patches set upon a little breach
Discredit more in hiding of the fault
Than did the fault before it was so patched.
Sal. To this effect, before you were new-crowned,
We breathed our counsel: but it pleased your highness
To overbear it, and we are all well pleased;
Since all and every part of what we would
Doth make a stand at what your highness will.
K. John. Some reasons of this double coronation
I have possessed you with, and think them strong;
And more, more strong, when lesser is my fear,
I shall indue you with: meantime, but ask
What you would have reformed that is not well;
And well shall you perceive how willingly
I will both hear and grant you your requests.
Pem. Then I, as one that am the tongue of these
To sound the purposes of all their hearts,
Both for myself and them, but, chief of all,
Your safety, for the which myself and them
Bend their best studies, heartily request
The enfranchisement of Arthur; whose restraint
Doth move the murmuring lips of discontent
To break into this dangerous argument:
If what in rest you have in right you hold,
Why then your fears,—which, as they say, attend
The steps of wrong,—should move you to mew up
Your tender kinsman, and to choke his days
With barbarous ignorance, and deny his youth
The rich advantage of good exercise?
That the time's enemies may not have this

To grace occasions, let it be our suit
That you have bid us ask, his liberty;
Which for our goods we do no further ask
Than whereupon our weal, on you depending,
Counts it your weal he have his liberty.

Enter HUBERT

K. John. Let it be so: I do commit his youth
To your direction.—Hubert, what news with you?
[*Hubert whispers the King*

Pem. This is the man should do the bloody deed:
He showed his warrant to a friend of mine.
The image of a wicked heinous fault
Lives in his eye: that close aspect of his
Does show the mood of a much troubled breast;
And I do fearfully believe 't is done,
What we so feared he had a charge to do.

Sal. The colour of the king doth come and go
Between his purpose and his conscience,
Like heralds 'twixt two dreadful battles set.
His passion is so ripe, it needs must break.

Pem. And when it breaks, I fear, will issue thence
The foul corruption of a sweet child's death.

K. John. We cannot hold mortality's strong hand.—
Good lords, although my will to give is living,
The suit which you demand is gone and dead:
He tells us, Arthur is deceased to-night.

Sal. Indeed, we feared his sickness was past cure.

Pem. Indeed, we heard how near his death he was,
Before the child himself felt he was sick.
This must be answered, either here, or hence.

K. John. Why do you bend such solemn brows on me?
Think you I bear the shears of destiny?
Have I commandment on the pulse of life?

Sal. It is apparent foul play; and 't is shame
That greatness should so grossly offer it.
So thrive it in your game! and so farewell.

Pem. Stay yet, Lord Salisbury; I'll go with thee,
And find the inheritance of this poor child,
His little kingdom of a forcéd grave.
That blood which owed the breadth of all this isle,
Three foot of it doth hold. Bad world the while!
This must not be thus borne: this will break out
To all our sorrows, and ere long, I doubt. [*Exeunt Lords*

K. John. They burn in indignation. I repent.
There is no sure foundation set on blood,
No certain life achieved by others' death.

Enter a Messenger

A fearful eye thou hast. Where is that blood
That I have seen inhabit in those cheeks?
So foul a sky clears not without a storm:
Pour down thy weather.—How goes all in France?
Mess. From France to England. Never such a power,
For any foreign preparation,
Was levied in the body of a land.
The copy of your speed is learned by them;
For when you should be told they do prepare,
The tidings comes that they are all arrived.
K. John. O, where hath our intelligence been drunk?
Where hath it slept? Where is my mother's care,
That such an army could be drawn in France,
And she not hear of it?
Mess. My liege, her ear
Is stopped with dust: the first of April, died
Your noble mother; and, as I hear, my lord,
The Lady Constance in a frenzy died
Three days before; but this from rumour's tongue
I idly heard; if true, or false, I know not.
K. John. Withhold thy speed, dreadful Occasion!
O, make a league with me, till I have pleased
My discontented peers.—What! mother dead!
How wildly then walks my estate in France!
Under whose conduct came those powers of France,
That thou for truth giv'st out are landed here?
Mess. Under the Dauphin.

Enter the BASTARD, *and* PETER *of Pomfret*

K. John. Thou hast made me giddy
With these ill tidings.—Now, what says the world
To your proceedings? do not seek to stuff
My head with more ill news, for it is full.
Bast. But if you be afeard to hear the worst,
Then let the worst, unheard, fall on your head.
K. John. Bear with me, cousin, for I was amazed
Under the tide; but now I breathe again
Aloft the flood, and can give audience
To any tongue, speak it of what it will.
Bast. How I have sped among the clergymen,
The sums I have collected shall express.
But as I travelled hither through the land
I find the people strangely fantasied,
Possessed with rumours, full of idle dreams,
Not knowing what they fear, but full of fear.
And here's a prophet that I brought with me
From forth the streets of Pomfret, whom I found

With many hundreds treading on his heels;
To whom he sung, in rude harsh-sounding rhymes,
That, ere the next Ascension-day at noon,
Your highness should deliver up your crown.
K. John. Thou idle dreamer, wherefore didst thou so?
Peter. Foreknowing that the truth will fall out so.
K. John. Hubert, away with him: imprison him;
And on that day at noon, whereon, he says,
I shall yield up my crown, let him be hanged.
Deliver him to safety, and return,
For I must use thee. [*Exit Hubert with Peter*
O my gentle cousin,
Hear'st thou the news abroad, who are arrived?
Bast. The French, my lord; men's mouths are full of it:
Besides, I met Lord Bigot and Lord Salisbury
With eyes as red as new-enkindled fire,
And others more, going to seek the grave
Of Arthur, who, they say, is killed to-night
On your suggestion.
K. John. Gentle kinsman, go,
And thrust thyself into their companies.
I have a way to win their loves again:
Bring them before me.
Bast. I will seek them out.
K. John. Nay, but make haste; the better foot before.
O, let me have no subject enemies,
When adverse foreigners affright my towns
With dreadful pomp of stout invasion.
Be Mercury, set feathers to thy heels,
And fly like thought from them to me again.
Bast. The spirit of the time shall teach me speed. [*Exit*
K. John. Spoke like a spriteful noble gentleman.
Go after him; for he, perhaps, shall need
Some messenger betwixt me and the peers,
And be thou he.
Mess. With all my heart, my liege. [*Exit*
K. John. My mother dead!

Re-enter HUBERT

Hub. My lord, they say five moons were seen to-night:
Four fixéd; and the fifth did whirl about
The other four, in wondrous motion.
K. John. Five moons?
Hub. Old men, and beldams, in the streets
Do prophesy upon it dangerously.
Young Arthur's death is common in their mouths;
And when they talk of him, they shake their heads
And whisper one another in the ear;
And he that speaks doth gripe the hearer's wrist,

Whilst he that hears makes fearful action,
With wrinkled brows, with nods, with rolling eyes
I saw a smith stand with his hammer, thus,
The whilst his iron did on the anvil cool,
With open mouth swallowing a tailor's news,
Who, with his shears and measure in his hand,
Standing on slippers (which his nimble haste
Had falsely thrust upon contrary feet),
Told of a many thousand warlike French,
That were embattelèd and ranked in Kent.
Another lean unwashed artificer
Cuts off his tale, and talks of Arthur's death.

K. John. Why seek'st thou to possess me with these fears?
Why urgest thou so oft young Arthur's death?
Thy hand hath murdered him:
I had a mighty cause to wish him dead,
But thou hadst none to kill him.

Hub. No hand, my lord?—Why, did you not provoke me?

K. John. It is the curse of kings to be attended
By slaves that take their humours for a warrant
To break within the bloody house of life,
And on the winking of authority
To understand a law, to know the meaning
Of dangerous majesty, when, perchance, it frowns
More upon humour than advised respect.

Hub. Here is your hand and seal for what I did.

K. John. O, when the last account 'twixt Heaven and earth
Is to be made, then shall this hand and seal
Witness against us to damnation.
How oft the sight of means to do ill deeds
Makes deeds ill done! Hadst not thou been by,
A fellow by the hand of nature marked
Quoted and signed to do a deed of shame,
This murder had not come into my mind;
But, taking note of thy abhorred aspect,
Finding thee fit for bloody villainy,
Apt, liable, to be employed in danger,
I faintly broke with thee of Arthur's death;
And thou, to be endearèd to a king,
Made it no conscience to destroy a prince.

Hub. My lord,—

K. John. Hadst thou but shook thy head, or made a pause,
When I spake darkly what I purposèd,
Or turned an eye of doubt upon my face,
As bid me tell my tale in express words,
Deep shame had struck me dumb, made me break off,

And those thy fears might have wrought fears in me:
But thou didst understand me by my signs,
And didst in signs again parley with sin;
Yea, without stop, didst let thy heart consent,
And consequently thy rude hand to act,
The deed which both our tongues held vile to name.
Out of my sight, and never see me more!
My nobles leave me, and my state is braved,
Even at my gates, with ranks of foreign powers:
Nay, in the body of this fleshly land,
This kingdom, this confine of blood and breath,
Hostility and civil tumult reigns
Between my conscience and my cousin's death.
Hub. Arm you against your other enemies,
I'll make a peace between your soul and you.
Young Arthur is alive: this hand of mine
Is yet a maiden and an innocent hand,
Not painted with the crimson spots of blood.
Within this bosom never entered yet
The dreadful motion of a murderous thought;
And you have slandered nature in my form,
Which, howsoever rude exteriorly,
Is yet the cover of a fairer mind
Than to be butcher of an innocent child.
K. John. Doth Arthur live? O haste thee to the peers,
Throw this report on their incensèd rage,
And make them tame to their obedience.
Forgive the comment that my passion made
Upon thy feature; for my rage was blind,
And foul imaginary eyes of blood
Presented thee more hideous than thou art.
O answer not; but to my closet bring
The angry lords, with all expedient haste.
I conjure thee but slowly; run more fast. [*Exeunt*

Scene III.—The Same. Before the Castle

Enter Arthur, *on the walls*

Arth. The wall is high; and yet will I leap down.
Good ground, be pitiful, and hurt me not!
There's few or none do know me; if they did,
This ship-boy's semblance hath disguised me quite.
I am afraid; and yet I'll venture it.
If I get down, and do not break my limbs,
I'll find a thousand shifts to get away:
As good to die and go, as die and stay. [*Leaps down*
O me! my uncle's spirit is in these stones.—
Heaven take my soul, and England keep my bones! [*Dies*

Enter PEMBROKE, SALISBURY, *and* BIGOT

Sal. Lords, I will meet him at Saint Edmund's Bury:
It is our safety, and we must embrace
This gentle offer of the perilous time.
Pem. Who brought that letter from the Cardinal?
Sal. The Count Melun, a noble lord of France;
Whose private with me, of the Dauphin's love,
Is much more general than these lines import.
Big. To-morrow morning let us meet him then.
Sal. Or rather then set forward; for 't will be
Two long days' journey, lords, or e'er we meet.

Enter the BASTARD

Bast. Once more to-day well met, distempered lords
The king by me requests your presence straight.
Sal. The king hath dispossessed himself of us.
We will not line his thin bestainèd cloak
With our pure honours, nor attend the foot
That leaves the print of blood where'er it walks.
Return, and tell him so: we know the worst.
Bast. Whate'er you think, good words, I think, were best.
Sal. Our griefs and not our manners reason now.
Bast. But there is little reason in your grief;
Therefore, 't were reason you had manners now.
Pem. Sir, sir, impatience hath his privilege.
Bast. 'T is true; to hurt his master, no man else.
Sal. This is the prison.—[*Seeing Arthur*] What is he lies here?
Pem. O death, made proud with pure and princely beauty!
The earth had not a hole to hide this deed.
Sal. Murder, as hating what himself hath done,
Doth lay it open to urge on revenge.
Big. Or when he doomed this beauty to a grave,
Found it too precious-princely for a grave.
Sal. Sir Richard, what think you? Have you beheld,
Or have you read, or heard, or could you think?
Or do you almost think, although you see,
That you do see? could thought, without this object,
Form such another? This is the very top,
The height, the crest, or crest unto the crest,
Of murder's arms: this is the bloodiest shame,
The wildest savagery, the vilest stroke,
That ever wall-eyed wrath, or staring rage,
Presented to the tears of soft remorse.
Pem. All murders past do stand excused in this:
And this, so sole and so unmatchable,

Shall give a holiness, a purity,
To the yet unbegotten sins of time,
And prove a deadly bloodshed but a jest,
Exampled by this heinous spectacle.
Bast. It is a damnéd and a bloody work;
The graceless action of a heavy hand,
If that it be the work of any hand.
Sal. If that it be the work of any hand?—
We had a kind of light what would ensue:
It is the shameful work of Hubert's hand;
The practice, and the purpose, of the king:
From whose obedience I forbid my soul,
Kneeling before this ruin of sweet life,
And breathing to his breathless excellence
The incense of a vow, a holy vow,
Never to taste the pleasures of the world,
Never to be infected with delight,
Nor conversant with ease and idleness,
Till I have set a glory to this hand
By giving it the worship of revenge.
Pem., Big. Our souls religiously confirm thy words.

Enter HUBERT

Hub. Lords, I am hot with haste in seeking you.
Arthur doth live: the king hath sent for you.
Sal. O, he is bold, and blushes not at death.—
Avaunt thou hateful villain! get thee gone.
Hub. I am no villain.
Sal. Must I rob the law!
[*Drawing his sword*
Bast. Your sword is bright, sir: put it up again.
Sal. Not till I sheathe it in a murderer's skin.
Hub. Stand back, Lord Salisbury, stand back, I say:
By Heaven, I think, my sword's as sharp as yours.
I would not have you, lord, forget yourself,
Nor tempt the danger of my true defence;
Lest I, by marking of your rage, forget
Your worth, your greatness, and nobility.
Big. Out, dunghill! dar'st thou brave a nobleman?
Hub. Not for my life; but yet I dare defend
My innocent life against an emperor.
Sal. Thou art a murderer.
Hub. Do not prove me so:
Yet, I am none. What tongue soe'er speaks false,
Not truly speaks; who speaks not truly, lies.
Pem. Cut him to pieces.
Bast. Keep the peace, I say.
Sal. Stand by, or I shall gall you, Faulconbridge.
Bast. Thou wert better gall the devil, Salisbury;

If thou but frown on me, or stir thy foot,
Or teach thy hasty spleen to do me shame,
I'll strike thee dead. Put up thy sword betime,
Or I'll so maul you and your toasting-iron,
That you shall think the devil is come from hell.

Big. What wilt thou do, renownéd Faulconbridge?
Second a villain, and a murderer?

Hub. Lord Bigot, I am none.

Big. Who killed this prince?

Hub. 'T is not an hour since I left him well:
I honoured him, I loved him; and will weep
My date of life out for his sweet life's loss.

Sal. Trust not those cunning waters of his eyes,
For villainy is not without such rheum;
And he, long-traded in it, makes it seem
Like rivers of remorse and innocency.
Away, with me, all you whose souls abhor
The uncleanly savours of a slaughter-house,
For I am stifled with this smell of sin.

Big. Away, toward Bury: to the Dauphin there!

Pem. There, tell the king, he may enquire us out.

[*Exeunt Lords*

Bast. Here's a good world!—Knew you of this fair work?
Beyond the infinite and boundless reach
Of mercy, if thou didst this deed of death,
Art thou damned, Hubert.

Hub. Do but hear me, sir,—

Bast. Ha! I 'll tell thee what;
Thou art damned as black—nay, nothing is so black;
Thou art more deep damned than Prince Lucifer:
There is not yet so ugly a fiend of hell
As thou shalt be, if thou didst kill this child.

Hub. Upon my soul,—

Bast. If thou didst but consent
To this most cruel act, do but despair;
And if thou want'st a cord, the smallest thread
That ever spider twisted from her womb
Will serve to strangle thee; a rush will be a beam
To hang thee on; or wouldst thou drown thyself,
Put but a little water in a spoon
And it shall be as all the ocean,
Enough to stifle such a villain up.
I do suspect thee very grievously.

Hub. If I in act, consent, or sin of thought,
Be guilty of the stealing that sweet breath
Which was embounded in this beauteous clay,
Let hell want pains enough to torture me.
I left him well.

Bast. Go, bear him in thine arms.

I am amazed, methinks, and lose my way
Among the thorns and dangers of this world.
How easy dost thou take all England up!
From forth this morsel of dead royalty,
The life, the right, and truth of all this realm
Is fled to heaven; and England now is left
To tug and scramble, and to part by the teeth
The unowed interest of proud-swelling state.
Now for the bare-picked bone of majesty
Doth doggéd war bristle his angry crest,
And snarleth in the gentle eyes of peace:
Now powers from home, and discontents at home,
Meet in one line; and vast confusion waits,
As doth a raven on a sick-fallen beast,
The imminent decay of wrested pomp.
Now happy he whose cloak and cinture can
Hold out this tempest.—Bear away that child,
And follow me with speed: I 'll to the king.
A thousand businesses are brief in hand,
And Heaven itself doth frown upon the land. [*Exeunt*

ACT FIVE

SCENE I.—The Same. A Room in the Palace

Enter KING JOHN, PANDULPH *with the crown, and Attendants*

K. John. Thus have I yielded up into your hand
The circle of my glory.
Pand. [*Giving John the crown*] Take again
From this my hand as holding of the Pope,
Your sovereign greatness and authority.
K. John. Now keep your holy word: go meet the French:
And from His Holiness use all your power
To stop their marches 'fore we are inflamed.
Our discontented counties do revolt,
Our people quarrel with obedience,
Swearing allegiance and the love of soul
To stranger blood, to foreign royalty.
This inundation of mistempered humour
Rests by you only to be qualified.
Then pause not; for the present time's so sick
That present medicine must be ministered,
Or overthrow incurable ensues.
Pand. It was my breath that blew this tempest up,
Upon your stubborn usage of the Pope;
But since you are a gentle convertite,

My tongue shall hush again this storm of war
And make fair weather in your blustering land.
On this Ascension-day, remember well,
Upon your oath of service to the Pope,
Go I to make the French lay down their arms. [*Exit*

K. John. Is this Ascension-day? Did not the prophet
Say, that before Ascension-day at noon
My crown I should give off? Even so I have.
I did suppose it should be on constraint;
But, Heaven be thanked, it is but voluntary.

Enter the BASTARD

Bast. All Kent hath yielded; nothing there holds out
But Dover Castle: London hath received,
Like a kind host, the Dauphin and his powers.
Your nobles will not hear you, but are gone
To offer service to your enemy;
And wild amazement hurries up and down
The little number of your doubtful friends.

K. John. Would not my lords return to me again,
After they heard young Arthur was alive?

Bast. They found him dead, and cast into the streets;
An empty casket, where the jewel of life
By some damned hand was robbed and ta'en away.

K. John. That villain Hubert told me he did live.

Bast. So, on my soul, he did, for aught he knew.
But wherefore do you droop? why look you sad?
Be great in act, as you have been in thought;
Let not the world see fear and sad distrust
Govern the motion of a kingly eye:
Be stirring as the time; be fire with fire;
Threaten the threatener, and outface the brow
Of bragging horror: so shall inferior eyes,
That borrow their behaviours from the great,
Grow great by your example and put on
The dauntless spirit of resolution.
Away! and glister like the god of war
When he intendeth to become the field:
Show boldness and aspiring confidence.
What, shall they seek the lion in his den,
And fright him there? and make him tremble there?
O, let it not be said. Forage, and run
To meet displeasure farther from the doors,
And grapple with him ere he comes so nigh.

K. John. The Legate of the Pope hath been with me,
And I have made a happy peace with him;
And he hath promised to dismiss the powers
Led by the Dauphin.

Bast. O inglorious league!

Shall we, upon the footing of our land,
Send fair-play orders, and make compromise,
Insinuation, parley, and base truce,
To arms invasive? Shall a beardless boy,
A cockered silken wanton, brave our fields,
And flesh his spirit in a warlike soil,
Mocking the air with colours idly spread,
And find no check? Let us, my liege, to arms:
Perchance, the Cardinal cannot make your peace;
Or if he do, let it at least be said,
They saw we had a purpose of defence.

K. John. Have thou the ordering of this present time.

Bast. Away, then, with good courage; yet, I know.
Our party may well meet a prouder foe. [*Exeunt*

SCENE II.—A Plain near Saint Edmund's Bury

Enter in arms, LEWIS, SALISBURY, MELUN, PEMBROKE, BIGOT, *and Soldiers*

Lew. My Lord Melun, let this be copied out,
And keep it safe for our remembrance.
Return the precedent to these lords again;
That, having our fair order written down,
Both they, and we, perusing o'er these notes,
May know wherefore we took the sacrament,
And keep our faiths firm and inviolable.

Sal. Upon our sides it never shall be broken.
And, noble Dauphin, albeit we swear
A voluntary zeal and unurged faith
To your proceedings, yet, believe me, prince,
I am not glad that such a sore of time
Should seek a plaster by contemned revolt,
And heal the inveterate canker of one wound
By making many. O, it grieves my soul
That I must draw this metal from my side
To be a widow-maker; O, and there,
Where honourable rescue, and defence,
Cries out upon the name of Salisbury.
But such is the infection of the time
That, for the health and physic of our right
We cannot deal but with the very hand
Of stern injustice and confuséd wrong.—
And is 't not pity, O my grievéd friends,
That we, the sons and children of this isle,
Were born to see so sad an hour as this;
Wherein we step after a stranger march
Upon her gentle bosom, and fill up
Her enemies' ranks,—I must withdraw, and weep,

Upon the spot of this enforcéd cause,—
To grace the gentry of a land remote,
And follow unacquainted colours here?
What, here?—O nation, that thou couldst remove!
That Neptune's arms, who clippeth thee about,
Would bear thee from the knowledge of thyself
And grapple thee unto a pagan shore,
Where these two Christian armies might combine
The blood of malice in a vein of league,
And not to spend it so unneighbourly!
Lew. A noble temper dost thou show in this;
And great affections wrestling in thy bosom
Do make an earthquake of nobility.
O, what a noble combat hast thou fought
Between compulsion and a brave respect!
Let me wipe off this honourable dew,
That silverly doth progress on thy cheeks.
My heart hath melted at a lady's tears,
Being an ordinary inundation;
But this effusion of such manly drops,
This shower blown up by tempest of the soul,
Startles mine eyes, and makes me more amazed
Than had I seen the valley top of heaven
Figured quite o'er with burning meteors.
Lift up thy brow, renownéd Salisbury,
And with a great heart heave away this storm:
Commend these waters to those baby eyes
That never saw the giant world enraged,
Nor met with fortune other than at feasts
Full warm of blood, of mirth, of gossiping.
Come, come; for thou shalt thrust thy hand as deep
Into the purse of rich prosperity
As Lewis himself:—so, nobles, shall you all.
That knit your sinews to the strength of mine.

Enter PANDULPH, *attended*

And even there, methinks, an angel spake:
Look, where the holy Legate comes apace,
To give us warrant from the hand of Heaven,
And on our actions set the name of right
With holy breath.
Pand. Hail, noble Prince of France!
The next is this:—King John hath reconciled
Himself to Rome; his spirit is come in,
That so stood out against the holy Church,
The great metropolis and see of Rome.
Therefore, thy threat'ning colours now wind up,
And tame the savage spirit of wild war,
That, like a lion fostered up at hand,

It may lie gently at the foot of peace
And be no further harmful than in show
Lew. Your grace shall pardon me; I will not back:
I am too high-born to be propertied,
To be a secondary at control,
Or useful serving-man and instrument
To any sovereign state throughout the world.
Your breath first kindled the dead coal of wars
Between this chastised kingdom and myself
And brought in matter that should feed this fire;
And now 't is far too huge to be blown out
With that same weak wind which enkindled it.
You taught me how to know the face of right,
Acquainted me with interest to this land,
Yes, thrust this enterprise into my heart;
And come ye now to tell me, John hath made
His peace with Rome? What is that peace to me?
I, by the honour of my marriage-bed,
After young Arthur, claim this land for mine;
And, now it is half-conquered, must I back,
Because that John hath made his peace with Rome?
Am I Rome's slave? What penny hath Rome borne,
What men provided, what munition sent,
To underprop this action? Is 't not I
That undergo this charge? who else but I,
And such as to my claim are liable,
Sweat in this business, and maintain this war?
Have I not heard these islanders shout out,
Vive le roy! as I have banked their towns?
Have I not here the best cards for the game,
To win this easy match played for a crown?
And shall I now give o'er the yielded set?
No, on my soul, it never shall be said.
Pand. You look but on the outside of this work.
Lew. Outside or inside, I will not return
Till my attempt so much be glorified
As to my ample hope was promiséd
Before I drew this gallant head of war,
And culled these fiery spirits from the world
To outlook conquest and to win renown
Even in the jaws of danger and of death.—
[*Trumpets sound*
What lusty trumpet thus doth summon us?

Enter the BASTARD, *attended*

Bast. According to the fair play of the world,
Let me have audience: I am sent to speak.
My holy Lord of Milan, from the king
I come, to learn how you have dealt for him;

And, as you do answer, I do know the scope
And warrant limited unto my tongue.
Pand. The Dauphin is too wilful-opposite,
And will not temporise with my entreaties:
He flatly says, he'll not lay down his arms.
Bast. By all the blood that ever fury breathed,
The youth says well.—Now, hear our English king;
For thus his royalty doth speak in me.
He is prepared; and reason too, he should:
This apish and unmannerly approach,
This harnessed masque, and unadviséd revel,
This unhaired sauciness, and boyish troops,
The king doth smile at, and is well prepared
To whip this dwarfish war, these pigmy arms,
From out the circle of his territories.
That hand which had the strength, even at your door,
To cudgel you and make you take the hatch;
To dive, like buckets, in concealéd wells;
To crouch in litter of your stable planks;
To lie like pawns locked up in chests and trunks;
To hug with swine; to seek sweet safety out
In vaults and prisons; and to thrill, and shake
Even at the crying of your nation's crow,
Thinking this voice an arméd Englishman:
Shall that victorious hand be feebled here,
That in your chambers gave you chastisement!
No! Know, the gallant monarch is in arms,
And, like an eagle, o'er his eyry towers
To souse annoyance that comes near his nest.
And you degenerate, you ingrate revolts,
You bloody Neroes ripping up the womb
Of your dear mother England, blush for shame:
For your own ladies and pale-visaged maids,
Like Amazons, come tripping after drums;
Their thimbles into arméd gauntlets change,
Their neelds to lances, and their gentle hearts
To fierce and bloody inclination.
Lew. There end thy brave, and turn thy face in peace;
We grant thou canst outscold us. Fare thee well;
We hold our time too precious to be spent
With such a brabbler.
Pand. Give me leave to speak.
Bast. No, I will speak.
Lew. We will attend to neither.
Strike up the drums! and let the tongue of war
Plead for our interest, and our being here.
Bas. Indeed, your drums, being beaten, will cry out;
And so shall you, being beaten. Do but start
An echo with the clamour of thy drum,
And even at hand a drum is ready braced,

That shall reverberate all as loud as thine;
Sound but another, and another shall,
As loud as thine, rattle the welkin's ear,
And mock the deep-mouthed thunder: for at hand—
Not trusting to this halting Legate here,
Whom he hath used rather for sport than need—
Is warlike John; and in his forehead sits
A bare-ribbed death, whose office is this day
To feast upon whole thousands of the French.
Lew. Strike up our drums, to find this danger out.
Bast. And thou shalt find it, Dauphin, do not doubt.
[*Exeunt*

SCENE III.—The Same. A Field of Battle

Alarums. Enter KING JOHN *and* HUBERT

K. John. How goes the day with us? O, tell me, Hubert.
Hub. Badly, I fear. How fares your majesty?
K. John. This fever that hath troubled me so long
Lies heavy on me: O, my heart is sick.

Enter a Messenger

Mess. My lord, your valiant kinsman, Faulconbridge,
Desires your majesty to leave the field,
And send him word by me which way you go.
K. John. Tell him, toward Swinstead, to the abbey there.
Mess. Be of good comfort; for the great supply,
That was expected by the Dauphin here,
Are wrecked three nights ago on Goodwin Sands.
This news was brought to Richard but even now.
The French fight coldly, and retire themselves.
K. John. Ah me! this tyrant fever burns me up,
And will not let me welcome this good news.
Set on toward Swinstead; to my litter straight:
Weakness possesseth me, and I am faint. [*Exeunt*

SCENE IV.—The Same. Another Part of the Same

Enter SALISBURY, PEMBROKE, BIGOT, *and others*

Sal. I did not think the king so stored with friends.
Pem. Up once again; put spirit in the French:
If they miscarry, we miscarry too.
Sal. That misbegotten devil, Faulconbridge,
In spite of spite, alone upholds the day.

Pem. They say, King John, sore sick, hath left the field.

Enter MELUN *wounded, and led by Soldiers*

Mel. Lead me to the revolts of England here.
Sal. When we were happy we had other names.
Pem. It is the Count Melun.
Sal. Wounded to death.
Mel. Fly, noble English; you are bought and sold;
Unthread the rude eye of rebellion
And welcome home again discarded faith.
Seek out King John, and fall before his feet;
For if the French be lord of this loud day,
He means to recompense the pains you take
By cutting off your heads. Thus hath he sworn,
And I with him, and many more with me,
Upon the altar at Saint Edmund's Bury;
Even on that altar, where we swore to you
Dear amity and everlasting love.
Sal. May this be possible? May this be true?
Mel. Have I not hideous death within my view,
Retaining but a quantity of life
Which bleeds away even as a form of wax
Resolveth from his figure 'gainst the fire?
What in the world should make me now deceive,
Since I must lose the use of all deceit?
Why should I then be false, since it is true
That I must die here, and live hence by truth?
I say again, if Lewis do win the day,
He is forsworn if e'er those eyes of yours
Behold another day break in the east:
But even this night, whose black contagious breath
Already smokes about the burning crest
Of the old, feeble, and day-wearied sun,
Even this ill night, your breathing shall expire,
Paying the fine of rated treachery
Even with a treacherous fine of all your lives,
If Lewis by your assistance win the day.
Commend me to one Hubert, with your king;
The love of him,—and this respect besides,
For that my grandsire was an Englishman,—
Awakes my conscience to confess all this.
In lieu whereof, I pray you, bear me hence
From forth the noise and rumour of the field;
Where I may think the remnant of my thoughts
In peace, and part this body and my soul
With contemplation and devout desires.
Sal. We do believe thee,—and beshrew my soul,
But I do love the favour and the form
Of this most fair occasion, by the which

We will untread the steps of damnéd flight;
And, like a bated and retiréd flood,
Leaving our rankness and irregular course,
Stoop low within those bounds we have o'erlooked,
And calmly run on in obedience
Even to our ocean, to our great King John.—
My arm shall give thee help to bear thee hence,
For I do see the cruel pangs of death
Right in thine eye.—Away, my friends! New flight;
And happy newness, that intends old right.
[*Exeunt, leading off Melun*

Scene V.—The Same. The French Camp

Enter Lewis *and his Train*

Lew. The sun of heaven, methought, was loath to set,
But stayed and made the western welkin blush,
When the English measured backward their own ground
In faint retire. O, bravely came we off,
When with a volley of our needless shot,
After such bloody toil, we bid good night,
And wound our tattering colours clearly up,
Last in the field, and almost lord of it!

Enter a Messenger

Mess. Where is my prince, the Dauphin?
Lew. Here.—What news?
Mess. The Count Melun is slain; the English lords,
By his persuasion, are again fallen off;
And your supply, which you have wished so long,
Are cast away, and sunk, on Goodwin Sands.
Lew. Ah, foul shrewd news! Beshrew thy very heart!
I did not think to be so sad to-night
As this hath made me.—Who was he that said,
King John did fly an hour or two before
The stumbling night did part our weary powers?
Mess. Whoever spoke it, it is true, my lord.
Lew. Well; keep good quarter and good care to-night:
The day shall not be up so soon as I,
To try the fair adventure of to-morrow. [*Exeunt*

SCENE VI.—An Open Place in the Neighbourhood of Swinstead Abbey

Enter the BASTARD *and* HUBERT, *severally*

Hub. Who's there? speak, ho! speak quickly, or I shoot.
Bast. A friend.—What art thou?
Hub. Of the part of England.
Bast. Whither dost thou go?
Hub. What's that to thee? why may not I demand
Of thine affairs, as well as thou of mine?
Bast. Hubert, I think.
Hub. Thou hast a perfect thought:
I will, upon all hazards, well believe
Thou art my friend, that know'st my tongue so well.
Who art thou?
Bast. Who thou wilt: and, if thou please,
Thou may'st befriend me so much as to think
I come one way of the Plantagenets.
Hub. Unkind Remembrance, thou, and endless night,
Have done me shame! Brave soldier, pardon me,
That any accent breaking from thy tongue
Should 'scape the true acquaintance of mine ear.
Bast. Come, come; sans compliment, what news abroad?
Hub. Why, here walk I in the black brow of night,
To find you out.
Bast. Brief then; and what's the news?
Hub. O, my sweet sir, news fitting to the night,
Black, fearful, comfortless, and horrible.
Bast. Show me the very wound of this ill news:
I am no woman; I'll not swoon at it.
Hub. The king, I fear, is poisoned by a monk:
I left him almost speechless, and broke out
To acquaint you with this evil, that you might
The better arm you to the sudden time
Than if you had at leisure known of this.
Bast. How did he take it? who did taste to him?
Hub. A monk, I tell you; a resolvéd villain,
Whose bowels suddenly burst out: the king
Yet speaks, and, peradventure, may recover.
Bast. Whom didst thou leave to tend his majesty?
Hub. Why, know you not? the lords are all come back.
And brought Prince Henry in their company;
At whose request the king hath pardoned them,
And they are all about his majesty.
Bast. Withhold thine indignation, mighty Heaven,
And tempt us not to bear above our power!

I'll tell thee, Hubert, half my power this night,
Passing these flats, are taken by the tide;
These Lincoln washes have devouréd them:
Myself, well mounted, hardly have escaped.
Away, before! conduct me to the king;
I doubt, he will be dead or e'er I come. [*Exeunt*

SCENE VII.—The Orchard of Swinstead Abbey

Enter PRINCE HENRY, SALISBURY, *and* BIGOT

P. Hen. It is too late: the life of all his blood
Is touched corruptibly; and his pure brain,
Which some suppose the soul's frail dwelling-house,
Doth, by the idle comments that it makes,
Foretell the ending of mortality.

Enter PEMBROKE

Pem. His highness yet doth speak; and holds belief
That being brought into the open air
It would allay the burning quality
Of that fell poison which assaileth him.
P. Hen. Let him be brought into the orchard here.
Doth he still rage? [*Exit Bigot*
Pem. He is more patient
Than when you left him: even now he sung.
P. Hen. O vanity of sickness? fierce extremes
In their continuance will not feel themselves.
Death, having preyed upon the outward parts
Leaves them, invisible? and his siege is now
Against the mind, the which he pricks and wounds
With many legions of strange fantasies
Which, in their throng and press to that last hold,
Confound themselves. 'T is strange that death should sing.
I am the cygnet to this pale faint swan
Who chants a doleful hymn to his own death.
And from the organ-pipe of frailty sings
His soul and body to their lasting rest.
Sal. Be of good comfort, prince; for you are born
To set a form upon that indigest
Which he hath left so shapeless and so rude.

Re-enter BIGOT *and Attendants, who bring in* KING JOHN *in a chair*

K. John. Ay, marry, now my soul hath elbow-room;
It would not out at windows, nor at doors,
There is so hot a summer in my bosom

That all my bowels crumble up to dust:
I am a scribbled form, drawn with a pen
Upon a parchment, and against this fire
Do I shrink up.

P. Hen. How fares your majesty?

K. John. Poisoned,—ill fare; dead, forsook, cast off:
And none of you will bid the winter come,
To thrust his icy fingers in my maw;
Nor let my kingdom's rivers take their course
Through my burned bosom; nor entreat the north
To make his bleak winds kiss my parchéd lips
And comfort me with cold.—I do not ask you much,
I beg cold comfort; and you are so strait
And so ingrateful, you deny me that.

P. Hen. O, that there were some virtue in my tears
That might relieve you!

K. John. The salt in them is hot.
Within me is a hell; and there the poison
Is as a fiend confined to tyrannise
On unreprievable-condemnéd blood.

Enter the BASTARD

Bast. O, I am scalded with my violent motion,
And spleen of speed to see your majesty.

K. John. O, cousin, thou art come to set mine eye:
The tackle of my heart is cracked and burned;
And all the shrouds wherewith my life should sail
Are turnéd to one thread, one little hair:
My heart hath one poor string to stay it by,
Which holds but till thy news be utteréd,
And then all this thou seest is but a clod,
And module of confounded royalty.

Bast. The Dauphin is preparing hitherward,
Where Heaven he knows how we shall answer him:
For, in a night, the best part of my power,
As I upon advantage did remove,
Were in the washes, all unwarily.
Devouréd by the unexpected flood. [*The King dies*

Sal. You breathe these dead news in as dead an ear.—
My liege! my lord!—But now, a king; now, thus.

P. Hen. Even so must I run on, and even so stop.
What surety of the world, what hope, what stay
When this was now a king, and now is clay?

Bast. Art thou gone so? I do but stay behind
To do the office for thee of revenge,
And then my soul shall wait on thee to heaven
As it on earth hath been thy servant still.
Now, now, you stars that move in your right spheres,
Where be your powers? Show now your mended faiths,

And instantly return with me again,
To push destruction and perpetual shame
Out of the weak door of our fainting land.
Straight let us seek, or straight we shall be sought:
The Dauphin rages at our very heels.
Sal. It seems you know not then so much as we,
The Cardinal Pandulph is within at rest,
Who half an hour since came from the Dauphin,
And brings from him such offers of our peace
As we with honour and respect may take,
With purpose presently to leave this war.
Bast. He will the rather do it, when he sees
Ourselves well sinewèd to our defence.
Sal. Nay, it is in a manner done already;
For many carriages he hath despatched
To the sea-side, and put his cause and quarrel
To the disposing of the Cardinal;
With whom yourself, myself, and other lords,
If you think meet, this afternoon will post
To consummate this business happily.
Bast. Let it be so. And you, my noble prince,
With other princes that may best be spared,
Shall wait upon your father's funeral.
P. Hen. At Worcester must his body be interred;
For so he willed it.
Bast. Thither shall it then.
And happily may your sweet self put on
The lineal state and glory of the land:
To whom, with all submission, on my knee,
I do bequeath my faithful services
And true subjection everlastingly.
Sal. And the like tender of our love we make,
To rest without a spot for evermore.
P. Hen. I have a kind soul that would give you thanks
And knows not how to do it but with tears.
Bast. O, let us pay the time but needful woe,
Since it hath been beforehand with our griefs,—
This England never did, nor never shall,
Lie at the proud foot of a conqueror,
But when it first did help to wound itself.
Now these her princes are come home again,
Come the three corners of the world in arms
And we shall shock them. Naught shall make us rue,
If England to itself do rest but true. [*Exeunt*